Anthony Storr

FEET OF CLAY

SAINTS, SINNERS, AND MADMEN:
A STUDY OF GURUS

The wisest men follow their own direction
And listen to no prophet guiding them.
None but the fools believe in oracles,
Forsaking their own judgement. Those who know,
Know that such men can only come to grief.

EURIPIDES, *Iphigenia in Tauris*

FREE PRESS PAPERBACKS
Published by Simon & Schuster
New York   London   Toronto   Sydney   Singapore

FREE PRESS PAPERBACKS
A Division of Simon & Schuster Inc.
1230 Avenue of the Americas
New York, NY 10020

First Free Press Paperbacks Edition 1997

FREE PRESS PAPERBACKS and colophon are trademarks
of Simon & Schuster Inc.

Manufactured in the United States of America

10 9 8 7 6 5 4 3 2 1

Library of Congress Cataloging-in-Publication Data

Storr, Anthony
      Feet of clay: saints, sinners and madmen: a study of gurus /
Anthony Storr
          p.   cm.
      Includes bibliographical references (p.   ) and index.
      ISBN 0–684–83495–2 (pbk. : alk. paper)
      1. Gurus–Biography.   2. Spiritual biography.   3. Cults—
Biography.   4. Gurus—Psychology.   5. Authoritarianism—Religious
aspects.   6. Control (Psychology)—Religious aspects.   7. Charisma
(Personality trait)   I. Title
BL72. S76   1997
291.6'1—dc21
                                                          97–14250
                                                             CIP

For my friend and colleague
Kay Redfield Jamison,
and in memory of our
mutual friend and publisher
Erwin Glikes.

Contents

LIST OF ILLUSTRATIONS   ix
ACKNOWLEDGEMENTS   x
INTRODUCTION   xi

I   Paranoid Enclosures   1

II   Georgei Ivanovitch Gurdjieff   21

III   Bhagwan Shree Rajneesh   45

IV   Rudolf Steiner   65

V   Carl Gustav Jung   83

VI   Sigmund Freud   107

VII   The Jesuit and Jesus   127

VIII   Sanity and Insanity   149

IX   Chaos and Order   173

X   Delusion and Faith   195

XI   To Whom Shall We Turn?   213

REFERENCES   235
BIBLIOGRAPHY   245
INDEX   249

List of Illustrations

Jim Jones and David Koresh   *page* 2

Georgei Ivanovitch Gurdjieff   22

Bhagwan Shree Rajneesh   46

Rudolf Steiner   66

Carl Gustav Jung   84

Sigmund Freud   108

Ignatius of Loyola   128

Paul Brunton   150

Mother Meera   214

Acknowledgements

My wife, Catherine Peters has read the whole typescript and made many percipient emendations. So have Stuart Proffitt and Arabella Quin of HarperCollins and Susan Arellano at The Free Press. I am also particularly grateful to Matthew Barton, Dr. Paul Bishop, Dr. Gordon Claridge, Dr. Kay R. Jamison, Dr. Kim Jobst, Dr. and Mrs. Irvine Loudon, Polly Lansdowne, Alan Ridout, and Margaret Wind, all of whom have made valuable comments and suggestions, or pointed my way to additional sources.

Introduction

SOME CHARACTERISTICS
OF GURUS

THIS IS A BOOK ABOUT GURUS. The Sanskrit word guru means 'heavy.' When applied to people, it means someone who commands respect. Professor R.F. Gombrich informs me that, in Sanskrit, the word is 'normally applied to one's father, and most commonly of all to a teacher.' He suggests that the closest English equivalent is 'respected teacher.' Today, anyone regarded as an expert in any field, from football to economics, is liable to be deemed a guru. In this book, I am restricting the term to teachers who claim special knowledge of the meaning of life, and who therefore feel entitled to tell others how life should be lived. *Chambers Twentieth Century Dictionary* defines guru as 'a spiritual teacher: a venerable person.' Not all gurus are venerable; but the definition 'spiritual teacher' is sufficiently accurate to indicate what is meant by the term in this book.

Gurus differ widely from each other in a variety of ways, but most claim the possession of special spiritual insight based on personal revelation. Gurus promise their followers new ways of self-development, new paths to salvation. Since there are no schools for gurus, and no recognized qualifications for becoming one, they are, like politicians, originally self-selected. Anyone can become a guru if he or she has the hubris to claim special spiritual gifts. Both recent and earlier history demonstrate that many gurus are, or become, unscrupulous wielders of power who exploit their followers in a variety of ways. Yet there have also been gurus whose holiness, lack of personal ambition, and integrity are beyond question. Jesus, Muhammad, and the Buddha were gurus who are still venerated and whose teachings have changed the lives of millions of people. Some of Muhammad's injunctions concerning legal punishment and the treatment of women, as recorded in the Koran, are repugnant to modern Western ideas, but both Jesus and the Buddha compel our admiration, even if we are neither Christians nor Buddhists.

Since this book is concerned with some gurus who were less than admirable, I want to affirm at the outset that I recognize that morally superior individuals exist whose integrity, virtue, and goodness are far beyond the reach of most of us. Such people, unlike gurus, usually influence others by their examples in daily life rather than by swaying crowds with rhetoric, surrounding themselves with adoring disciples, or claiming access to esoteric wisdom which the ordinary person cannot reach unaided. Most of us have encountered people who can be described as 'good' without being priggish. Perhaps they visit the sick, or adopt deprived children, or devote themselves to charitable enterprises without hope of reward or public recognition. They do not preach; they *do*. Genuine virtue is usually unobtrusive, although it may be perceived as something less admirable when exposed to the glare of publicity, as happened with Albert Schweitzer and Mother Teresa.

Gurus are in a different category. I do not mean to suggest that *all* gurus have feet of clay. Yet many gurus have been entirely unworthy of veneration: false prophets, madmen, confidence tricksters, or unscrupulous psychopaths who exploit their disciples emotionally, financially, and sexually. In the light of history, we may think it easy to distinguish the saints from the madmen and the crooks; but it is clear that those who seek a guru to give their lives meaning find it difficult to make this distinction. This is partly because their urgent need blinds them to the true characteristics of the guru; a distortion familiar to psychoanalysts who are accustomed to the phenomena accompanying transference. It is also because the best and worst prophets, though varying greatly in intelligence and personality, have a number of characteristics in common.

A person becoming a guru usually claims to have been granted a special, spiritual insight which has transformed his own life. This revelation is sometimes believed to come direct from God or from his angels; but may also be attributed to mysterious beings residing in the Himalayas or even to the inhabitants of other planets. Often, this purely personal revelation is claimed to be universally, or at least widely, applicable. In other words, gurus generalize from their own experience. Some gurus are inclined to believe that all humanity should accept their vision: others allege that, when the last trump sounds, their own followers will be saved, whilst the majority of mankind will remain unredeemed. This apparently arrogant assumption is closely connected with certain features of personality displayed by a variety of gurus.

Many gurus appear to have been rather isolated as children, and to have remained so. They seldom have close friends. They are more interested in what goes on in their own minds than in personal relationships, perhaps because they do not believe that anyone else really cares for them. In other words, they tend to be introverted and narcissistic. As Freud wrote:

> The man who is predominantly erotic will give first preference to his emotional relationships to other people; the narcissistic man, who inclines to be self-sufficient, will seek his main satisfactions in his internal mental processes.[1]

Many painters, writers, and composers are narcissistic in that they value their own creative pursuits more than human relationships, and are often predominantly solitary. I wrote about such people in my book *Solitude*.[2] But, although they may spend much of their time alone, most creative artists want to communicate with others through their work and gain self-esteem from those who appreciate it. They may be very sensitive to criticism, but many are prepared to learn from it, and to exchange ideas with people who do not wholly agree with them.

Gurus tend to be intolerant of any kind of criticism, believing that anything less than total agreement is equivalent to hostility. This may be because they have been so isolated that they have never experienced the interchange of ideas and positive criticism which only friends can provide. It is also because revelations are in a different category from works of art, in that they cannot be criticized, only accepted or rejected.

Gurus tend to be élitist and anti-democratic, even if they pay lip-service to democracy. How could it be otherwise? Conviction of a special revelation must imply that the guru is a superior person who is not as other men are. Gurus attract disciples without acquiring friends. Once established, gurus must exercise authority, which again precludes making friends on equal terms. Indeed, friendship may undermine the guru's power. One of the favourite sayings of Gurdjieff's father was: 'If you want to lose your faith, make friends with the priest.' The relationship which the guru has with his followers is not one of friendship but of dominance. This again derives from a previous lack of friendships on equal terms. A guru's conviction of his own worth depends upon impressing people rather than upon being loved. Gurus seldom discuss their ideas; they only impose them.

It is frequently the case that the guru's new insight follows a period of mental distress or physical illness, in which the guru has been fruitlessly searching for an answer to his own emotional problems. This change is likely to take place in the subject's thirties or forties, and may warrant the diagnosis of mid-life crisis. Sometimes the revelatory answer comes gradually; at other times, a new insight strikes like a thunderbolt. As we shall see, the distress of chaos followed by the establishment of a new order is a typical course of events which takes place in all creative activity, whether in the arts or the sciences. This *Eureka* pattern is also characteristic of religious revelation and the delusional systems of people we label insane. Relief comes with the solution of problems; and I shall argue that both revelation and delusion are attempts at the solution of problems. Artists and scientists realize that no solution is ever final, but that each new creative step points the way to the next artistic or scientific problem. In contrast, those who embrace religious revelations and delusional systems tend to see them as unshakeable and permanent.

When the guru's 'dark night of the soul' has been ended by his new vision of reality, he usually appears to become convinced that he has discovered 'the truth'. The fervent certainty with which he proclaims this accounts to a large extent for his powerful effect upon others; his persuasiveness, his charisma. Gurus must possess charisma. The Greek word χάρισμα (charisma) originally meant the gift of grace. Max Weber introduced it into sociology to denote a special magical quality of personality by virtue of which the individual possessing it was set apart from ordinary men and women, and treated as if endowed with supernatural or superhuman powers. Such people have the capacity of immediately impressing and influencing others and of attracting devoted followers. Charisma is closely linked with intensity of conviction. The ability to speak fluently in public and good looks are helpful additional assets. Some of the gurus discussed in this book were so fluent that, without reference to notes, they could hold an audience entranced for hours at a time.

Eileen Barker, a leading expert in the sociology of religion, has written: 'Almost by definition, charismatic leaders are unpredictable, for they are bound by neither tradition nor rules; they are not answerable to other human beings.'[3] If a leader is accepted as having charismatic authority, he is often accorded the right to direct every aspect of his followers' lives. For example, he may dictate where they live, with whom they form sexual relationships, and what should be done with their money or other possessions.

Intensity of conviction is necessary if a guru is to attract disciples. This is not to say that all gurus believe everything they preach; but an initial conviction of having special insight is probably necessary if a new sect is to be born. Many people go through conversion experiences and hold strong religious or other convictions without being impelled to preach or to convert others, but gurus require disciples just as disciples require gurus. We must consider the possibility that the conviction expressed by gurus is less absolute than it appears in that their apparent confidence needs boosting by the response of followers. As we shall see, some gurus avoid the stigma of being labelled insane or even of being confined in a mental hospital because they have acquired a group of disciples who accept them as prophets rather than perceiving them as deluded. Some historians have proposed that all messianic characters have secret doubts about their missions, and that this is why they strive to gain disciples. It is difficult to sustain a belief in the authenticity of a new revelation if no one else shares it.

Because they claim superior wisdom, gurus sometimes invent a background of mystery. Travels to parts of Central Asia or Tibet inaccessible to ordinary mortals have, in the past, been promoted as prologues to the acquisition of esoteric knowledge and mystical experiences. Now that most of the world is mapped, explored, and, like Everest, cluttered with western rubbish, it is harder to find places which are sufficiently remote to be mysterious. But there are always other worlds. Perhaps other planets are inhabited by creatures of infinite wisdom who send messages to selected mortals? Some gurus appear to believe so.

Like other humans, gurus risk becoming corrupted by power. Although a guru may begin his mission in ascetic poverty, success often brings about a revision of values. It is intoxicating to be adored, and it becomes increasingly difficult for the guru not to concur with the beliefs of his disciples about him. If a man comes to believe that he has special insights, and that he has been selected by God to pass on these insights to others, he is likely to conclude that he is entitled to special privileges. For example, he may feel, along with his followers, that he cannot be expected to carry out his exhausting spiritual mission if he has to worry about money, and that he is therefore entitled to demand and make use of any money which his followers can raise. Gurus sometimes end up living in luxury.

Gurus who feel entitled to be relieved of financial responsibility also often engage in sexual behaviour which would be condemned as irresponsible in an ordinary person. If a man is surrounded by adoring and attractive women, it is difficult for him to avoid sexual involvements. But the guru who seduces disciples who look up to him as a spiritual guide may do them as much harm as the psycho-analyst who seduces his patients, or the father who sexually assaults his children.

Gurus not infrequently exploit their followers in other ways. Subservient disciples are all too willing to undertake the chores of life, so that the guru may be spared involvement with trivia. Gurus often get pleasure from this exercise of power, and some carry it to the point of making their followers perform meaningless and unnecessary tasks, ostensibly as spiritual exercises, but in fact as a proof of the guru's power over them. Some enjoy inflicting cruel punishments upon transgressors. Gurus vary greatly in personal integrity and the ability to resist the corruption which power over others usually brings with it.

Because a guru professes a bizarre cosmology or becomes corrupt it does not necessarily follow that all his insights are nonsense. I have never believed R. D. Laing's theory that psychosis is a path to higher wisdom, but the period of intense distress or mental illness which so often precedes a new revelation may open doors of perception which are closed to the ordinary person. Manic-depressives sometimes claim that their experiences of the depths of despair and the heights of elation have so intensified their lives that, if offered the choice, they would choose to have their illness rather than suffer the tedium of conventional normality. Even those who passed through an acute episode of schizophrenia and who have emerged intact are sometimes grateful for this experience. I shall often refer to Ellenberger's concept of 'creative illness' which is applicable to a number of gurus.

Some gurus pass through a period of definable mental illness from which they recover: others deteriorate to the point at which most psychiatrists would diagnose them as psychotic; that is, insane rather than neurotic or suffering from temporary emotional instability. Still others remain socially competent and reasonably well-balanced throughout their lives. Critical examination of the lives and beliefs of gurus demonstrates that our psychiatric labels and our conceptions of what is or is not mental illness are woefully inadequate. How, for example, does one distinguish an unorthodox or bizarre faith from a delusion?

In what follows, I want to examine a few gurus who differ markedly from each other, but who all display some of the features which I have just described as characteristic. No guru exhibits all these features; but even the best and worst of gurus have something in common which distinguishes them from ordinary human beings. Contemporary cults like the Unification Church, the Church of Scientology, International Society for Krishna Consciousness (ISKCON), and the Children of God have been extensively studied and written about during the last twenty years because so many parents and others became anxious about the effects that membership of these new religious movements was having on their children. My particular interest is in the personalities of the gurus themselves, although some characteristics of their followers will be mentioned in passing. I have deliberately chosen to study a number of gurus who, ranging as they do from saints to crooks, appear to be quite dissimilar. I hope to show that they have more in common than meets the uncritical eye.

I

PARANOID
ENCLOSURES

JIM JONES

DAVID KORESH

THE INFAMOUS DICTATORS of the twentieth century, Hitler, Mussolini, Stalin, Ceausescu, and Mao Tse-tung were all unscrupulous in the pursuit of power and ruthless in eliminating enemies. Dictators cannot afford the luxury of friends. Although they may marry and rear families, they depend primarily upon the plaudits of the unknown multitude rather than on true affection from intimates to maintain their self-esteem. It is not surprising that leaders of this type become suspicious, often to the point of paranoia. The crowd is fickle and easily swayed. Dictators who depend upon popular acclaim and propaganda alone can be unseated by the adverse events which plague all political leaders. If a dictator is to hold on to power even when the country is in trouble, he must ensure that he is totally in control and that no rival has a chance of supplanting him. To do so requires the apparatus of informers, secret police, and spies which is so characteristic of dictatorial regimes. The number of people who have been banished, imprisoned, tortured, or executed for no reason other than that a dictator perceived them as possible threats to his position is beyond computation. Moreover, it is those who are high in the dictator's hierarchy who are most likely to be seen as threatening. Paradoxically, the 'friends' and allies on whom a normal leader might depend for advice and support during crises, often constitute the greatest threat to the paranoid dictator. Hitler's purge of Ernst Röhm and his Stormtrooper lieutenants in 1934 is a typical example. Hitler owed a great deal to Röhm, who had supported him from his earliest days in Munich, but this did not save him when he became a threat. Both Stalin and Mao Tse-tung disposed of their closest associates without hesitation.

As we shall see, some gurus are dictators on a small scale. Although their message is ostensibly religious rather than political, they behave like dictators, thrive on adulation, have no true friends, attempt

3

to exercise absolute power, and are afflicted by the same kind of paranoid suspicions. Let us look at two gurus who fit this description.

On November 18, 1978, over nine hundred people, including two hundred and sixty children, drank or were injected with cyanide in Jonestown, Guyana. This self-annihilation of the members of the People's Temple was ordered by its founder, Jim Jones, who himself died of a gunshot wound to the head. On April 19, 1993, eighty-six people, including twenty-two children, perished in the flames of Ranch Apocalypse, Waco, Texas. This self-immolation was at the instigation of the cult leader David Koresh, who also died of a gunshot wound to the head.

There are other remarkable resemblances between the two gurus. In childhood, both were rather isolated boys who had few friends amongst contemporaries. Both became eloquent, fluent preachers who could harangue their listeners for hours at a time, battering their audiences into submission by the apparently endless flow of words. Both were entirely unscrupulous sexually; Jim Jones with both sexes, David Koresh with young children as well as with adults. Both were physically cruel, inflicting vicious punishments upon any member of their respective cults who was deemed guilty of infringing the arbitrary rules which they had instituted. Both did all they could to prevent their disciples leaving the cult, by undermining family ties, by threatening dire punishments, and by posting armed guards who were as much concerned with keeping people in as with protecting the enclosures from intruders, although very few disciples wanted to leave. Both exhibited obsessional traits of character and paranoid anxieties which led to their stockpiling weapons against the attacks which they were expecting. Both hovered on the brink of insanity for a considerable part of their lives, and both ended up as demonstrably psychotic.

I have no doubt that, in the course of history, there have been other gurus as repellent as these two, but it is difficult to imagine any who were more so. The fact that so many people worshipped them to the point of being prepared to commit suicide at their behest is terrifying. Their aim was absolute power, and the ultimate expression of power over others is to bring about their death. Perhaps

4

a closer look at these two monsters can teach us something about gurus and the fanaticism which they inspire.

Jim Jones was born in Lynn, Indiana on May 13, 1931. His early childhood was somewhat isolated, since his father was a partial invalid, and his mother had to go out to work. He described himself as always being alone, and he became a fanatical reader. A neighbour, Mrs. Kennedy, acted as a mother substitute and inculcated the boy with religious ideas from an early age. At high school he did well, and was rated as having an IQ of 115–118. He developed an extraordinary verbal fluency. When he was still quite young he abandoned Methodism and joined the Pentecostal Church. This may have been because of some crisis of faith of the kind characteristic of gurus, but it seems equally likely that Jones believed that the Pentecostal Church would offer him more opportunity to display his talents as a preacher and 'spiritual healer'. He was allowed to address the congregation of the Pentecostal church when he was still quite young. As he was handsome as well as persuasive, he soon discovered that he could hold an audience. He was reported as appearing entirely certain of himself, with an air of authority and complete conviction. Even as a schoolboy of ten, Jones claimed special powers. In Indianapolis, he became known as a charismatic preacher who championed the rights of the underprivileged. In 1953, he said: 'I've come into the realization of the Holy Spirit'; but his beliefs were anything but orthodox.[1] Although Jones claimed divine inspiration and was a persuasive preacher, his actual message was more political than religious, being principally concerned with racial integration and what he called socialism. He did promise a new way of life to his followers; but this was based upon a primitive Marxist vision rather than upon religious revelation. In fact he attacked the Bible as an aggressive text supporting capitalism, slavery, and racial discrimination. He also poured scorn upon the 'sky God' of conventional Christianity, claiming that his followers had no need of such a God when he came as 'your socialist worker God'. 'The only thing that brings perfect freedom, justice and equality, perfect love in all its beauty and holiness, is socialism.'[2] He prided himself on having delivered the goods to his followers which the 'sky God' had failed to deliver.

No doubt his powers of oratory went some way to compensate

him for his isolation, but Jones remained pathologically anxious about being deserted by such friends as he had, and later by his disciples. As a youth, he invited an acquaintance for dinner. When the lad said that he must leave before Jones wished him to do so, Jones fired a gun at him, narrowly missing him.

Jones, who was always a neat dresser, was obsessionally preoccupied with cleanliness, and avoided anything which might make him sweat. Like many people of obsessional personality, he had a strong wish to bring everything under his own control, including those around him. His wife Marceline, whom he married in June 1949, soon regretted her choice because she found him so dominant and overbearing.

In 1956, he set up his People's Temple in Indianapolis. The emphasis was on racial equality. Jones and his wife were the first white couple in Indianapolis to adopt a black child. At the time, mixed congregations were a rarity, and many of his black congregation felt that their status had been enhanced by Jones's refusal to discriminate. Much of his early preaching was concerned with calling up individuals from the congregation and 'touching them in the name of the Lord', at which point some entered a trance-like state. In the early days of the People's Temple, Jones undoubtedly did some good. He established soup kitchens for the poor, and also provided coal and clothes for them. When he moved the Temple to Redwood Valley in California in 1965, Jones operated a ranch for mentally handicapped boys, nursing homes for the elderly, homes for foster children, and a day-care centre. These enterprises apparently provided excellent services. Jones was skilful at cultivating important people, and succeeded in impressing Jane Fonda, Angela Davis, Daniel Ellsberg, and Rosalynn Carter, with whom he once shared a platform.

Jones claimed divinely inspired clairvoyance, which he invoked as explaining his knowledge of the personal histories and secrets of those whom he called up. In reality, he employed spies who discovered these secrets by passing on information gleaned from personal enquiries, unauthorized entries to homes, and even from combing through dustbins.

Jones specialized in services of healing, for which he claimed he had a divine gift. Many of his so-called cures were faked. People brought in in wheelchairs would be told they were healed and could walk. In fact, these were disguised members of the People's Temple who had been trained for the role. Jones had no hesitation in claiming to cure cancer. An individual would be told that he had cancer of the bowel and instructed to go to the lavatory. Then, a bloody mass of animal intestine would be produced as evidence that the cancer had been miraculously evacuated. Complicity in his deceptions as a healer was one way in which Jones gained control over the members of his cult. Sexual confessions were another. Some were compelled to sign confessions to crimes which they had not committed. Members of the Temple had to abrogate anything which ministered to their sense of individuality: possessions, children, spouses, and ownership of their own bodies. Everything was to be held in common. Jones, like many other gurus, was good at raising money. By 1975 the Temple's assets were rated at $10 million.

Jones was more obviously a confidence trickster than many gurus, but this did not prevent Eugene Chaikin, a Californian attorney who became a member of the Temple, from describing him as the most loving, Christ-like human being he had ever met. Another law graduate, Tim Stoen, called Jones 'the most compassionate, honest and courageous human being the world contains'. In 1972, Stoen signed a paper requesting that Jones sire a child by his wife, since he himself was unable to do so. As lawyers are not generally noted for being particularly gullible, these opinions are impressive testimony to Jones's powers of persuasion. Jones acceded to Stoen's request, and a later legal conflict about the custody of the ensuing child was one factor leading to the exposure and downfall of Jonestown. Because Jim Jones would not give up John Victor Stoen, as a San Francisco judge ordered, the little boy perished in Jonestown along with the others.

In 1972, Jones again moved the Temple, this time to San Francisco; but disquieting rumours about his claims to heal the sick and raise the dead, combined with accusations of misappropriating funds, soon made him think it advisable to leave California. By 1974, an advance team was clearing an area of jungle in Guyana which Jones had bought from the government for what he called an agricultural project. In May 1977 a massive exodus of Temple members from

San Francisco and Los Angeles resulted in the establishment of Jonestown, a settlement so remote from the coastal capital, Georgetown, that it took thirty-six hours to reach it by steamer and river boat. Guyana was chosen because it had a history of offering sanctuary to a variety of fugitives, including a number of criminals and the black leader, Michael X.* Jones himself became permanently resident there from July 1977. About seventy per cent of those who followed Jones to Guyana were black; about two-thirds were female. As Eileen Barker has pointed out, the membership of the People's Temple was unlike the typical membership of most contemporary cults. Jonestown was originally called an agricultural commune, and the People's Temple was not classified as a new religious movement until after the mass death of its members.[3]

The settlement which Jones established was publicized as utopian; a place from which disease had all but vanished because of Jones's efforts as a divinely-gifted healer: a paradise of racial equality, economic equality and communal bliss. In fact, as some reported it, it was more like a concentration camp presided over by a cruel and ruthless commandant. Jones's need to bring everything and everyone under his own control came near to fulfilment in this remote place.

According to Deborah Blakey, a former financial secretary of the Temple, who managed to get out in April 1978, the commune lived under a reign of terror. She told Shiva Naipaul that most people were required to work in the fields for eleven hours a day on grossly inadequate rations.[4] As a result, extreme loss of weight, chronic diarrhoea, and recurrent fever affected half the inhabitants. Medical treatment was practically non-existent. One middle-aged ex-merchant seaman was forced to work until his shoulder was raw from humping lumber and he broke down sobbing. He was beaten up and forced to crawl in front of Jones to beg forgiveness. The settlement was constantly patrolled by armed guards. Jones threatened that anyone who tried to escape would be killed, forbade telephone calls to the outside world, ensured that mail was censored, and confiscated passports and money. He also told them that the

---

* A convert to Islam and Black Power, he was expelled from Britain for dope-dealing, fled back to Trinidad, and, after committing murder, fled to Guyana.

settlement was surrounded by mercenaries or by the Guyanese Army, who would capture and torture any defectors and castrate any males who attempted escape.

Jones himself, together with some favourites, enjoyed a varied and more than adequate diet from foods stored in his personal refrigerator. He considered himself entitled to have sexual relations with anyone of either sex, although it was noted by his son Stephan that nearly all his father's partners were white. Some were undoubtedly given drugs to make them more amenable. Jones affirmed that he was the only truly heterosexual male in the settlement, and alleged that many of the other males had not come to terms with their homosexual feelings. To demonstrate this, he found it advisable to bugger some of them. One such victim is reported as saying: 'Your fucking me in the ass, was, as I see it now, necessary to get me to deal with my deep-seated repression against my homosexuality'.[5] This man seems to have had no realization of being exploited, no consciousness that Jones might be exercising power over him and, at the same time, gaining personal sexual satisfaction. 'Father' could do no wrong, and sex with Father was generally reported as an incomparable experience.

Punishments were generally carried out in public on the stage of the church. Beatings were inflicted with a three-foot paddle, and some beatings lasted half-an-hour. Grace Stoen saw her son John Victor beaten in public, but when she finally escaped from the settlement in July 1976, she had to leave the child behind. Victims of beatings had their cries amplified by microphones held to their lips. A child who soiled his pants was forced to wear them on his head, forbidden food, and made to watch others eating. Children were sometimes tossed into a well near Jones's bungalow and pulled down into the water by aides who were already swimming there. Their screams of fear could be heard all over the settlement. Another punishment was a boxing match in which the offender was made to fight with a much stronger adversary who beat him semi-conscious. Other offenders were forced to eat hot peppers, or had a hot pepper stuffed up the rectum. Jones's son Stephan recalled that his sixteen-year-old friend, Vincent Lopez, was forced to chew a pepper. To save him from being compelled to chew another, Stephan caught his friend's vomit in his hand so that he could swallow it again.

9

Another punishment was to be confined in a crate too small to permit standing for days at a time. Some offenders were given electric shocks from a machine known as Big Foot. As Jones himself deteriorated, both mentally and physically, Jonestown appears to have come close to resembling Belsen.

Yet, as Shiva Naipaul indicates in his book *Journey to Nowhere*, there was another side to Jonestown. Some reported that their lives had been radically changed for the better; that Jonestown, because of its insistence on racial integration, had removed the stigma of being black, and had given them a new dignity. Others who had previously been alcoholic or drug addicts claimed to have been 'saved' by the Temple or by Jones himself. Dr. James S. Gordon, a psychiatrist who interviewed a number of survivors over a period of ten years, was impressed with the fact that none regretted their stay in Jonestown. It is evident that some people who had been alienated from conventional society felt themselves part of a new community in which they were for the first time accepted and valued. Naipaul writes that some experienced Jonestown as a paradise, while others found it a nightmare.

Jim Jones's confidence in himself was not based, as it is with most of us, on feeling loved and appreciated by friends and family, but on his ability to impress others with his fluent oratory. I have no doubt that this isolated youth early convinced himself, as he convinced others, that he was endowed with special powers and spiritual insight. Like the dwarf Alberich in Wagner's *Das Rheingold*, Jones abandoned the search for love in favour of the acquisition of power. The savage punishments described earlier are a demonstration of his misuse of power. It is hardly credible that mothers could have tolerated such physical abuse of their children, or that adults would submit to such public pain and humiliation; but, as we shall see, Jones was not unique in his punitive methods. His sexual behaviour indicates that he used sex as a way to dominate others rather than as an expression of love. His corrupt sexual behaviour went hand in hand with his élitist conviction of his own superiority. Jones felt entitled to be well fed when his followers were half-starving, and was better housed than they were; but, although the People's Temple accumulated considerable funds, he does not seem to have been attracted by conventional trappings of wealth in the shape of Rolls-Royces, yachts, or gold trinkets. What fascinated him was the exercise of power over other people.

Jones perfectly illustrates the difficulty in defining the borderlines between conviction, delusion, confidence trickery, and psychosis. Perhaps more overtly than any guru with whom I am concerned except Gurdjieff, Jones was a confidence trickster. He had no scruples about faking cures of illness, or himself pretending to collapse when it appeared desirable, or in inventing attacks from imagined enemies. He once broke a window and claimed that a brick on the floor had been thrown at him. Unfortunately for him, the absence of broken glass within the room demonstrated that the window had been broken from inside. In Jonestown, he claimed that enemies had fired at him, and produced bullets in evidence. In fact, his adopted son Jimmy had fired the shots, and was seen to do so by Vincent Lopez, whose punishment by forced eating of a hot pepper was referred to earlier. Jones was always inclined to suspect that he was being persecuted by agents of the United States Government including the Internal Revenue and the CIA, no doubt because he was in reality guilty of financial misdemeanours, and also because he outspokenly condemned the administration as fascist and racist. However, as he got older, his suspicions took on more and more the colouring of paranoid delusions, until, in Jonestown, his tediously long broadcast harangues amounted to the ramblings of a psychotic. This mental deterioration was undoubtedly promoted by the large quantities of drugs, including both amphetamines and anti-depressants, which he took for a variety of ailments, both real and imagined. During the 1970s, Jones drove home his paranoid message with increasing force. He alleged that the San Francisco authorities were preparing concentration camps for ethnic minorities and, by the mid–1970s, he had accumulated at least two hundred guns. In Jonestown, he added to this armoury by smuggling more weapons in crates containing machinery. These were generally obtained from the San Francisco Gun Exchange (or 'Bible Exchange' as it was known in Jonestown).

Jones began to announce himself as God around 1974. Before this, he had generally claimed to be a messenger from God with a divine gift of healing: later, he said, 'I come as God socialist'. Drugs made him more inclined to claim divine status but how far he believed in his own divinity is an open question. According to the

New Yorker of 22 November 1993, his wife Marceline tried to persuade their son Stephan to talk his father into giving up drugs. Stephan replied: 'You're talking about going to God and telling him he's a drug addict?'

The inhabitants of Jonestown were well prepared in advance for their eventual death. Jones kept on telling them that he expected the settlement to be attacked by a variety of foes, and that if this happened, the only way out might be suicide. He announced that the community must exist together or die together rather than be split up. If death was to be the final solution, this would not be in vain, for it would vividly demonstrate to the world the evil nature of the U.S. Government. In spite of this, there is some doubt about how many people actually committed suicide and how many may have been murdered. Reports by survivors, and examination of the site of injection in the corpses suggest that more were murdered than was originally supposed. The sheer scale of the Jonestown disaster shocked the world; but tragic events of a similar kind have occurred since and more can certainly be expected.

Let us turn from Jonestown to Ranch Apocalypse. Vernon Howell, as Koresh was originally named, was born on August 17, 1959 to a fourteen-year-old girl. When her lover left her two years later, she placed the baby in the care of her mother and sister. In 1964, she married a former merchant seaman and reclaimed Vernon, telling him for the first time that she was his real mother. According to his own account, Vernon Howell did not get on with his stepfather, who frequently thrashed him. He did poorly at school, where he was put into a special class, and teased for being 'retarded'. He also claimed that a group of older boys had raped him. He was said to have been dyslexic rather than mentally handicapped; but this does not seem to have prevented him from reading the Bible, since his mother stated that he knew the whole of the New Testament by heart by the age of twelve. Later, this slow learner was to boast that he had more knowledge than all the great scholars could learn in a lifetime.

This is certainly an unfortunate background, but others have suffered worse childhoods without becoming psychotic or monsters of cruelty. By the time he dropped out of school at the age of fourteen,

Howell had attained success as an athlete and had overcome his early unpopularity. His reaction was to become arrogant and patronizing; attitudes which precluded his keeping many of the odd jobs which he attempted. Howell was always hypersensitive to rejection, as was Jim Jones. At the age of nineteen, a sixteen-year-old girl whom he had got pregnant refused to live with him on the grounds that he was unfit to bring up a child. This shattered his confidence, and he began to suffer from mood swings of pathological intensity, sometimes believing himself to be uniquely evil, sometimes thinking that he was especially favoured by God. After various abortive attempts to find consolation in religion, Howell joined the Seventh Day Adventist Church in Tyler, Texas, and was baptized in 1979. He became infatuated with the pastor's daughter, claiming that God had spoken to him in a vision and said that he would give the girl to him. Howell's behaviour became so outrageous that, in 1981, the pastor and his congregation expelled him.

Howell's reaction to these rejections is interesting, and follows the pattern of stress or illness succeeded by a new vision which is characteristic of most gurus. His initial periods of depression were succeeded by an ever mounting confidence that he had been specially selected by God; a conviction which may have been reinforced by the drug LSD, which he started to use in his late teens. Following his expulsion from the official Seventh Day Adventist Church, Howell joined a splinter group called the Branch Davidian Seventh Day Adventists. The story of how he became leader of this sect can be read in David Leppard's book, *Fire and Blood*, but need not detain us here. In 1988, Koresh managed to establish himself and his followers on a site originally called the New Mount Carmel Center, which occupied some seventy-seven acres ten miles east of Waco, Texas. Within four years, Howell, who had now changed his name to David Koresh, had established a regime closely resembling that instituted by Jim Jones in Guyana. With the aid of his associate, Marc Breault, whose home was in Hawaii, a number of rich businessmen were persuaded to finance the cult. The funds raised were used by Koresh for two main purposes: musical equipment to further his ambition of becoming a rock star, and weapons to protect his cult against enemies. By the time the cult was being investigated by the U.S. authorities, Koresh had spent around $200,000 on

13

weapons.[6] His annual income amounted to about $500,000. It was because a delivery man reported that pineapple hand grenades were being delivered to Koresh's commune that the train of events which culminated in its siege by the FBI and its ultimate destruction by fire was set in motion.

Koresh resembled Jim Jones in being a fluent speaker who could hold his listeners for hours at a time. Jones's vision was of a communist society in which private property was abolished and racial equality established. Koresh's vision was apocalyptic. As other apocalyptic prophets have done, Koresh laid hold upon the Book of Revelation and claimed that he alone could interpret it correctly. He especially emphasized his unique insight into the Seven Seals. According to David Leppard, Koresh said: 'If you don't know the Seven Seals, you really don't know Christ . . . The Seven Seals are the acid test for who knows God and who doesn't.'[7]

The Book of Revelation was probably written around 95–96 A.D. In it, Jesus is portrayed as a warrior who leads a host of angels to defeat the Satanic forces ranged against him. Following the final defeat of evil, a Kingdom is established in which selected human beings, rendered immortal, live for ever in perfect peace and harmony. The opening of the book or scroll, which is sealed with seven seals, heralds a series of terrible events which, as in other apocalyptic visions, are bound to precede the final establishment of peace and order. When the first seal is broken, a white horse appears ridden by a rider armed with a bow and given a crown, who goes forth to conquer. The breaking of the second seal heralds a red horse and rider who is given a great sword and the power to make men slaughter each other. Breaking the third seal releases a rider on a black horse who carries a pair of scales and who appears to be the herald of famine. When the fourth seal has been broken, a sickly pale horse appears whose rider is Death. He is given power over a quarter of the earth, with the right to kill by sword, famine, epidemics, or wild beasts. After the fifth seal has been broken, the souls of those who have been slaughtered for the faith complain; but they are reassured, provided with white robes and told to wait until the tally of those destined to be killed for Christ's sake is complete. The breaking of the sixth seal is followed by a violent earthquake. The sun turns black, the moon red, and the stars fall out of the sky.

Following the breaking of the seventh seal by the Lamb of God, silence reigns in Heaven for half-an-hour. Then comes the destruction of a third of mankind, followed by the final defeat of the powers of darkness.

Koresh seems to have convinced his followers that he himself had the power to break the seventh seal, thus precipitating the catastrophes described in The Book of Revelation. He taught that God would return to earth with fire and lightning and establish a new kingdom in Israel, with Koresh on the throne. He persuaded his followers that death was only a prelude to a better life to come, in which they would be among the army of élite immortals who were destined to slaughter all the wicked on earth, beginning with the Christian church.

Koresh's delusional system, like that of Jim Jones, took time to develop. At first, he alleged himself to be no more than a prophet, armed with special understanding of the Seven Seals. As his power increased, so did his claims for himself. When his defected disciple Marc Breault was asked whether Koresh believed himself to be the Son of God, Breault was emphatic that he did. When asked what control this gave Koresh over his followers, Breault replied: 'Absolute control. I know it's hard for you to understand this. But just imagine you believe someone is Jesus Christ. He can tell you anything. If you argue, you go to Hell. He's the Son of God. Who wants to fight against God?'[8] By the time that his Texan prairie retreat was undergoing its terminal siege in April 1993, Koresh was claiming that he was God, and signing his letters Yahweh Koresh.

Ranch Apocalypse, as Koresh now re-named the Mount Carmel property, was a squalid enclosure. There was hardly any heating and no running water or proper plumbing. Members of the cult had to excrete into chamber pots and bury the contents in the ground. Water was supplied from a container brought in by truck. As in Jonestown, cult members soon developed a variety of ailments, including Hepatitis B. Koresh considered that seeking medical help was a threat to his authority, and forbade visits to doctors. He constantly imposed a string of varied dietary injunctions of an irrational kind. During one month, bananas were the only fruit allowed. It was forbidden to eat oranges and grapes at the same meal. On some days only vegetables were allowed; on others, food was restricted to fruit and popcorn. There was no hot food, and buying food from outside without Koresh's direct permission was forbidden. Koresh used starvation as a punishment, and many members of the cult suffered from malnutrition, as members of Jones's cult had done in Guyana. And, as in the case of Jones, Koresh himself was exempt from all dietary restrictions. His ridiculous rules and prohibitions were merely an added proof of his almost absolute power; on a par with the senseless and meaningless tasks which other gurus require of their followers. Another arbitrary exercise of power was Koresh's practice of waking the entire compound at night, and compelling them to listen to his protracted expositions of the Bible, which sometimes went on for as long as fifteen hours.

The punishments instituted by Koresh were as savage as those employed by Jones. He taught that children as young as eight months old should receive corporal punishment for misbehaviour, and told their mothers that they would burn in hell if they refused to beat their children. Children were punished for the slightest misdemeanour by being beaten with a piece of wood known as a 'helper'. Each child had his own 'helper' with his name written on it. A special room was set aside for these beatings. Koresh beat his own three-year-old son Cyrus so severely that it sickened Marc Breault, and no doubt contributed to Breault's eventual disillusion. Several of the twenty-one children who were eventually released bore the marks of recent beatings. Another punishment was to immerse the offender in sewage and not allow him or her to bathe. Derek Lovelock, an English survivor of the terminal siege, nevertheless insisted that Koresh was 'a very caring compassionate man,' and denied the accusations of cruelty and sexual abuse, although he did admit that parents some-times beat their children.[9] He told William Shaw that the months he spent at the ranch were the happiest days of his life. '"We were one big family," he says. "We all believed in the one belief, and agreed on the same points. We were all one community."'[10]

Koresh was as sexually rapacious as Jim Jones, but his tastes were different. In 1983, Koresh married Rachel, the daughter of an official of the Branch Davidian Church. She was only fourteen years old, but no one objected. She bore him three children. In 1986, Koresh began sleeping with her younger sister, then twelve years old. When Koresh took command of Ranch Apocalypse, he split up families by ensuring that the men slept on one floor, the women on another. Severing family ties was one way of reinforcing allegiance to himself, and also made it easier for him to seduce the women he wanted. Koresh considered himself entitled to have sexual relations with any of the females in the compound, including girls of twelve and thirteen. One child who was too small for penetration was urged to use large tampons in order that her vagina might become able to accommodate him.[11]

Koresh, like Jones, deteriorated mentally. He took a variety of vitamins and herbal remedies to cure what he called impotence, but drugs cannot be blamed for the development of his delusions as they can in the case of Jones. He was less obviously a confidence trickster than Jones; but when Breault was asked whether Koresh really believed what he was teaching or was just a con man, Breault replied: 'I think a little of both. Vernon gets a craving. Then he finds the theology to justify that craving. When others buy into his doctrine, he starts believing it himself.'[12]

By 1986 he was teaching that he was entitled to a hundred and forty wives. When Ranch Apocalypse finally went up in flames, seventeen of the twenty-two children who perished had been fathered by Koresh, who claimed that only he was allowed to procreate, and that part of his mission was to fill the world with righteous children.

At the beginning of the FBI siege, Koresh allowed those children who were not fathered by him to be released. The psychiatrists who interviewed them repeatedly heard stories about dead babies. Some children alleged that the bodies of babies were stored in a freezer until they could be got rid of. It is possible, though unproven, that Koresh sacrificed the children of cult members because he himself was not their father. He certainly tried to persuade his followers that ritual sacrifices of children might be necessary. It is fair to add that reports about the condition of the children who were released varies. In his book *The Ashes of Waco*, Dick J. Reavis is chiefly concerned with attacking the clumsy way in which the Bureau of Alcohol, Tobacco and Firearms and the FBI handled the siege, which he considered entirely unjustified. He claims that there is evidence that the children within the compound were well cared for and quotes one psychiatrist who examined the released children as saying that there was no evidence of sexual abuse. When the FBI blasted holes in the compound buildings, they assumed that the mothers of small children would take the opportunity to escape with their offspring. None did so. The final holocaust was initiated by members of the cult, who used kerosene lamps to start the blaze. Not everyone who died was burned alive. Twenty-seven cult members, including Koresh himself, were shot.

Constructing or adopting a belief system in which one is either God's prophet or God himself inflates the ego to monstrous proportions. Koresh was more deeply concerned with religion, Jim Jones with racial equality and an egalitarian society. But both compensated for isolation and lack of love in childhood by becoming infatuated with power, and both ended up with delusions of their own divinity.

It seems almost incredible that either of these gurus could have retained the allegiance of their followers for so long. Koresh made some ineffective attempts to conceal the identity of the children whom he took to bed, but most of the outrageous sexual behaviour and the appalling cruelty of each guru were paraded rather than concealed. There were very few defectors from either camp. It appears that once a guru has convinced a follower of his Messianic status, his actual behaviour, as judged by ordinary human standards, becomes largely irrelevant. Belief in a guru, while it persists, entirely overrules rational judgement. Dedicated disciples are as impervious to reason as are infatuated lovers.

There is a well-known psychiatric phenomenon called *folie à deux*. If two people live together and one is mad, the other may become convinced by at least some of the delusions expressed by the psychotic partner. If the psychotic partner is removed to hospital, the other partner usually recovers his or her sanity. Shared delusions are mutually reinforcing, and membership of a sect led by a psychotic leader reassures both the leader and the disciple who has fallen under his spell of the truth of their beliefs. Both Jim Jones and David Koresh kept their followers under close surveillance and made it difficult for anyone to leave. Fortunately, this is exceptional. Contrary to popular belief, most of those who join 'New Religious Movements' are not subject to coercion, and many leave such movements without difficulty. But communities like Jonestown which are isolated from normal sources of information become more dependent on whatever information is given them by their leaders, and are less able to question what they are told. Research into so-called 'sensory deprivation' has shown that individuals who are cut off from most varieties of sensory input by being placed in sound-proof, light-proof rooms become more suggestible, and tend to be less critical of any information which is fed to them. The same is true of isolated communities. In addition, anyone within the community who dares to doubt the pronouncements of the guru is likely to be treated as a traitor by his fellows. Jones and Koresh, to all except their disciples, appear to have been evil madmen. They exhibited, in exaggerated form, with very few redeeming features, all the worst possible characteristics of gurus. Fortunately, the majority of gurus are not as bad as they were. We need to examine some other varieties.

II

GEORGEI IVANOVITCH GURDJIEFF

GEORGEI IVANOVITCH GURDJIEFF

GURDJIEFF CLAIMS OUR INTEREST because he, or his doctrines as propounded by his disciple Ouspensky, bewitched so many interesting and intelligent people, including the writer Katherine Mansfield, A. R. Orage, the distinguished socialist editor of *The New Age*, Margaret Anderson, the editor of the *Little Review*, and her friend and co-editor Jane Heap; the surgeon and sexologist Kenneth Walker; Olgivanna, the third wife of Frank Lloyd Wright; John Godolphin Bennett, later to become something of a guru himself. The psychiatrists James Young and Maurice Nicoll, and the psychoanalyst David Eder were also followers. T. S. Eliot, David Garnett and Herbert Read intermittently attended Ouspensky's meetings. Ouspensky, who first encountered Gurdjieff in 1915, became chiefly based in London and was therefore more accessible to interested English people than the guru himself.

The date of Gurdjieff's birth is uncertain. Some say 1866; others quote one óf his several passports, which showed December 28, 1877. James Moore,[1] Gurdjieff's latest biographer and the author of *Gurdjieff and Katherine Mansfield,* argues that the earlier date is the more probable. Gurdjieff was secretive about this as he was about so many features of his background. He died on October 29, 1949. His birthplace was Alexandropol (formerly Gumru) in Russian Armenia, in the land lying between the Black Sea on the West and the Caspian Sea on the East, south of the Caucasus mountains. His father was Greek, his mother Armenian. Armenian was spoken at home, but he also learned some Greek, some Turkish, and the local dialects. In his autobiographical memoir, *Meetings with Remarkable Men*, he claimed to know eighteen languages, but there is no evidence to support this. Throughout his life, he continued to speak both Russian and English incorrectly.

Gurdjieff was the eldest of six children; he had a brother and four

23

sisters. One of the sisters died young. In Gurdjieff's early childhood, the family moved to the near-by city of Kars, shortly after the defeat of the Turkish forces there in 1878 by the Grand Duke Michael Niklayevich, brother of the Russian Tsar. The boy Gurdjieff was accepted as a chorister at Kars military cathedral, and being obviously intelligent, attracted the notice of Father Dean Borsh, who helped to educate him. He developed a passion for learning, read widely in Greek, Armenian, and Russian, and began to harbour a wish to find some answer to the problem of 'the meaning of life'. He resembles other gurus in going through a period of doubt which was succeeded by the revelation which manifested itself in his new cosmogony and his teaching. Why his perplexity was so extreme as to propel him into a search for truth which lasted twenty years is not apparent.

Gurdjieff's esoteric knowledge and status as a guru were attributed to his discoveries during his travels in Central Asia, but we are entirely dependent upon his own inaccurate account. The period 1887–1911 remains unsubstantiated and mysterious. Gurdjieff claimed to have learned much from a three months' stay in 'the chief Sarmoung monastery', belonging to a brotherhood which he said taught him secret wisdom derived from traditions dating back to 2500 B.C., including physical techniques for self-transformation, and sacred dances. Gurdjieff was careful never to be specific about the exact location of these teachers of secret knowledge, although he later stated that he had a teacher from whom he was never separated, and with whom he constantly communicated, presumably tele-pathically. The Sarmoung monastery cannot be identified, and even disciples of Gurdjieff regard his account of it as an allegory rather than literal truth. His own autobiographical account, in *Meetings with Remarkable Men*, is contradictory and chronologically unreliable. What does emerge from that book is his resourcefulness and his capacity to survive, both physically and financially. He sold carpets and antiques; repaired sewing-machines; bought quantities of old-fashioned corsets and remodelled them to suit current taste; traded in oil and fish, and claimed that he cured drug addicts by hypnosis. His prowess as a healer was, he wrote, unprecedented (Gurdjieff never exhibited false modesty). When asked by Ouspensky about his studies and discoveries, he said that he travelled with a group of specialists in various subjects who eventually pooled their knowledge; but he did not vouchsafe their names or say where they were, nor did he answer direct questions about where he had been. 'About schools and where he had found the knowledge he undoubtedly possessed he spoke very little and always superficially.'[2] It is hardly surprising that there were rumours that he was a secret agent employed by the Russians.

Gurdjieff established himself as a guru in Moscow in 1912. His principal contention was that man does not know himself, and is therefore not what he should be. He considered that modern civilization had made it difficult to co-ordinate the physical, emotional, and intellectual aspects of personality, which he believed were controlled by three separate centres. He thought that the majority of people were 'asleep', and behaved like machines reacting blindly to external forces. His training was designed to awaken selected followers to a higher level of consciousness and a new perception of reality.

A modern man lives in sleep, in sleep he is born and in sleep he dies. About sleep, its significance and its role in life, we will speak later. But at present just think of one thing, what *knowledge* can a sleeping man have? And if you think about it and at the same time remember that *sleep* is the chief feature of our being, it will at once become clear to you that if a man really wants knowledge, he must first of all think about how to wake, that is, about how to change his *being*.[3]

By participating in what became known as 'The Work', the fortunate few might become more able to co-ordinate the three centres through self-observation. Instead of living in a dream in which a series of fleeting 'I's' succeeded one another, the awakened individual would cease living 'in quotation marks', achieve a new unity, and, by means of this, direct his own destiny, or become able to *do*, as Gurdjieff phrased it. 'To do means to act consciously and according to one's will.'[4] This change in consciousness, like everything else, has a material basis, which in this case manifests itself as a trace chemical compound in the brain.

The keystone of his teaching, of course, was that no progress – no human progress, that is – can be accomplished except on an individual basis. Group work is valuable only in the sense that it helps the individual to achieve individual self-perfection.[5]

J. G. Bennett, who died in 1974, first met Gurdjieff in 1920. In his book *Gurdjieff: Making a New World*, Bennett devoted three chapters to Gurdjieff's travels and search for esoteric wisdom. Both J. G. Bennett and James Moore have to admit that it is impossible to trace Gurdjieff's travels with any degree of accuracy. Although careful never to commit himself whole-heartedly, Bennett clearly believed in the literal truth of the tradition that, somewhere in Central Asia, there is a group of wise men or 'Masters of Wisdom' who watch over the destiny of mankind and intervene from time to time to alter the course of events by introducing new ideas and new modes of thinking. Bennett suggests that Gurdjieff made contact with such a group; an 'Inner Circle of Humanity', perhaps the Sarmoun brotherhood, whose members were highly developed spiritually and able to generate higher energies. Bennett wrote:

> The true significance of such a group must lie in its mission. The more that one becomes aware of the spiritual realities, the more convinced does one become that a very great action is now proceeding in the world. The task before us is to help mankind to make the difficult and dangerous transition to a new epoch. If we find evidence that Gurdjieff was concerned in this task and moreover that he opened the way for us to participate in it, we shall have gone a long way to connecting him with the 'Inner Circle'.[6]

We shall again encounter the idea that mankind is on the threshold of a new epoch when discussing the ideas of Jung.

Bennett was a long-term disciple of Ouspensky, and was therefore at one remove from the master himself. But he remained intermittently in touch with Gurdjieff, and saw him frequently during the last two years of his life. Bennett believed that Gurdjieff's ideas and teaching had transformed his own life, and himself ran groups along Gurdjieffian lines in London, sometimes with dire effects upon participants, as I remember from seeing one or two of them as psychiatric patients. Nevertheless, Bennett followed a path characteristic of those who constantly search for esoteric wisdom without ever quite finding what they want.

> Bennett . . . broke from the Gurdjieffian mainstream in 1955 to pursue eclectic affiliations (being *inter alia* 'opened' into *Subud* by Hosein Rofé, initiated by the Maharishi Mahesh Yogi, received into the Roman Catholic Church, and introduced to the 'Invisible Hierarchy' by Idries Shah).[7]

The Russian revolution of 1917 caused Gurdjieff to move to Tiflis in Georgia and then to Constantinople and on to Berlin. His exhausting and sometimes dangerous journeys are chronicled by his biographer, James Moore. His close associates Thomas and Olga de Hartmann joined him in one of his stopping places; Essentuki in the Caucasus. This was in August 1917, not long after Kerensky had been announced as Prime Minister of the coalition government which followed the abdication of the Tsar. Gurdjieff then suddenly announced that he was going to Tuapse, on the Black Sea. The dutiful de Hartmanns followed. Their account of an exhausting nocturnal walk forced on them by Gurdjieff in spite of the fact that they were unsuitably clad and also dead tired is a striking example of the autocratic and unreasonable demands which Gurdjieff made on his followers which they nevertheless slavishly obeyed. Olga de Hartmann's feet were so swollen and bleeding that she could not put on her shoes and had to walk barefoot. Thomas de Hartmann had missed a night's sleep because he had been ordered to stay on guard. Their limbs ached and they were both exhausted; but they went on nevertheless.

> Mr. Gurdjieff demanded from us a very great effort, especially difficult because we did not know when it would end. We suffered and would have been only too happy to rest; but there was no protest in us, because the one thing we really wished to do was to follow Mr. Gurdjieff. Beside that, everything else seemed unimportant.[8]

It was a recurrent pattern of behaviour. The de Hartmanns claim that these demands were made upon them as a way of teaching them to overcome emotional and physical difficulties. Gurdjieff certainly pushed people to the limit of their physical capacities; and some discovered that they had more powers of endurance than they had ever suspected.

When short of money, he survived by dealing in caviar and carpets. He had hoped to settle in England, but the Home Office were suspicious of him and would not permit him to stay unless he did so as a private individual, which would have meant abandoning his nucleus of followers. Eventually, the generosity of Lady Rothermere, the estranged wife of the newspaper magnate, together with funds from other wealthy supporters, made it possible for him to set up his Institute for the Harmonious Development of Man at the Château du Prieuré, a large estate near Fontainebleau, in France.

'The Work' was carried out in groups and included special exercises and dances, exhausting physical work, training in memory and self-observation, together with lectures given by Gurdjieff at irregular intervals. Some of those who participated in the so-called 'Sacred Dances' found them more valuable than Yoga or any other training affecting physical awareness. Complete concentration on whatever was being carried out at the time was an essential part of Gurdjieff's message and of his own behaviour. Insistence on living intensely in the present moment and discarding the concern with past or future which interferes with fully experiencing the here-and-now, is not confined to Gurdjieff's teaching. Zen also treats the past and future as fleeting illusions. It is only the present which is eternally real.[9]

Gurdjieff was a dictator. He had the capacity so completely to humiliate his disciples that grown men would burst into tears. He might then show the victim special favour. He demanded unquestioning obedience to his arbitrary commands. For example, he once suddenly announced that none of his followers might speak to each other within the Institute. All communication must be by means of the special physical movements he had taught them. Gurdjieff sometimes imposed fasting for periods up to a week without any lessening of the work load. His authority was such that his followers convinced themselves that these orders were for their own good. Those less infatuated are likely to think that, like other gurus, Gurdjieff enjoyed the exercise of power for its own sake. There were also dinners at which large quantities of alcohol were drunk, and large sums of money extracted from the diners.

Gurdjieff also developed an elaborate cosmology. His picture of the universe and man's place in it is complex, and unsupported by any objective evidence. It is deliberately obscure and often incoherent. Yet, because Gurdjieff was a powerful guru whose followers included some sophisticated, intelligent people, attempts have been made by his followers to make sense out of what appears to the sceptical reader to be a psychotic delusional system. The task is rendered more difficult by the numerous ludicrous neologisms which Gurdjieff introduced. It is appropriate to remind the reader that chronic schizophrenics often invent words which carry a special meaning for them but which others find hard to understand. Eugen Bleuler, the famous director of the Burghölzli mental hospital in Zurich and the originator of the term 'schizophrenia', quotes a patient who wrote:

At Apell plain church-state, the people have customs and habits partly taken from glos-faith because the father wanted to enter new f. situation, since they believed the father had a Babeli comediation only with music. Therefore they went to the high Osetion and on the cabbage earth and all sorts of malice, and against everything good. On their inverted Osetion valley will come and within thus is the father righteousness.[10]

Another patient referred to being tormented by 'elbow-people'. As Bleuler notes, wording is preferably bombastic. 'The patients utter trivialities using highly affected expressions as if they were of the greatest interest to humanity.'[11] I am not suggesting that Gurdjieff was schizophrenic, but his use of language resembled that employed by some psychotics.

For example, Gurdjieff is said to have believed in God, to whom he referred as 'Our Almighty Omni-Loving Common Father Uni-Being Creator Endlessness'.[12] This description may fairly be described as bombastic. In the beginning was the 'Most Most Holy Sun Absolute' in space which was also endless, but which was charged with a primordial cosmic substance *Etherokilno*. 'Because this nebulous *Etherokilno* was in static equilibrium, the super-sun existed and was maintained by our Common Father, quite independently of outside stimulus, through the internal action of his laws and under the dispensation termed *Autoegocrat* (I keep everything under my control).'[13]

However, Time, that villain who attacks us all, appeared in the shape of the merciless *Heropass*, which so threatened to diminish the volume of Sun Absolute that steps had to be taken to forestall this action. Thereupon Common Father issued from himself a creative Word-God named *Theomertmalogos* which interacted with *Etherokilno* to produce our universe *Megalocosmos*. This creation is maintained by a principle or law named *Trogoautoegocrat* – by eating myself, I am maintained: 'In the cosmic sense, God feeds on the Creation and the creation feeds on God.'[14] So God and his creation become separate entities, which are only distantly related to each other, and creation is maintained by new laws; *Triamazikamno*, the law of Three, and *Heptaparparashinokh* or *Eftalogodiksis*, the law of Seven.

The law of Three is relatively straightforward. 'The higher blends with the lower in order to actualise the middle.' For example, sperm and ovum merge to create the embryo. This formula can be applied to many situations in which opposites require a third – Moore gives as an example a judge resolving a case between plaintiff and defendant.

The law of Seven is more complex, and, in my view, incoherent. Gurdjieff tried to relate cosmology with the musical scale, believing that every completing process has seven discrete phases corresponding to an ascending or descending series of notes, including the two semitonal intervals, which constitute necessary irregularities. Gurdjieff represented the universe in a diagram called the *Ray of Creation* which begins with the Absolute and ends with the moon.

Gurdjieff taught that a collision between a comet named *Kondoor* and the earth gave rise to two orbiting bodies, *Loondeiperzo* (later known as the moon) and *Anulios*. After the shock 'a whole commission consisting of Angels and Archangels, specialists in the work of World-creation and World-maintenance, under the direction of the Most Great Archangel Sakaki, was immediately sent from the Most Holy Sun Absolute to that solar system "Ors".'[15] Gurdjieff's beliefs about the moon were even more eccentric. He claimed that the moon was still an unborn planet which was gradually becoming warmer and more like earth, just as the earth was becoming warmer and more like the sun. *Anulios* became forgotten, but the moon required energy to assist its evolution. *Sakaki* therefore arranged that the planet earth should send to the moon the 'sacred vibration *askokin*'. *Askokin* was liberated when organic life on earth dies. According to Ouspensky's report in *In Search of the Miraculous*, Gurdjieff said:

> The process of the growth and the warming of the moon is connected with life and death on the earth. Everything living sets free at its death a certain amount of the energy that has 'animated' it; this energy, or the 'souls' of everything living – plants, animals, people – is attracted to the moon as though by a huge electromagnet, and brings to it the warmth and the life upon which its growth depends, that is, the growth of the ray of creation. In the economy of the universe nothing is lost, and a certain energy having finished its work on one plane goes to another.[16]

He then went on to say that the moon influences everything that happens on earth.

> Man, like every other living being, cannot, in the ordinary conditions of life, tear himself free from the moon. All his movements and consequently all his actions are controlled by the moon. If he kills another man, the moon does it; if he sacrifices himself for others, the moon does that also. All evil deeds, all crimes, all self-sacrificing actions, all heroic exploits, as well as all the actions of ordinary life, are controlled by the moon.[17]

And J. G. Bennett wrote:

> At a certain point in the history of the earth it was perceived by the Higher Powers that a very undesirable and dangerous situation was developing on the planet earth which could endanger the equilibrium of the entire solar system and, in particular, the evolution of the Moon.[18]

If men realized that, because they were controlled by the moon, their personal efforts were unavailing, might they not be tempted to mass suicide, and so deprive the moon of the *askokin* needed for its development? To guard against this possibility, the Higher Powers implanted an organ at the base of man's spine delightfully named by Gurdjieff 'the organ *Kundabuffer*'.* This had the effect of ensuring that man would base his values solely on satisfying his own desires and the pursuit of happiness by making him perceive reality as topsy-turvy. So man would serve the moon blindly, unaware that, by embarking on the path of self-development, he could free himself from the moon altogether. Once the moon crisis had passed, the organ *Kundabuffer* was removed; but the majority of mankind still behave blindly, selfishly, and without insight as if the organ was still there. This is actually necessary if the purposes of nature are to be fulfilled. According to Ouspensky, Gurdjieff said that the evolution of humanity as a whole might be injurious.

> For instance, the evolution of humanity beyond a certain point, or, to speak more correctly, above a certain percentage, would be fatal for the *moon*. The moon at present *feeds* on organic life, on humanity.
>
> Humanity is part of organic life; this means that humanity is *food* for the moon. If all men were to become too intelligent they would not want to be eaten by the moon.[19]

The majority of human beings provide *askokin* for the moon after death, and are then condemned to obliteration. However, some few who follow the path of self-development and self-realization prescribed by Gurdjieff create *askokin* during life. Such people may finally develop a soul which can survive and may even reach Objective Reason and attain a form of immortality by being reunited with the Most Most Holy Sun Absolute.

How can anyone ever have taken this kind of thing seriously? Some have referred to Gurdjieff's teachings as myths, and Bhagwan Shree Rajneesh claimed that Gurdjieff was joking about the moon, but J. G. Bennett wrote that Gurdjieff certainly intended his account

---

* Many of Gurdjieff's neologisms have fairly obvious derivations. Since the organ *Kundabuffer* is supposed to have been inserted at the base of the spine, it appears probable that the name is derived from Kundalini yoga, in which a serpent is pictured as coiled in a similar position.

of the historical appearance and disappearance of the organ *Kunda-buffer* to be taken literally.[20] He also quotes the author Denis Saurat, then Director of the French Institute in London, as believing that Gurdjieff's teaching 'could not be of terrestrial origin. Either Gurdjieff had revelations vouchsafed only to prophets or he had access to a school on a supernatural level.'[21] Although writers about Gurdjieff tend to distance themselves from his most extravagant propositions, Philip Mairet, an intelligent literary figure who was editor of the *New English Weekly*, and who was also well acquainted with the works of Freud, Jung, and Adler, is reported as saying: 'No system of gnostic soteriological philosophy that has been published to the modern world is comparable to it in power and intellectual articulation.'[22] Having read Ouspensky's exposition of Gurdjieff's teaching in his book *In Search of the Miraculous*, and having attempted to read Gurdjieff's own book *All and Everything*, I can only wonder at Mairet's opinion. Perhaps I have extracted enough to give the reader some idea of Gurdjieff's picture of the cosmos, and to demonstrate that Gurdjieff's own writings are both voluminous and obscure. Even his devotees say that *All and Everything* has to be read several times if its meaning is to be grasped; and some claim that Gurdjieff's obscurity was deliberate; a device adopted to ensure that the disciple would have to make a considerable effort at understanding on his own account rather than be spoon-fed with clear statements and doctrines.

At first sight, it is difficult to believe that Gurdjieff's elaborate cosmology was anything other than a planned, comical confidence trick designed to demonstrate how far the gullibility of his followers could be tested. His own account of how he survived his early wanderings reveals how expert he was at deception. Gurdjieff wrote that he coloured sparrows with aniline dyes and sold them as 'American canaries' in Samarkand. He tells us that he had to leave quickly in case rain washed the sparrows clean. When people brought him sewing machines and other mechanical objects for repair, he was often able to see that the mere shift of a lever would cure the problem. However, he was careful to pretend that such repairs were time-consuming and difficult, and charged accordingly. He also wrote that he found out in advance which villages and towns the new railway would pass through, and then informed the local authorities that he had the power to arrange the course of the railway. He boasted that he obtained large sums for his pretended services, and said that he had no pangs of conscience about doing so.[23]

We know from J. G. Bennett that, when he and his followers were in danger from the conflict between the Cossacks and the Bolsheviks, Gurdjieff managed to get transport from the Provincial Government by spreading a rumour that he knew of enormously rich deposits of gold and platinum in the Caucasus mountains which would fill the Government's coffers. Bennett wrote:

> In all this, he was also demonstrating to his pupils the power of suggestion and the ease with which people could be made to 'believe any old tale'.[24]

Fritz Peters recounts an elaborate hoax in which Gurdjieff diluted a bottle of *vin ordinaire* with water, and then covered it with sand and cobwebs. Two distinguished women visitors were tricked into believing that Gurdjieff was serving them with wine of a rare vintage, and dutifully pronounced it the most delicious which they had ever tasted.[25]

Fritz Peters recalled an occasion on which a rich English lady approached Gurdjieff as he was sitting at a café table and offered him a cheque for £1,000 if he would tell her 'the secret of life'. Gurdjieff promptly summoned a well-known prostitute from her beat in front of the café, gave her a drink, and proceeded to tell her that he was a being from another planet called Karatas. He complained that it was very expensive to have the food he needed flown in from this planet, but urged the prostitute to taste some which he gave her. When asked what she made of it, she replied that he had given her cherries, and went on her way with the money Gurdjieff pressed upon her, obviously believing that he was mad. Gurdjieff turned to the English lady and said: 'That is the secret of life.' She appeared to be disgusted, called him a charlatan, and went off. However, she reappeared later on the same day, gave Gurdjieff the cheque for £1,000, and became a devoted follower.[26]

He became skilled at extracting money from Americans to support his enterprises at the Château du Prieuré, and referred to this activity as 'shearing sheep'. For example, an American woman travelled from the United States to the Prieuré to seek Gurdjieff's advice about her chain smoking, which she said was a phallic activity connected with her marital sexual difficulties. After a pause for thought Gurdjieff suggested that she should change her brand of cigarette to *Gauloises Bleus*, and charged her a large fee for this advice, which she gladly and gratefully paid. There is no doubt that Gurdjieff could be a convincing confidence trickster when he so wished and that he did not hesitate to mislead the gullible when it suited him. He was always a wonderful story teller who held his audiences entranced.

He told Peters, 'I not make money like others make money, and when I have too much money I spend. But I never need money for self, and I not *make* or earn money, I *ask* for money and people always give and for this I give opportunity study my teaching.'[27] However, he contradicted himself a moment later by saying that he owned a business making false eyelashes and another business selling rugs. When he went to New York in 1933, he demanded coaching in the use of four-letter words in English from Fritz Peters before giving a dinner for some fifteen New Yorkers. When the diners had drunk a certain amount, Gurdjieff began to tell them that it was a pity that most people – especially Americans – were motivated only by genital urges. He picked out a particularly elegant woman and told her in crude terms that she took so much trouble with her appearance because she wanted to fuck. The guests were soon behaving in an uninhibited fashion and becoming physically entangled with each other. Gurdjieff then announced that he had proved his point that Americans were decadent and demanded that he be paid for his lesson. According to Peters, he collected several thousand dollars.

Yet confidence trickery cannot be the whole explanation of Gurdjieff's teaching. If Gurdjieff could support himself so easily by deception, why should he bother to invent a cosmogony? Gurdjieff found writing a burden. He was much more impressive as a lecturer than he was as a writer. *All and Everything* is enormously long, and, although it was dictated to Olga de Hartmann rather than written, it must have demanded considerable dedication to complete. Gurdjieff began his dictation on 16 December 1924. He completed the dictation of *Beelzebub's Tales to his Grandson* (the first part of *All and Everything*) in November 1927. Could anyone devote so much time and energy to creating something in which he did not believe himself, with the deliberate intention to deceive? We hover on the borderline between confidence trickery and psychosis. Gurdjieff's propositions about the universe were totally at variance with the discoveries of astronomers and other scientists, and can only be compared with science fiction, but I think he believed in them, just as paranoid psychotics believe in their delusional systems.

Gurdjieff's arrogance and disregard of established experts were extraordinary. When he visited the caves of Lascaux, he told J. G. Bennett that he did not agree with the Abbé Breuil's dating of the rock paintings at thirty thousand years ago because he had concluded that the paintings were the work of a brotherhood that existed after the loss of Atlantis some seven or eight thousand years ago. He also told Bennett that he intended that his Institute would become 'a centre of training and research not only into the powers of man himself, but into the secrets of the solar system. He said he had invented a special means for increasing the visibility of the planets and the sun and also for releasing energies that would influence the whole world situation.'[28]

Gurdjieff's complete disregard for science and for the views of generally accepted experts is narcissistic in the extreme. But he did, at times, show considerable interest in other people, and compassion for those who were suffering. He sometimes exhibited a capacity for intense concentration upon individuals, which was certainly one component of his undoubted charisma. Fritz Peters, whose parents were divorced, was legally adopted by his mother's sister, Margaret Anderson and her friend Jane Heap, who were mentioned earlier as adherents of Gurdjieff. Peters, who was brought to Le Prieuré when he was a boy of eleven and stayed there until he was fifteen, described Gurdjieff's behaviour to himself.

> Whenever I saw him, whenever he gave me an order, he was fully aware of me, completely concentrated on whatever words he said to me; his attention never wandered when I spoke to him. He always knew exactly what I was doing, what I had done. I think we must all have felt, certainly I did, when he was with any one of us, that we received his total attention. I can think of nothing more complimentary in human relations.[29]

This intense concentration, as we have seen, was an important part of Gurdjieff's teaching. It entered in to everything he did. His ability to mobilize and direct attention may have accounted for his extraordinary effect on other people.

> When you do a thing, do it with the whole self. *One thing at a time*. Now I sit here and eat. For me nothing exists in the world except this food, this table. I eat with the whole attention. So *you* must do – in everything ... To be able to do *one* thing at a time ... this is the property of Man, not man in quotation marks.[30]

In movement, he gave the impression of complete co-ordination and integrated power. 'His gait and his gestures were never hurried, but flowed in unison with the rhythm of his breathing like those of a peasant or a mountaineer.'[31] Peters writes that Gurdjieff's presence and physical magnetism were 'undeniable and generally overwhelming'. When, in the late summer of 1945, long after he had left the Prieuré, Peters suffered from severe depression with insomnia, anorexia, and loss of weight, he sought Gurdjieff in Paris. Gurdjieff realized that he was ill, forbade him to talk and at once offered him a bedroom for as long as he needed it. He made Peters drink strong, hot coffee, and concentrated upon him intensely. It seemed to Peters that a violent electric blue light emanated from Gurdjieff and entered himself. Whatever the reason, Peters promptly recovered from his depression.

However, not everything about Gurdjieff was so impressive. His personal habits could be disgusting. One of the jobs that Peters was given when he was still resident at the Prieuré, was to clean Gurdjieff's rooms.

> What he could do to his dressing room and bathroom is something that cannot be described without invading his privacy; I will only say that, physically, Mr. Gurdjieff, at least so I gathered, lived like an animal ... There were times when I would have to use a ladder to clean the walls.[32]

Gurdjieff generalized from his own experience in that he set himself up as a teacher who could train others to attain the wisdom and autonomy which he believed himself to possess. But such teaching could only be assimilated by the chosen few. As we saw earlier, Gurdjieff did not believe that mankind as a whole was capable of development, or that it was desirable that any attempt should be made in this direction, lest the development of the moon might suffer. Gurdjieff, like many other gurus, was unashamedly élitist and authoritarian.

Gurdjieff's sexual behaviour was unscrupulous, in that he coupled with any female disciple whom he found attractive, and not infrequently made her pregnant. When Fritz Peters went to the Château du Prieuré at the age of eleven, there were about ten other children there, some of whom were undoubtedly fathered by Gurdjieff.

Like other gurus whom we have encountered, Gurdjieff enjoyed the exercise of power. We saw earlier what physical demands he made on the de Hartmanns. He was not directly cruel, but the regime he imposed upon his disciples was rigorous to the point of physical exhaustion.

> The daily routine was exacting in the extreme. We woke up at five or six in the morning and worked for two hours before breakfast. Afterwards there was more work: building, felling trees, sawing timber, caring for the animals of almost every domestic species, cooking, cleaning, and every kind of domestic duty. After a quick light lunch and a period of rest, one or two hours were devoted to 'exercises' and 'rhythms' accompanied by music usually played by Thomas de Hartmann on the piano. Sometimes there would be fasts lasting one, two, three or even up to seven days during which all the work continued as usual. In the evening, there would be classes in rhythms and ritual dances which might go on for three, four or five hours until everyone was totally exhausted.[33]

It is not surprising that one disciple who was fixing trusses twenty-five feet above the ground fell asleep whilst precariously balanced on a narrow beam and had to be rescued by Gurdjieff.

Bennett does not point out that, whether or not this regime assisted spiritual development, it was certainly a convenient way of obtaining free labour to run the Prieuré. Moreover, Gurdjieff, as an experienced hypnotist, would have realized that physical exhaustion makes people more suggestible, although one of his avowed aims was to discover some means of 'destroying in people the predilection for suggestibility'.[34] He once ordered Orage to dig a ditch to drain water from the kitchen garden. Orage worked extremely hard for several days. He was then told to make the edges of the ditch quite equal, and did so after more labour. Immediately after he had finished, Gurdjieff ordered him to fill in the ditch because it was no longer needed.

One of Gurdjieff's disciples was Olgivanna Ivanovna Lazovich, who became the third wife of the American architect, Frank Lloyd Wright. She first encountered Gurdjieff in Russia in 1917 at a time of crisis in her life. She was nineteen years old and was just about to have a child. Her first marriage was failing, her father was ill, her mother far distant. When Gurdjieff moved to the Prieuré, she joined him, became one of his best dancers, and an assistant instructor in The Work. In 1924, Gurdjieff suggested that she join her brother in America for no obvious reason. Shortly after her arrival, she encountered Frank Lloyd Wright at a ballet performance in Chicago and fell in love with him. Gurdjieff visited the Wrights on more than one occasion. Finding that Wright was seriously worried about his digestion, Gurdjieff invited them both out to dinner and served a series of extremely hot and indigestible dishes followed by the inevitable draughts of Armagnac. Wright felt terrible, but woke the next morning to find that his fears about his digestion had disappeared.[35] On another occasion,

Wright grandly remarked that perhaps he should send some of his pupils to Gurdjieff in Paris. 'Then they can come back to me and I'll finish them off.'

'*You* finish! You are idiot,' said Gurdjieff angrily. '*You* finish! No. *You* begin. I finish.' It was clear that Wright had met his match.[36]

Wright had many guru-like characteristics himself, so that it is not surprising to learn that these two autocrats found themselves in competition. Even so, Gurdjieff won Wright over. Shortly after

Gurdjieff's death, when Wright was receiving a medal in New York, he interrupted proceedings to announce: 'The greatest man in the world has recently died. His name was Gurdjieff.'[37]

Olgivanna appears to have acquired or developed a number of Gurdjieff's less engaging traits. Draftsmen, apprentices and their wives were supposed to sit at Olgivanna's feet whilst she gave them instructions and mercilessly criticized their failings. They even had to undergo the ordeal of listening to Wright reading from Gurdjieff's writings.[38] As she became older, she became more and more dictatorial, and, after Wright's death, became a 'despotic and jealous' widow with whom scholars and institutions preferred not to negotiate.[39]

Adherents of Gurdjieff's teaching recount with satisfaction that he did not bring pressure upon followers to stay with him, and in fact often dismissed them. This is interpreted as indicating his desire that they should become independent of him. In some cases, it may rather have been his perception of impending apostasy: gurus generally prefer to rid themselves of potential dissidents rather than be deserted. Ouspensky, Gurdjieff's most devoted disciple and interpreter, began to lose confidence in him as a person as early as 1917. This seems to have been precipitated by Gurdjieff's arbitrary dispersal of the group he had assembled around him in Essentuki. Ouspensky continued to believe in the authenticity of Gurdjieff's vision and teaching which he accepted as having been handed down from some ancient, esoteric source, but found the man himself more and more intolerable. Ouspensky formally broke off relations in January 1924, and forbade his own pupils to communicate with Gurdjieff or refer to him.[40]

A. R. Orage, the talented editor of the *New Age*, had abandoned literary life in London for life at the Prieuré, and later moved to New York, where he set up his own Gurdjieffian groups, and whence he sent large sums of money to Gurdjieff. During the seven years of his close involvement with Gurdjieff, he produced practically no work of his own. As John Carswell puts it: 'The most notable English editor of his time had become a mysterious exile owing obedience to an Armenian magus.'[41] Orage's devotion was tested to the limit by Gurdjieff's incessant demands for money, and by the abuse heaped upon him when he did not instantly obey. His allegiance was further undermined by his wife, Jessie Dwight, whom he married in 1927, and who had hated her visit to the Prieuré. Eventually, Gurdjieff, realizing Orage's disillusion, turned up in New York when Orage was temporarily absent, assembled Orage's group, denounced Orage and required each member to sign a written declaration that they would have nothing further to do with their instructor. Some did so; others refused. Orage, summoned back from England, demanded to see Gurdjieff, and, after remarking that he too repudiated the Orage created by Gurdjieff, signed the document denouncing his own teaching.

J. G. Bennett gives a list of close adherents whom Gurdjieff deliberately dismissed. Bennett himself left the Prieuré in 1923 and did not see Gurdjieff again until 1948, the year before he died. Even Fritz Peters, who had been greatly influenced by Gurdjieff in childhood, and who, as we have seen, turned to Gurdjieff when he was seriously depressed as an adult, wrote: 'He began to seem to me in a very excellent phrase "a real, genuine phony." '[42]

By the beginning of 1932, it became clear that the Château du Prieuré was no longer financially viable. Gurdjieff habitually overreached himself financially and American support fell away after the crash of 1929. The Institute for the Harmonious Development of Man finally closed in May. But Gurdjieff himself continued to flourish. He lived in Paris throughout the German occupation of the city during the Second World War. Characteristically, he obtained credit from various food shops by persuading them that an American pupil had given him an oil well in Texas which would ensure that their bills would be settled as soon as the war was over.

Gurdjieff's cosmogony can only be described as fantastic. Reviewing his picture of the universe, it is hard to understand that any intelligent, educated person could believe in it. Yet disciples struggled to read *All and Everything* as if its incoherence must contain esoteric wisdom; as if it was their fault if they did not understand it rather than the author's inability to construct a credible picture of man and the universe or to write intelligibly. When Gurdjieff had a car accident in July 1924 which nearly killed him, he said that this accident was 'the manifestation of a power hostile to his aim, a power with which he could not contend'.[43] This suggests an underlying paranoid belief system. In reality, he was so dangerous a driver that his followers avoided being driven by him whenever possible. Perhaps he was referring to the adverse planetary influences which, he claimed, had caused the First World War. Gurdjieff had the bizarre notion that, from time to time, planets might approach each other too closely. The resulting tension would cause human beings to slaughter each other without their realizing that they were merely pawns in a cosmic game.

Although Gurdjieff's picture of the universe can confidently be dismissed as rubbish, it is possible to salvage a few valuable ideas from what he taught. Gurdjieff believed that man had obligations as well as rights. He did not think that the world was made for man, or that progress consisted in further technological domination of the environment. He considered that man had lost touch with the meaning of his existence, which was to fulfil a cosmic purpose rather than merely to satisfy his desires. Now that we realize that we are destroying the earth we live on, Gurdjieff's view that man should serve the world rather than exploit it seems apposite. His notion that most people are 'asleep' and are driven by their instincts to behave automatically rather than with conscious intention is probably true of the majority. Some of the charisma which Gurdjieff undoubtedly manifested sprang from his own capacity to live intensely in the moment. One pupil recalled his saying:

> You live in the past. The past is dead. Act in the present. If you live as if you have always lived, the future will be like the past. Work on yourself, change something in yourself, then the future perhaps will be different.[44]

Some of those who practised Gurdjieff's techniques for awakening people and transforming them into beings who could direct their own destinies certainly claimed benefit, but Claire Tomalin, in her biography of Katherine Mansfield, is almost certainly right in her summing up.

> Whether Gurdjieff's methods for righting the internal balance of his disciples had much, or any, merit is another matter. Since the whole thing depended on his personality, and made no scientific claims (as psychoanalysis did) or cosmological and moral claims

(as most brands of Christianity did), it remained an amateur, ram-
shackle affair, and although Gurdjieff aroused passionate hate as
well as love, his system seems to have done little lasting damage,
and obviously allowed some people to change direction in a way
that seemed helpful to them.[45]

As we have seen, Gurdjieff was, by his own admission, an accomplished confidence trickster who had no hesitation in deceiving other
people and extracting money from them when he needed to do so.
Confidence tricksters are successful at deception because they are
more than halfway to believing in their own fictions. Was Gurdjieff
anything more than this? I suggested earlier that he could not have
constructed his elaborate cosmogony merely in order to deceive.
Gurdjieff's picture of the universe, whether learned from esoteric
sources or constructed by himself, provided him with his own myth,
his own answer to the problem of the meaning of life for which he
had sought a solution during his twenty years of travel. This myth
was akin to a religious revelation. It gave him the certainty of faith.
It was his own conviction that he had discovered *the answer* which
made him charismatic and persuasive. Even if some of his followers
could not accept or understand all his cosmic doctrines, they still
believed that he *knew*; a phenomenon which we shall encounter
when discussing other gurus.

III

BHAGWAN SHREE
RAJNEESH

BHAGWAN
SHREE
RAJNEESH

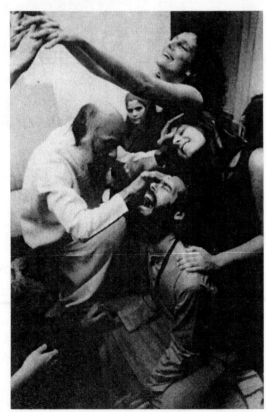

RAJNEESH IS BEST KNOWN TO the general public as the guru who owned ninety-three Rolls-Royces and who celebrated sex as a path to enlightenment. Any guru who promotes technology, capitalism, and free love is likely to win support, and Rajneesh was hugely successful in attracting followers, especially from the white middle class. Eileen Barker wrote that, in the early 1980s, there were between three and four thousand disciples in the UK alone in 'what was possibly the most fashionable and fastest-growing alternative spiritual/religious movement in Britain.'[1] Rajneesh resembled other gurus in many particulars which we shall explore, but differed from them in being so eclectic that what was personal in his teaching is hard to determine. He was certainly influenced by the writings of Gurdjieff, to whom he frequently referred, and whom he partly resembled. Both gurus affirmed that it was their mission to rouse people from sleep, and both relied more upon personal charisma than upon any coherent body of doctrine.

Rajneesh, like Gurdjieff, was personally extremely impressive. Many of those who visited him for the first time felt that their most intimate feelings were instantly understood; that they were accepted and unequivocally welcomed rather than judged. He seemed to radiate energy and to awaken hidden possibilities in those who came into contact with him. Professor Ralph Rowbottom wrote that he found in Rajneesh 'a teacher whose words made sense of all the basic issues of life, one whose presence touched me deeply.'[2] Hugh Milne, a Scottish osteopath who became his bodyguard, wrote of his first meeting: 'I had the overwhelming sensation that I had come home. He was my spiritual father, a man who understood everything, someone who would be able to convey sense and meaning into my life.'[3] In her introduction to Rajneesh's book *The Supreme Understanding*, Ma Yoga Anurag wrote: 'Only a Master to whom you can

47

entrust your very being – physical, mental and spiritual – is capable of taking you on such a journey. Listening to Bhagwan, I gradually came to realize that he knows, he has the power, that if I can only say, "Yes, I leave everything to you," everything will be taken care of.'⁴ The psychiatrist James S. Gordon, who has written the best book on Rajneesh, said that the phrase which his disciples repeatedly used of him was 'This man knew.'⁵

Yet Rajneesh, like so many other gurus, became corrupted by wealth and power and deteriorated both physically and mentally. He was finally imprisoned in, and then expelled from, the United States. After being refused entry by various countries, he eventually returned to India. He died in 1990. It is a sad story; for it appears from his discourses that, at the beginning of his career, he had much to offer.

Rajneesh was born on December 11, 1931 in the small town of Kuchwada in the state of Madhya Pradesh at the house of his maternal grandparents with whom he spent much of his childhood. They seem to have adored him, and it is alleged that he was so graceful and beautiful a child that his grandfather believed that he must have been a king in some previous existence. This is why he was called 'Raja' which later became 'Rajneesh'. When he was five years old, a younger sister died. He was distressed by her death, but by far the most traumatic event of his early childhood was the death of his grandfather in 1938, when he was seven. The grandfather's terminal illness, which followed a stroke, was prolonged and painful; and Rajneesh claimed that it had the effect of persuading him never to form any more close attachments for fear that a similar tragedy would follow. It is reported that after watching his grandfather die, Rajneesh refused to eat or leave his bed for three days. After this bereavement, he moved back to live with his parents in Gadarwara and went to school there.

As a boy, Rajneesh was isolated, self-absorbed, and obviously clever. It is typical of gurus to attract followers rather than make friends; and this characteristic manifested itself very early. He led other children into mischief and constantly challenged authority. He was also a sickly child who suffered from asthma and who came close to death on several occasions. He played with death, taking risks in order to come to terms with his fear of it. For example, he would dive into whirlpools in the river Shakkar and let himself be sucked down until, at the bottom of the whirl, he was thrown free. Like other intelligent isolates with poor health, he read enormously widely and continued to do so for many years. He became familiar with both the sacred scriptures of the East and with the major philosophers of the West. But his search for religious truth always ended in rebellion and mockery. He was as incapable of accepting any ideology as he was of obeying authority. He was turbulent, aggressive, and arrogant. A contemporary described him as being very bright, but also as being an habitual liar. There were also early doubts about his financial honesty. He toyed with socialism and atheism, and joined the youth branch of the Indian National Army. In 1951 he graduated from high school and went to Hitkarini College in Jabalpur. He was so argumentative and difficult that he was asked to leave. He was admitted to another college, but preferred to stay at home rather than attend classes.

He then appears to have experienced an extended period of mental illness in which he suffered from disabling headaches, anorexia, depersonalisation, and severe loss of confidence. On one occasion he felt as if the connection between his body and his spiritual being had disintegrated. He ran up to sixteen miles a day in order to try and feel himself again, and started to meditate. His parents, believing that he was mentally ill, took him to see a number of different doctors; but an Ayurvedic physician, in R. D. Laingian fashion, reassured them that he was passing through an important personal crisis from which he would emerge.

On March 21, 1953, when he was twenty-one years old, Rajneesh's illness terminated with what he called 'enlightenment'. This was the end-point of seven days during which he ceased to strive, seek, or struggle, but passively let go and waited. He entered an ecstatic state in which 'everything became luminous, alive and beautiful,' and he himself felt 'mad with blissfulness'. He sat under a Maulshree tree, as the Buddha, reputedly, had sat under the bodhi tree; but the ecstatic enlightenment which he experienced seems very different from the calm, composed, dispassionate state of mind in which the Buddha came to his conclusions about the human condition.

This series of events sounds like a psychotic episode. It appears

49

probable that Rajneesh suffered from a fairly severe depressive illness between the ages of nineteen and twenty-one which came to an end with a hypomanic state in the form of an ecstatic experience. Although this period of mental distress followed by revelatory recovery took place rather earlier in Rajneesh's life than it did with other gurus, it still conforms to the characteristic pattern. There are strong hints that he suffered from further periods of depression after he had become established as a guru. Twenty-one years later, in March 1974, he withdrew from all activities and went into complete silence for the next few weeks. In 1981, he also went through a period of some months in which he failed to respond to those caring for him, and apparently did not even read. Rumour also suggested that from time to time he drank heavily, and took valium, hashish, and other drugs including nitrous oxide. These could have been used to alleviate or ward off periods of depression which, naturally enough, would have been concealed by those close to him. I think it reasonable to conclude that, as in the cases of many other leaders, his personality was both narcissistic and manic-depressive, manifesting itself in actual illness from time to time.

His physical health remained poor throughout his life. He suffered from diabetes, asthma, and a variety of allergies; and was also treated for a herniated intervertebral disc which caused recurrent back pain.

However, it appears that his youthful ecstatic experience led to a permanent change in that he became more content to live in and for the moment. He obtained a B.A. in philosophy in 1955, and an M.A. from Saugar University in 1957. By 1960, he was an assistant professor teaching philosophy at the University of Jabalpur. At the same time, he began to travel round India giving controversial lectures which gained him a reputation as a debater and iconoclast, although many Indians were shocked by his arrogance and by his attacks on traditional values. He instituted his first 'meditation camp' in 1964. In 1966 he resigned from academic life in response to pressure from the university administration at Jabalpur. When the centenary of Gandhi's birth was celebrated throughout India in 1969, Rajneesh seized the opportunity to outrage conventional opinion by alleging that Gandhi's fasting was masochism, and his abstinence from sex a form of perversion. Later, he would pour scorn on Mother Teresa, whom he called a charlatan.

By the end of the decade, Rajneesh had settled in an apartment in Bombay with a few followers. It remained his centre of operations until 1974. He began to recruit more disciples; *sannyasins*, as they called themselves. To qualify, the potential disciple had to engage in meditation, wear orange or red clothes, wear a *mala*, a necklace of 108 wooden beads carrying a picture of Rajneesh, use a new name given to him or her by Rajneesh, discard the past, and accept Rajneesh's authority. By 1971, 419 people had become initiates.

Most gurus acknowledge a debt to previous teachers, living or dead; but Rajneesh, though clearly influenced by Gurdjieff, did not admit owing anything to anyone. He said that he had never had a master, although he claimed to have studied a great deal in past incarnations. His remarkable range of reading ensured that his teaching was a pot-pourri of all the great religious leaders of the past, including Lao Tzu, the Buddha, Jesus and Muhammad. He could quote – not always accurately – from every well-known western thinker from Plato to Freud. When Bernard Levin visited his ashram in 1980, he reported that Rajneesh talked for an hour and three-quarters without hesitation, repetition, pauses, or notes. His voice was 'low, smooth and exceptionally beautiful'.[6] He leavened the seriousness of his discourse with parables which were often funny. He also told sexually explicit and scatological stories of a rather childish kind.

Rajneesh wrote nothing himself; but devoted disciples recorded his discourses and commentaries and made books out of them. Assuming that the edited discourses are accurate, one can understand that Rajneesh must have been a riveting as well as a fluent speaker. Reading discourses given in 1974 and 1975, I began to understand that Rajneesh, in spite of his terminal decline and fall, did convey a vision which could bring new meaning to life for those who were in search of it. The main thrust of his teaching was what he called a 'religionless religiousness'; by which he meant a religious attitude to life without commitment to any particular creed or church. Jung shared the same outlook. However, Rajneesh regarded religion as a luxury available only to those who had fulfilled their material needs and who could therefore afford to think about the meaning of life. 'In a poor society religion cannot be meaningful because people have not yet failed':[7] that is, they have not yet discovered that getting a house or becoming rich or whatever material advantage they have set their hearts on will not bring happiness. Rajneesh always hated and despised poverty, and unashamedly claimed to be the rich man's guru. On the other hand, in one of his discourses on the sayings of Jesus, he said: 'The more things accumulate the more life is wasted because they have to be purchased at the cost of life.'[8] He signally failed to follow his own teaching in this respect.

He divided people into three types: those who collect things and were outward-orientated; those who collect knowledge and who are less outward-orientated; those who cultivate awareness and who are inner-orientated. Their goal is to become more and more conscious. He announced that he wanted those aspects of human beings personified by Gautama the Buddha and Zorba the Greek to come closer to one another in his followers. The most basic requirement was to cast off the shackles of the past, live in the moment, and obey the most fundamental commandment; to love oneself. 'You are not sent as beggars into the world, you are sent as emperors.'[9]

Drawing on Tantric doctrines which give spiritual significance to sex, Rajneesh affirmed that sex was a way to enlightenment. All inhibitions and possessiveness must be discarded and sexual experimentation and free love with different partners should be encouraged. The sexual act should be prolonged as long as possible in order to reach what he called 'valley orgasm' as opposed to 'peak orgasm'. Orgasm of the whole body was incompatible with thinking, and so was one valuable experience in which the subject just existed, without thought for the morrow. This is one example of intense living in the here-and-now to which reference was made in the chapter on Gurdjieff. Sexuality could be a path to the divine, and religions which exalted celibacy and tried to suppress sexuality were, in his view, merely producing frustration and neurosis. Rajneesh once said that, of all the problems which people brought to him, 99% were sexual. But his teaching only applied to heterosexual encounters, since he regarded homosexuality as a disease. This seems a curiously old-fashioned attitude in one who was so intolerant of sexual restrictions. It was also possible to transcend sexuality by looking for the opposite within – for a man, the inner woman – but this could be done only under the guidance of a Master.[10] This closely resembles Jung's notion of the *anima*.

Rajneesh had no hesitation in asserting his own identity as a Master, although in one passage he denies being a guru. I think he meant by this that he was aware that he didn't preach a coherent body of doctrine.

> I have only devices – only psychological answers. And the answer does not depend on me; it depends on you. Because of you, I have to give a particular answer.
>
> That is why I cannot be a guru – never! Buddha can become one, but I never can. Because you are so inconsistent, every individual is so different, how can I become consistent? I cannot. And I cannot create a sect because for this consistency is very needed . . .
>
> So I am less a guru and more like a psychiatrist (*plus* something).[11]

Some of his remarks echo those attributed to Jesus. 'While I am here, a little while more, don't miss the opportunity.'[12] Repeatedly, he advises his hearers to be empty, loose, and natural. They must distinguish between action and activity. Action is goal-orientated and fulfils needs. It is comparable with Gurdjieff's ability to *do*. Activity is a restless inability to *be* without engaging in futile pursuits like re-reading the same newspaper. Morality and religion must be separated, for morality is concerned with denial and fighting against impulses, whereas religion is concerned with increasing consciousness and awaking the light within. A man possessed with anger is no longer aware. Full consciousness and anger are incompatible. People should be able to detach themselves from their thoughts through increased consciousness, just as they can distance themselves from their emotions. It is possible to become a witness to one's own thoughts if the right degree of consciousness is attained. A notice at the entrance of the hall in which he spoke read: 'Shoes and minds to be left here.' Conventional ways of thinking must be abandoned if the subject is to become open to God.

According to Rajneesh, there are three main approaches to reality:

the scientific, based on experiment; the logical, based on reasoning; and the metaphorical, manifesting itself in poetry and religion. 'Poetry is a golden bridge, it bridges the object with the subject.'[13] Religion is essentially poetry. The Tantric teaching is always to say 'Yes' to life. 'The real atheist is one who goes on saying "No" to life.'[14] 'Man is the only unnatural animal – that's why religion is needed.'[15] Rajneesh resembled Jung in thinking that some varieties of neurotic symptoms were valuable because they compelled the individual to look within, to face his real problems.

Rajneesh did not claim that his teaching was original, although he did say that his way of expressing it was modern. However, he introduced a technique of meditation based on hyperventilation which I have not encountered elsewhere. 'Dynamic Meditation' consisted of ten minutes of rapid, irregular overbreathing to repetitive music. This is followed by ten minutes of catharsis in which the subject is required to release tension by shouting, weeping, dancing – expressing whatever comes to mind in the most uninhibited way possible. Dr. Gordon found himself screaming abuse and obscenities against hated figures from the past; teachers, parents, nurses, playmates. The third ten minute stage is occupied by jumping as high as possible whilst shouting the Sufi mantra 'Hoo, hoo, hoo'. Rajneesh described this. 'As you jump, land hard on the souls (sic) of your feet so that the sound reaches deep into the sex center. Exhaust yourself completely.'[16] Following this, the subject stops doing anything at all for another ten minutes during which physical cramps and pains induced by the overbreathing and violent exercise begin to subside. The last stage is dancing to more music until the mind becomes quiet and the body relaxed.

In 1971 Rajneesh adopted the title of *Bhagwan*. This alienated some of his Indian followers, because the appellation means *The Blessed One* and implies an incarnation of God. His disciple Laxmi told Bernard Levin that many of the *sannyasins* regarded Rajneesh as God, but that he himself only claimed to be a conduit transferring divine energy. I think it possible that Rajneesh came to believe in his own divinity. He used to give out boxes containing cuttings from his hair or nail clippings in case carrying his photograph was not enough to persuade his disciples that he was always with them. His narcissism also manifested itself in his insistent concern that any photographs of himself should be carefully posed and lit in order to bring out his best features.

In early 1974, Rajneesh sent some thirty or forty *sannyasins* to work on a farm belonging to his family in Kailash. This was an appalling place, overrun with rats and scorpions, extremely hot, and almost infertile. Gurdjieff's technique of persuading disciples that exhausting, futile work was a path to enlightenment was employed and used as a test of commitment to Rajneesh. The *sannyasins* were grossly underfed and overworked. They were forbidden to leave the farm or take time off and many became ill with amoebic dysentery and other diseases, including hepatitis, tuberculosis, and dengue fever. Some suffered permanent impairment of their health. After some months the experiment was abandoned.

As more and more disciples joined the movement, more space was needed. Some Indian business men set up a trust which became the Rajneesh Foundation. They bought a six acre estate at 17 Koregaon Park, Poona, in which the Shree Rajneesh Ashram grew and flourished. From 1974 onward, around six thousand followers of Rajneesh would be living there at any one time. The ashram became so famous that thirty thousand people a year from all over the world came as visitors. Large donations had launched the ashram; charges for rooms and meals, sales of books, fees for admission to discourses, and fees for group and individual therapy generated a regular income of somewhere between $100,000 and $200,000 per month which served to sustain it.

The ashram day started with dynamic meditation from 6 a.m. to 7 a.m. This was followed by a spontaneous discourse given by Rajneesh lasting two hours, in English and Hindi alternately. In 1975, encounter groups of various kinds were introduced. So many varieties of group and individual therapies were employed that Frances Fitzgerald described the Poona ashram as 'a spiritual garage for anyone with a method';[17] while Bernard Levin referred to it as a 'spiritual supermarket'.[18] The group techniques employed became notorious for the expression of uninhibited sex and aggression. In the course of expressing anger, so many fractures occurred that suspicious local hospitals were fobbed off with euphemistic tales that injuries had been caused by falling off ladders or bicycles. The sexual freedom offered in Poona is described by Hugh Milne as 'quite phenomenal'. The girls wore transparent dresses with no under-clothes, since Rajneesh had said that underclothes interfered with the passage of energy. There were groups in which people were forced to watch their beloved having intercourse with someone else, ostensibly to free them from over-attachment to sex. There were groups in which oral sex predominated. One favoured sexual activity was for males to eat ripe mangoes which had been introduced into the women's vaginas.

Rajneesh himself seems to have been an indifferent sexual per-former, in spite of claiming that he had had intercourse with more women than any man in history. Like some other gurus, he helped himself to any female delights which were on offer. Becoming Bhagwan's sexual partner was, of course, a highly prized distinction. But the experience itself was usually disappointing, since he appears to have suffered from premature ejaculation. He was more of a voyeur than a lover. Sometimes a couple would be encouraged to make love in front of him. A new recruit might be told to strip naked and be closely inspected without necessarily being touched. Others would be masturbated without intercourse taking place.

Yet his teaching about love demonstrates that he recognized that it could have another dimension.

> In deep love, somehow your desire ceases. The very moment is enough: There is no desire for the future. If I love someone, there in that very moment of love the mind is not. This moment is eternity . . . So love has many glimpses of the divine.[19]

He constantly reiterated that the person who does not love himself or who is asking for love cannot be loved by anyone else.

Among his beliefs was the notion that most people were unfit to have children, and that there were far too many children in the world. He felt that a twenty year world-wide ban on childbirth would solve many of the world's problems. Pregnant women were encouraged to have abortions and then be sterilized. Vasectomy and tubal ligation were made easily available at the ashram, and it became a sign of commitment to Rajneesh to have oneself sterilized. As many as two hundred people complied. Some later bitterly regretted having done so.

Ma Satya Bharti, a disciple from New York who edited Rajneesh's book on meditation, abandoned her three children to the care of her former husband in order to be with Rajneesh, and was told that she had done the right thing. When compared with the disciple's relationship with the guru, all other relationships were deemed unimportant. Rajneesh is reported as saying: 'The greatest relationship is between a Master and a disciple . . . Struggle is not the key with the Master, surrender is the key.'[20]

As the number of his adherents increased, Rajneesh himself became less and less accessible. From about 1979, the quality of his addresses deteriorated, and, in April 1981, he 'entered into silence' and stopped speaking in public. Instead, he sat silently with his disciples for one hour every day. As I suggested earlier, he probably suffered a period of depressive illness. His physical illnesses – diabetes, asthma, and various allergies – were apparently worsening, and the orthopaedic surgeon James Cyriax was flown from London to see if he could cure Rajneesh's back pain. Hugh Milne, who became his bodyguard, records that Rajneesh was so sensitive about needing medication that Milne had to pretend that prescriptions were for himself rather than for the guru.

The *sannyasins* had made themselves unpopular in Poona by behaving obnoxiously and offending the Indians by the indecency of their dress. Some became involved in drug running; others supported themselves by prostitution. Some were beaten up by the local inhabitants. The sexual freedom encouraged by Rajneesh was the very opposite of traditional Hindu teaching and caused offence. Eventually the Indian Government revoked the tax exempt status of the Rajneesh Foundation and attempted to collect $4,000,000 in back taxes. Rajneesh was forbidden to purchase a still larger site for a new commune, and there were rumours that he might be arrested for inciting religious unrest. After illegally moving millions of dollars out of India, preparations were made to leave Poona for the United States. It was announced that Rajneesh needed medical treatment in the US which he could not get in India. He was flown to New Jersey on May 31, 1981, where he announced on arrival: 'I am the Messiah America has been waiting for.'

An advance guard had chosen and bought the second largest ranch in Oregon, paying $5,750,000 for 64,229 acres. This was to become

Rajneeshpuram, Rajneesh's new commune. Rajneesh himself arrived there in July 1981, ostensibly as a visitor or guest in order not to arouse the suspicions of the US Immigration and Naturalization Service. By 1985, there were 2,500 permanent residents and another 2,000 long-term visitors. Rajneesh adopted the tactic used by Gurdjieff of affirming that work was a form of meditation or worship, or else a form of play. In either case work was a necessary part of the road toward enlightenment. The *sannyasins* worked such long hours – a hundred hours per week or more – that they had little time or inclination for any intellectual or artistic activities. Their favourite author seems to have been Louis L'Amour, a prolific writer of Westerns. This was surprising in view of their educational status. Eighty-three per cent were college educated; sixty-four per cent had bachelor's degrees, thirty-six per cent had advanced degrees, including twelve per cent with doctorates, They were nearly all white, fifty-four per cent female, forty-six per cent male, and eighty per cent were rated as middle-class. The average age was just over thirty. Sheela, the *sannyasin* who was now the chief administrator of the whole enterprise, repeatedly alleged poverty, and would not hesitate in persuading *sannyasins* to telephone their parents for money on spurious grounds; for example, claiming to need $20,000 for a kidney operation. One fund raiser alleged that there was not enough money to feed Rajneesh on the very day on which he had taken delivery of his eleventh Rolls-Royce. In four years, some $120 million was spent on the ranch.

Many disciples undoubtedly enjoyed themselves. There was a lot of hugging and a lot of laughter. Frances Fitzgerald described the ranch as 'a year-round summer camp for young urban professionals'.[21] The dark side of the idyll was the prevalence of sexually transmitted diseases, including gonorrhoea, herpes, non-specific urethritis, and finally AIDS. In 1984 orders were issued that no one in the commune should make love unless equipped with both a condom and rubber gloves. Eleven *sannyasins* were told that they had positive HIV tests and were segregated in a remote part of the ranch; but it was later suggested that the administration wanted an excuse to remove them from the centre of ranch life because they knew too much about the telephone tapping and electronic bugging which had by then been instituted.[22] One *sannyasin* is thought to have died of AIDS, but may have been poisoned. Rajneesh affirmed that AIDS was the scourge foretold by Nostradamus and would become a huge epidemic which might kill two-thirds of the world's population before the end of the century. He also prophesied nuclear war in the 1990s and an earthquake along the San Andreas fault. Only those who had achieved peace and strength of mind through meditation would be able to survive the coming chaos.

Rajneesh himself continued to deteriorate. Whereas he had previously spent nearly all his day reading, he now watched videos instead. His favourite films were *Patton* and *The Ten Commandments*. His passion for collecting Rolls-Royces continued until he had accumulated ninety-three. He shared with Gurdjieff the characteristic of being an exceedingly dangerous driver, who crossed red lights, accumulated speeding tickets, and often drove his cars off the road so that they had to be sent away for expensive repairs. Rajneesh had always been a compulsive collector. As a boy, he had collected stones from the beach; so many that his mother sewed extra pockets in his clothes. As an adult he collected pens, cuff-links, and watches; always the most expensive, often encrusted with diamonds and emeralds. Rajneesh's accumulation of thousands of disciples was another collection designed to boost his self-esteem. In 1985, he boasted that he had one million disciples throughout the world; but this was a gross exaggeration.

In studying gurus, one constantly encounters the paradox that people who appear so supremely self-confident that they radiate charisma are also those who have an especial need for disciples to reassure them. Whatever devices Rajneesh employed to ward off depression and bolster his ego failed in the end. He was said to be taking 60 mgm. of valium a day, and his dentist gave him inhalations of nitrous oxide, ostensibly to relieve his asthma, but probably to cause temporary euphoria. If this is true, it would explain his deterioration.

His former bodyguard, Hugh Milne, wrote that, when Rajneesh was rambling after having inhaled nitrous oxide, he once said: 'I am so relieved that I don't have to pretend to be enlightened any more. Poor Krishnamurti – he still has to pretend.'[23] This is so comical an admission that it leads one to wonder whether Hugh Milne was an entirely reliable witness. He was entranced by Rajneesh when he first encountered him in 1973, but became so disillusioned that he left the ranch in the autumn of 1982. Milne was greatly disturbed by his own defection, although he continued to affirm that he had gained a great deal from his encounter with the movement. He attempted suicide in 1983 and received psychiatric treatment as an in-patient. Even if there are one or two doubtful passages, his book *Bhagwan: The God that Failed* is an invaluable account of the movement by an observer who was close to Rajneesh.

In Oregon, as in Poona, the Rajneeshees succeeded in making themselves unpopular by being high-handed and contemptuous of the local population. Antelope, the small town nearest the ranch, had few inhabitants, mostly retired, some born-again Christians. They were shocked by what they heard of the sexual and violent behaviour of their new neighbours. Legal battles were instituted to prevent the Rajneeshees building and expanding; but the local people were defeated, because the Rajneeshees packed their meetings and out-voted them. They succeeded in taking over the Antelope city government, even changing the names of the streets from those of American heroes to those of Indian and other sages, and eventually re-naming Antelope itself as Rajneesh. The local inhabitants complained of being harassed, both verbally and in other ways.

In the spring of 1984 the ranch increased security and accumulated weapons, just as Jim Jones had done in Guyana, and David Koresh was to do in Texas. There were assault rifles, riot guns, semi-automatic carbines, and various other firearms. A special Rajneeshpuram police force was created. Gradually the ranch became more and more like a police state. The residents of the ranch were forbidden to leave temporarily unless some dire emergency required them to do so. Rajneesh created a system in which he spoke to no one except his chief administrator, Sheela, who became a virtual dictator with absolute power and an increasingly paranoid attitude.

An elaborate system of telephone-tapping and electronic bugging was introduced with the aim of detecting possible rebels within the commune. Large quantities of the drug haloperidol were ordered. This is a powerful neuroleptic drug used in the treatment of schizophrenia which has the advantages of being colourless, odourless, and tasteless. Recalcitrant *sannyasins* who wanted to leave were given this drug in potatoes and beer to make them more compliant, and it is believed that one died from being over sedated with it. Sheela resented the fact that Rajneesh's British doctor Devaraj was close to him and feared that the doctor might try to replace her with his own wife. She repeatedly poisoned Devaraj, making him ill with diarrhoea, vomiting and cramps, and finally attempted to kill him with an injection that resulted in his admission to hospital for two weeks after coughing blood. There were many other instances of *sannyasins* being poisoned.

Further attempts were made to increase the political power of the commune by rigging the votes in Wasco county elections. Large numbers of homeless were imported into the ranch, ostensibly as a charitable enterprise, but in reality to provide extra voters. Fraudulent voting cards with the names of people who had either died or left found their way into the county offices. In September 1984 Sheela and her aides caused an outbreak of salmonella in the main population centre of Wasco county by deliberately infecting salad bars in several large restaurants: this was a practice run to see if they could diminish the number of voters when it came to election day. When three local commissioners visited the ranch, two of them became ill and one nearly died after being given glasses of water.

The United States Immigration and Naturalization Service (I.N.S.) had always been suspicious of the Rajneeshees' intentions because, although their leader had declared himself opposed to marriage, so many of them contracted marriages with U.S. citizens. Most of them had only tourist visas. In December 1982, the Portland branch of I.N.S. had issued orders refusing permission for Rajneesh to become a permanent resident and also denying his classification as a religious worker. The ranch's lawyers at once opposed this, and managed to get him recognized as a religious teacher although unable to get the ruling about residence reversed. Rajneesh's lawyers were expert at employing delaying tactics, but, in the end, violations of immigration laws were used to arrest Rajneesh.

On September 14 and 15, 1985, Sheela and nineteen others took flight from Oregon and went to Germany. They were arrested there on October 28 and held for extradition. Sheela later pleaded guilty to immigration fraud, wire-tapping, and engineering the outbreak of salmonella infection: also to arson at the county planner's office, attempted murder of Devaraj, and assaults on the Wasco commissioners. She was given two twenty-year and two ten-year sentences to run concurrently. Since she had reportedly deposited millions of dollars in Swiss banks, the sum of $69,000 demanded to restore what her arson had destroyed and the imposition of a $400,000 fine probably meant very little to her.

Meanwhile a thirty-five count indictment, chiefly concerning violations of immigration laws, was to be used as a reason for arresting Rajneesh himself. He got wind of this and flew to Charlotte, North Carolina, whence he hoped to get to Bermuda, but U.S. marshals were waiting for him and arrested him. He was carrying thirty-five platinum and gold watches, worth around $400,000 as well as $58,000 in cash. He spent twelve days in jail before being released on bail. In November, he pleaded guilty to infringing immigration laws. A bargain was struck with the prosecuting attorney, and he was given a ten-year suspended prison sentence, paid a fine of $400,000, and agreed to leave the country within five days. He was forbidden to return within five years without written permission from the U.S. Attorney General. He then left for India. Many people think that he escaped extremely lightly.

Almost immediately after Sheela's flight in September, Rajneesh denounced her and claimed that he had been entirely ignorant of what she had been doing, which was completely opposed to his teachings. This apparently unnecessary denunciation took place because Rajneesh feared that Sheela would implicate him in exchange for immunity from prosecution. If he made her crimes public, this could not happen, and so she would be less likely to reveal his own complicity. It seems certain that Rajneesh did know what was going on and that he ordered some, if not all, of the crimes which Sheela committed. This explanation also accounts for Rajneesh's attempted flight, which, if he was only going to be accused of offences against the immigration laws, was quite unnecessary.

Rajneesh was an extremely gifted man whose discourses given in the early days at Poona demonstrate that he did have special insights and something of value to teach. It is easy to understand that those who were searching for a guru thought that they had found one in him, as indeed they had, for a time. Bernard Levin, who was impressed with the liveliness and apparent happiness of the *sannyasins* in Poona was sure that Rajneesh's teachings had 'enabled them to find a meaning for their lives and a place in the universe'.[24] But Rajneesh is surely a telling example of the truth of Lord Acton's maxim: 'Power tends to corrupt and absolute power corrupts absolutely.' Rajneesh degenerated into a monster of greed. He was always a leader; arrogant, intolerant of authority, self-taught, and acknowledging no debt to any Master. No wonder that he became inflated with his own importance. Even the Pope has his own confessor; but Rajneesh had no-one to whom to confess, no-one to point out his faults or restrain his excesses. Nor does it appear that he had faith in a personal God to whom he could pray for guidance or from whom he could ask forgiveness. I am sure that he had had ecstatic experiences (*satori,* to use the Zen phrase), and that he knew that love of another person can sometimes transcend desire; but I think he ended, as he had begun, isolated, narcissistic, and unable to relate to anyone on equal terms at an ordinary human level. Reading his discourses made me realize that Rajneesh was a sad loss. He had an extraordinary range of knowledge and a vision of how life should be lived, but he proved incapable of following his own precepts.

IV

RUDOLF STEINER

RUDOLF STEINER

RUDOLF STEINER WAS the founder of a spiritual movement which is still active in both Europe and the United States. The Anthroposophical Society, which continues to promote his ideas, was instituted by him in 1913. Its headquarters in England is at Rudolf Steiner House in north London which houses a book shop and a library as well as the offices of the Society. Unlike the gurus so far discussed, Rudolph Steiner was closer to being a saint than a villain.

The word 'Anthroposophy' was coined by the Swiss physician and philosopher Ignaz Troxler, a friend of Beethoven, who meant by it 'a cognitive method, which, taking as a starting point the spiritual nature of man, investigates the spiritual nature of the world.'[1] This, rather than the literal meaning – knowledge of human nature – is the sense in which Steiner employed the term. The Anthroposophic Press and the Rudolf Steiner Publishing Company have kept in print many of Steiner's varied and voluminous writings. He had a passion for education, and inaugurated the Waldorf School Movement at the end of the First World War. The movement took its name from the first Steiner school to be founded, which was for the benefit of the children of workers in a cigarette factory owned by Waldorf-Astoria. Steiner schools, which continue to flourish in many countries, try to ensure that children realize whatever potentials they have at different ages, both physical and mental, without stressing competition, examination results, or the particular skills required for success in a competitive, materialistic society. Steiner's concern was with the whole person, not with the one-sided development of the intellect. In many respects, his attitude to personal growth resembled that of Jung, who emphasized the one-sidedness of many of those who became neurotic, and who pointed out their need to become more 'whole' by developing neglected aspects of their personalities.

Steiner also instituted therapeutic education for mentally and physically handicapped children. Steiner's beliefs, which we shall discuss later, made him able to value the personalities of such children in a way which many people find difficult. In 1884, when he was twenty-three, he became private tutor in a family which included a handicapped boy aged ten, who was said to be suffering from hydrocephalus (so-called 'water on the brain'). The boy was so backward as to be considered almost ineducable; but Steiner succeeded in teaching him so effectively that he became able to attend an ordinary school and later to qualify as a doctor. Steiner stayed with the family until 1890, when he moved from Vienna to Weimar. I don't think that anyone who has visited a Steiner home for the handicapped could come away without being deeply impressed with the care given to children who may be brain damaged, mentally retarded, and, to a varying degree, paralyzed; but who are all perceived as possessing both individuality and potential for development, and who are never dismissed as hopeless.

Steiner is an example of a guru who was much beloved for his warmth, sensitivity, kindness, and generosity. One man who knew him well described him as 'the spirit of kindness incarnate'.[2] Steiner's effect upon people depended in part upon his capacity to devote himself entirely to understanding the other person without at first obtruding himself or his opinions. He manifested an attitude of acceptance and respect for each individual without forming premature conclusions or passing judgement. He was a highly intelligent polymath who had read biology, chemistry, physics, and mathematics, and who was therefore well aware of the requirements of scientific proof. But Steiner claimed that he, and anyone who cared to follow his lead, could transcend the conventions of natural science by a technique of directly apprehending the spiritual reality which he believed to underlie material appearances.

Steiner gave a vast number of lectures about his ideas: transcripts of more than six thousand have been printed. He certainly had charisma, for his listeners are reported as feeling that they were at some form of divine service rather than at a conventional lecture. The French writer Edouard Schuré, who heard Steiner lecture in 1906 wrote: 'I would have crossed the Atlantic to hear him.'[3] But his charisma did not depend upon devices of oratory or forceful harangues. It sprang from his own faith, his honesty, and his capacity to sense the mood of his audience and relate to it. His lectures were generally unprepared, spontaneous reactions to the audience as he perceived it. Yet Steiner presents us with a paradox. His belief system is so eccentric, so unsupported by evidence, so manifestly bizarre, that rational sceptics are bound to consider it delusional.

Steiner was born in 1861, the eldest son of an Austrian railway worker, at a village on the Hungarian-Croatian border. He was baptised as a Roman Catholic, although his father was a freethinker. When he was eight, the family moved to Neudörfl, a village near both Wiener-Neustadt and the famous shallow lake, Neusiedlersee, which is beloved by ornithologists because of its rich bird-life. From his own account, it is clear that, from childhood onward, Steiner was notably introverted; much more preoccupied with what went on in his own mind than with the external world. One biographer concludes that, after the move, 'the boy must have felt isolated, set apart from others.'⁴ This was partly because most of his childhood companions belonged to farming families, whereas his father had become a telegraphist and worked on the railway. It was also because, from an early age, he had 'clairvoyant' experiences which made him feel that he was different in other ways. One which he related in a lecture given in Berlin in 1913 is of seeing the figure of a woman in a railway waiting room who appeared to come through the door, demand help, and who then disappeared. It was later revealed that a distant relative had committed suicide at the precise time at which he had this vision. Steiner was convinced that he had seen the soul of the departed relative, and remained sure that he had a special faculty of communicating with the souls of the dead. Since he could not share his beliefs with the majority of his contemporaries without risking rebuff, Steiner's isolation continued into the early years of his adult life. But he did acquire one friend who was also interested in the occult, a herbalist called Felix Koguzki. Steiner was a precocious scholar, who read Kant when he was only fifteen, and who went on to study Fichte, Hegel, Schelling, Schopenhauer, and other philosophers. Steiner had little in common with either Bertrand Russell or Einstein, but it is worth pointing out that, in childhood, all three men became infatuated with geometry. Russell describes his first encounter with Euclid at the age of eleven as being as dazzling as first love. Einstein, when given a textbook of geometry at the age of twelve, was transported by realizing that 'man was capable, through the force of thought alone, of achieving the degree of stability and purity which the Greeks, before anybody else, demonstrated to us in geometry.'[5] Steiner came across a geometry book at the age of nine and was equally enthusiastic. Einstein's declared aim was to perceive the world by thought alone, omitting everything subjective. In similar fashion, Steiner describes geometry as bringing him happiness because he could grasp its propositions purely in the mind, without reference to the external world. To a non-mathematician, it seems odd to select geometry from among the other branches of mathematics as exemplifying the delights of abstraction, for geometry appears to have more connection with the external world and more practical applications than, for example, algebra. However this may be, geometry became a justification for Steiner's conviction that an inner, spiritual world existed which was just as real as the external world.

> As a child I felt, without of course expressing it to myself clearly, that knowledge of the spiritual world is something to be grasped in the mind in the same way as geometrical concepts. For I was as certain of the reality of the spiritual world as of the physical world. But I needed in some way to justify this assumption.[6]

But, whereas Einstein's way of perceiving the world by thought became confirmed by experiment and mathematical proof, Steiner's remained intensely subjective and insusceptible of objective confirmation.

Einstein, in an attempt to define what he meant by *thinking* referred to it as 'a free play with concepts; the justification for this play lies in the measure of survey over the experience of the senses which we are able to achieve with its aid.'[7] This is easy enough to follow. Einstein perceives that, in order to form new concepts about the world, one must separate oneself from direct perception of the world, and be able to play around 'in one's head' with concepts already there from which new combinations may arise. His ability to imagine how the world might appear to an observer travelling at near the speed of light took origin from just such play, and from it emerged the theory of relativity.

Einstein's description of thinking as playing with concepts is supported by the famous French mathematician Henri Poincaré and other creative thinkers, who appear to agree that finding solutions to mathematical and physical problems requires that concentrated work needs to be followed by a period of passivity. The thinker must allow ideas to simmer and, as it were, form themselves into new combinations from which the solution will be born. A well-known example was furnished by Friedrich August von Kekulé, Professor of Chemistry in Ghent, who was dozing in front of the fire one afternoon in 1865. Kekulé had a vision of chains of atoms coiling themselves into snakes eating their own tails which led to his discovery of the ring structure of organic molecules, and hence to the development of modern organic chemistry. The same sequence occurs in the arts. Writers and composers describe how new ideas 'come to' them as solutions to artistic problems, often after long periods of playing around with different possibilities.

Steiner's view of thinking was entirely different, and, to my mind, extremely eccentric. Most educated people consider thinking to be a form of abstraction, a withdrawal from involvement with objects into a state of mind in which 'playing with concepts' becomes possible. Steiner regarded thinking as a way of becoming more deeply involved with objects. His book *The Philosophy of Freedom* is subtitled *Some results of introspective observation following the methods of Natural Science*. Experimental scientists would regard this subtitle as a contradiction in terms, since one of their aims is to examine the phenomena of the natural world objectively, without allowing introspection or subjective experience to contaminate their observations. In contrast, Steiner claimed that thinking can reach the spiritual reality which he believed to underlie the phenomena of the natural world. He considered that the spiritual always preceded the physical; that material objects were formed from the spiritual, just as ice is formed from water. Steiner thought that the world was given to us as a duality which he called 'spirit' and 'nature', and that knowledge transforms this duality into a unity. 'The act of knowing overcomes this duality by fusing the two elements of reality, the percept and the concept gained by thinking, into the complete thing.'[8] He wrote that 'The history of our spiritual life is a continuing search for the unity between ourselves and the world.'[9]

In thinking, we have that element given us which welds our separate individuality into one whole with the cosmos. In so far as we sense and feel (and also perceive), we are single beings; in so far as we think, we are the all-one being that pervades everything.[10]

Similar claims were made by the early Christian gnostics, who believed that knowing oneself led to knowing both God and human destiny.

According to both Kant and Schopenhauer, the construction of the perceptual apparatus and the human brain demands that we perceive objects in the external world as existing in space and time, and as being governed by causal relations. The existence of these constraints implies that the way we see objects and the relations between them may not correspond to the way those objects actually are. We are seeing the world through distorting spectacles which we cannot remove. This is why Kant and Schopenhauer were convinced that human beings can never perceive 'things-in-themselves'.

Steiner would have none of this. 'If, however, we regard the sum of all percepts as the one part and contrast with this a second part, namely the things-in-themselves, then we are philosophising into the blue. We are merely playing with concepts.'[11] Thus, in two short sentences, Steiner dismisses Kant and Schopenhauer as wrong about perception, and Einstein's view of creative thinking as trivial. Steiner was convinced that what he called 'thinking' did reveal 'things-in-themselves'.

Thinking all too readily leaves us cold in recollection; it is as if the life of the soul had dried out. Yet this is really nothing but the strongly marked shadow of its real nature – warm, luminous, and penetrating deeply into the phenomena of the world. This penetration is brought about by a power flowing through the activity of thinking itself – the power of love in its spiritual form.[12]

Steiner's ideas about science and the natural world are originally derived from Goethe, whose scientific works he began to edit when he was still only twenty-one years old. The first volume appeared in 1884. From the autumn of 1890 until 1897 he was working at the Goethe and Schiller Archives in Weimar. He performed his task conscientiously, and met a number of distinguished people. But, according to his own account in letters, he became more and more isolated in Weimar, feeling that no one understood his motives or what went on in his mind. This stressful period was terminated by what Ellenberger calls 'a deep-reaching psychological metamorphosis' in 1896, at the age of thirty-five, which might equally be called a mid-life crisis or creative illness.[13] According to his own account, his perception of the material world and his relations with other people changed at this point. His one-sided emphasis upon his inner world had made him regard external reality as a dream. Now, he became more acutely aware of the material world and more open to his fellow men. The experience included the gradual realization that what Steiner called 'the Mystery of Golgotha', the passion, death and resurrection of Jesus, occupied a central place in his view of the universe. Steiner believed that Christ's essence was eternal, that Christ had always existed in the spiritual realm and had been worshipped by pre-Christian cultures under a variety of other names. At the baptism of Jesus in the river Jordan, this eternal Christ had entered into a man called Jesus and remained there until his death on the cross. The metamorphosis of the shy, introverted student into the guru who would found his own movement of Anthroposophy had begun.

Goethe remained his guiding light; more especially, those scientific writings of Goethe which he had been editing, which most subsequent writers have dismissed as prejudiced and clearly wrong. Goethe, claiming Spinoza as his mentor, led a movement in Germany called *Naturphilosophie*, which rejected the analytic dissection of the world by Newtonian science in favour of a holistic vision of nature. This led to his bitter, mistaken rejection of Newton's theory of light and colour which, to his mind, destroyed the phenomenon of light as perceived by a human observer. William Blake shared this opinion of science as a dehumanizing activity and denounced 'The Atoms of Democritus and Newton's Particles of Light.' Goethe seems to have believed that direct contemplation of individual phenomena could lead from the particular to the general; for instance, that close observation of a single plant could lead to the perception of the primal plant, which he conceived as being the original model for all plants. He condemned the neutral, detached, objective observation required by science as a partial, unnatural use of human faculties. The whole man should be engaged in the act of observation, just as the whole object should be studied without dissection into components which could not be directly perceived. Although the doctrines of *Naturphilosophie* may have inspired a few valuable scientific hypotheses, including the idea of the conservation of energy, the achievements of modern science triumphantly depend upon detachment, objectivity, analysis, experiment, and reduction of structures to their elementary constituents.

But what Goethe and Steiner proposed is interesting even if modern scientists find it misguided. The kind of observational understanding which Goethe and Steiner advocated does in fact provide knowledge which cannot be reached by detached scientific observation when we consider knowledge of ourselves and other human beings. Although experimental psychologists accumulate valuable information about human behaviour by scientific scrutiny and rigorous experiment, this is a special example of human interaction far removed from what happens between people in ordinary social circumstances. If a man were to treat his wife 'objectively', as if she were a participant in a psychological study, he would soon lose her. In our ordinary day-to-day encounters with other people, we are bound to rely upon our own subjective experience if we wish to grasp what others are thinking and feeling. We must assume that they possess an inner life of feelings, thoughts, desires, intentions, and beliefs which are similar to, though not identical with, our own, even if there is no objective evidence that such an inner life exists. Meeting a new person, we make assumptions about what he or she is thinking and feeling, about what kind of person this is, based upon the signals with which we are presented. Getting to know another person partly consists in correcting these first impressions, and intimacy, if it supervenes, may bring surprises. But most of us develop antennae of varying degrees of sensitiveness, which tell us how others are feeling, and which serve us well enough in social life. We have the capacity, more or less developed in different individuals, of putting ourselves in another person's shoes; of *identifying* with him or her. This subjective reaction to other human beings may have no place in the psychological laboratory, but is biologically adaptive. At the most basic level, it enables us to distinguish friend from foe. At higher levels it enables us to comprehend, co-operate, empathize, and love. Understanding another person really is a different enterprise from understanding an object in the external world.

However, Goethe and Steiner would have disagreed. They wanted to bring to bear on objects the same intuitive, subjective understanding which is actually only appropriate when applied to other human beings. Zoologists warn us against anthropomorphism: we must not attribute human characteristics to animals when we study them. Steiner tried to anthropomorphise the whole world; to identify with flowers, animals, and all other phenomena as well as with other people. Goethe's *Naturphilosophie* rejected scientific objectivity as insufficient, but Goethe could never have accepted Steiner's wilder flights of fancy.

Steiner believed that patient observation of physical reality led to an awareness of the spiritual reality behind physical appearances. For instance, he wrote that, if one looked at a seed for long enough, the seed would appear to be enveloped in a small luminous cloud. 'In a sensory-spiritual way it will be felt as a kind of flame. The centre of this flame evokes the same impression as that made by the colour lilac.'[14] In like fashion, every flower, when properly observed, would reveal secrets. This power of seeing through objects could be developed by concentrated, meditative thought. Steiner gives perfectly sensible advice about withdrawing from mundane concerns to practise meditation which many people will find helpful, without necessarily sharing the experiences which he says will follow. He describes how development of the inner life can be achieved by tranquil self-contemplation in which the person concerned learns to look at his experience and actions as though they were those of others. Rajneesh also advocated the development of such detachment that the subject could learn to become a witness to his own emotions and thoughts, rather than identifying himself with them. For Steiner, the attitude thus induced reveals that even the most insignificant experience or action is connected with 'cosmic beings and cosmic happenings.'[15] Perseverance in meditation and contemplation leads, so Steiner wrote, to a time 'when spiritual light will be all around him and a whole new world will be revealed to an inner eye of which he had previously been unaware.'[16]

When the initiate had sufficiently developed supersensible perception and 'organs of clairvoyance,' there was no definable limit to the knowledge of the spiritual world which he could obtain. Steiner, in line with his early conviction that he could communicate with the dead, alleged that he knew what happened to the soul after death. Each individual perceives his past life spread out in a vast series of pictures. He then goes through everything experienced in his past life in order, so that a kind of purgation takes place through suffering. The Beings of the spiritual world then convert the fruit of the individual's former life into the seed of his new one. Reincarnation remained a central tenet of Rudolf Steiner's faith. In the book in which he set forth his personal version of this ancient belief, he quoted no earlier authorities. In company with other gurus, Steiner *knew*. In a letter he wrote:

I will never say anything about spiritual matters that I do not know from direct spiritual experience. This is my guiding star. And this has enabled me to see through every illusion.[17]

He taught that the human spirit must be repeatedly re-incarnated, and that it brought to each incarnation a destiny which depended on actions in previous incarnations. In the new life, a man was able to make good the injuries he had inflicted in the previous life. Steiner's concern for mentally and physically handicapped children originated from his belief that damaged brains and twisted bodies were but temporary homes for spirits which, in their next incarnation, might inhabit normal frames.

Steiner, before he broke away to establish Anthroposophy, had originally been a member of the Theosophical Society founded by Madame Blavatsky in 1875. Madame Blavatsky claimed that she was instructed in esoteric wisdom by a brotherhood of Masters residing in the Himalayas. The Theosophical Society, which still exists, was at first enormously successful and attracted converts of the intellectual stature of the inventor Thomas Edison and Darwin's friend and collaborator Alfred Russel Wallace. But Theosophy's attempt to infuse western religion with eastern wisdom did not accord Christ the central position which he occupied in Steiner's belief system, and he parted company with Theosophy in 1910. However, he retained some of Blavatsky's beliefs, including her idea that the universe was permeated by a kind of psychic ether called *akasa* through which clairvoyance and telepathy could operate and in which were preserved 'Akashic Records' of the whole of man's history. Access to these records could be obtained through spiritual perception.

Steiner's belief that there is a spiritual world inhabited by Higher Beings sounds fantastic to sceptics; but is not far removed from Plato's postulate of an eternal realm of perfect, ideal Forms of which the material world is a derivative or imitation. Jung also believed in a spiritual world which, following the gnostics, he called the *pleroma*. The dictionary definition of *pleroma* is 'the abode of God and of the totality of Divine powers and emanations.' Steiner considered that here was 'a world of formative forces, imperceptible by the physical senses, but objectively perceptible at the first level of higher consciousness as giving life, movement, and form to the material world.'[18]

Although Steiner claimed that everything he taught sprang from his own direct spiritual experience, he took into account the possibility that his spiritual perceptions might be subjective; but he had no hesitation in affirming that methodical practice and scrupulous honesty could distinguish phantasy from fact.

> It is by healthy inner experience that one knows a spiritual 'Imagination' to be no mere subjective picture but the expression of a spiritual reality in picture-form. Just as in sensory perception anyone sound in mind and body can discriminate between mere fancies and the perception of real facts, so a like power of discernment can be attained by spiritual means.[19]

This is a difficult claim to sustain in the absence of any supporting evidence, and only those who are already convinced that Steiner's picture of spiritual reality is true will be able to accept his statement.

Steiner espoused a variety of vitalism in that he argued that, since the physical body begins to decay immediately after death, there must be some force operative during life which stops this. He named this force or principle the Etheric body, and said that every organ in the body had an underlying etheric equivalent which, to spiritual perception, was even more real than the physical. In addition to the physical body and the Etheric body, he postulated a third Astral body, which was responsible for rousing the unconscious sleeper to wakefulness. This Astral body gives rise to consciousness by permeating the Etheric body. The fourth member is the Ego or I. Although the Astral body experiences pain and pleasure, it has no memory, no sense of anything permanent. During sleep the Astral body 'returns into the harmony of the Universe, whence on awakening he brings sufficient force into his bodies to enable him for a time once more to forgo the sojourn there'.[20] The Ego is that part of the human being which has conscious experience because it has memory. Although Steiner uses the term 'bodies' for these subdivisions of the human being, it is probably easier for most people to picture them as fields of force rather than as 'subtle bodies'.

This division of the human being will undoubtedly sound bizarre to those who are not Theosophists or Anthroposophists, but it must be remembered that Freud's division into Ego, Superego and Id has been widely accepted as an authentic model of the mental apparatus, although these entities have no anatomical or physiological existence.

Steiner also claimed occult knowledge about the evolution of the world: 'Our Earth has passed through three previous planetary conditions, with intermediate states of spiritualization in between.'[21] So the inanimate, as well as the animate, undergoes reincarnation. Steiner regarded the present solar system as the fourth incarnation of the cosmic bodies which constitute it. The previous three are named *Old Saturn*, *Old Sun*, and *Old Moon*. Man's physical body began its evolution on *Old Saturn*.

Old Saturn incorporated the whole solar system.

Old Saturn consisted of interweaving, surging warmth. There was no air; the space in which this primal sphere existed was permeated with regular streams of warmth. These streams were the predecessors of human beings. At that time our body consisted of streams of flowing warmth.[22]

After separating from *Old Saturn*, the sun, moon, and earth remained together as one body. When the moon separated, the difference between waking and sleeping was instituted. At night, the moon stimulated the life of the soul. Mankind became aware of forces which worked upon them from the moon and made them clairvoyant. Man began to evolve his etheric body on *Old Sun*; his astral body on *Old Moon*. The evolution of the Ego has begun on the current planetary incarnation; the stage of Earth. Readers may recall that Gurdjieff also expressed bizarre beliefs about the moon of a quite different variety.

Steiner believed that there were seven epochs of Earth evolution: the *Polarian*, the *Hyperborean*, the *Lemurian*, the *Atlantean*, the *Post-Atlantean*, and the *sixth and seventh epochs*.[23] He believed that the Atlantean age had been brought to an end by a catastrophic flood, and that there would be a final 'war of all against all' which is foretold in the apocalyptic visions described in the Book of Revelation. After this catastrophe, man would enter upon a new epoch in which conquest of the body by the spirit would be finally accomplished.

We must understand the difference between the evolution of souls and the evolution of bodies. From epoch to epoch human souls find themselves again and again in different bodies. These souls will one day see the strife that will reign among the human souls who will be born in the last post-Atlantean age. This experience will be a lesson for them and will help to free them from egotism. Then they will be able to grow into an era where they will have the fruits of selfhood but without its disadvantages. An age will come with clairvoyant conditions similar to those prevailing in ancient Atlantis, but with this difference: human beings will have a free consciousness of self. We will then have learned, in these seven cultures of the post-Atlantean age, what can be achieved in the physical world. This self-perception or consciousness of self can only awaken in a physical body; but the human being must again subjugate the physical body. After the war of all against all, we will have achieved a stage of evolution where we live in a bodily nature in such a way that we are no longer slaves of our physical bodies.[24]

Steiner wrote some forty books. Even if I had read them all there would be no possibility of summarizing them here. I think enough has been said to illustrate my main point. Steiner was undoubtedly a guru with a spiritual message, a charismatic presence, persuasive powers as a lecturer, and benign intentions. Steiner thought that his capacity for spiritual perception added another dimension to conventional techniques and disciplines. For example, he lectured to doctors and medical students on therapeutics, and wrote a book on how spiritual science could be applied to medicine, without in any way criticizing or opposing the scientific principles on which modern medicine is based. Many doctors in Germany and Italy follow Steiner's teaching, and there are a number of clinics and research centres in which Steiner's therapeutic principles are applied. Steiner also taught a new style of architecture, exemplified by the Anthroposophical centre at Dornach in Switzerland which he designed and called the Goetheanum. The first building so-named was dedicated in 1914 but unfortunately burned down in 1922. However, Steiner lived long enough to design its successor, which was completed and opened three years after his death. It is still a centre for lectures, seminars, and dramatic performances, including Goethe's *Faust* and mystery plays written by Steiner himself.

Steiner's legacy in education has been fruitful. At the time of his death in 1925, there were two Steiner schools in Germany and one each in the Netherlands and Great Britain. Now there are about 500 schools throughout the world. Steiner's view of education as a way of developing individual physical and mental potentials with little emphasis on conventional examination results has already been mentioned. Steiner was an early advocate of co-education. He also believed that, instead of competing with each other, children should be encouraged to help one another with whatever subjects they were studying. By staying together in the same class over a period of several years, a miniature community is created in which children can learn the social skills of tolerance and mutual co-operation. Particularly welcome is Steiner's insistence that the arts should play an important part in education. Music, painting, and manual skills such as carving and modelling are part of every child's education, not 'extras' as they so often are in conventional schools.

Steiner's acceptance of the brain-damaged and mentally handicapped as individuals capable of spiritual development has inspired those who care for them with new hope and a new capacity for dedication. The Camphill homes for the handicapped are based on Steiner's principles.

Steiner gave a course of lectures for agriculturists in 1924. This surprised some who thought of him as an intellectual, but Steiner always retained traces of his peasant origin and proved to be well-informed about country matters and practical in his recommendations even if these were based on an eccentric view of the relation between earth and the cosmos. He anticipated our present concern with the destruction of the environment by advocating organic farming and forbidding chemical fertilisers and other artificial aids, which have, as we know, often disturbed the balance of nature and been harmful to wild life.

Steiner was undoubtedly a man of high ideals and high intelligence who inspired other people and who certainly did far more good than harm. Yet his so-called 'thinking', his supposed power of supersensible perception, led to a vision of the world, the universe, and of cosmic history which is entirely unsupported by any evidence, which is at odds with practically everything which modern physics and astronomy have revealed, and which is more like science fiction than anything else. The claims which he made for himself are astonishing. He had complete confidence that his own subjective powers of 'spiritual perception' revealed the truth about the universe in ways beyond the reach of orthodox science, and that the discoveries which he made in this way could be applied to every department of life, from medicine and agriculture to the education of both normal and handicapped children. This mild, gentle, good, kindly man had, at some level of his personality, an unshakeable conviction that he 'knew'. It was this utter certainty, so characteristic of gurus, which brought him followers, and made it possible for his disciples to believe in his spiritual science and embrace his teaching as a philosophy of life. Steiner's belief system is both idiosyncratic and incredible; but what he achieved in humanitarian terms is remarkable and enduring.

V

CARL GUSTAV JUNG

CARL GUSTAV JUNG

THERE MAY STILL BE people who think of Carl Gustav Jung only as a distinguished psychiatrist who enlarged our understanding of the mind and who also made important contributions to psychotherapy. He did both, but his variety of analysis is not simply concerned with the relief of neurotic symptoms; it promises a secular form of salvation. Jung was a spiritual teacher as well as a physician. In many respects, he conformed to the pattern typical of gurus which I indicated in the introduction. He himself affirmed that all his most important insights originated from the long period of psychological disturbance which followed his parting from Freud. He emerged from this distressing mental illness toward the end of the First World War with a new revelation. In his later writings he made overt claims to be a prophet, because he believed that he had been granted special insight. He said that, for all those of middle-age or over, healing depended upon gaining or regaining a religious outlook on life. Jung did not directly aim at acquiring disciples; but he became surrounded with a group of close associates in Zürich who founded the C. G. Jung Institute there in 1948. Jungian centres at which analysts were trained and Jungian ideas propagated subsequently became established in many different parts of Europe and America.

Jung claimed to be a scientist, and no doubt wanted to be regarded in this light. In a letter written in 1935 to a lady seeking his view of Rudolf Steiner, Jung wrote:

> I have read a few books by Rudolf Steiner and must confess that I have found nothing in them that is of the slightest use to me. You must understand that I am a researcher and not a prophet. What matters to me is what can be verified by experience. But I am not interested at all in what can be speculated about experience without any proof.[1]

But many of Jung's own ideas. like those of Steiner, are directly derived from his own subjective experience, and cannot be objectively verified.

Jung was a distinguished psychiatrist before he met Freud, and had carried out experiments in word-association which can be regarded as more 'scientific' than any work carried out by Freud after he left Brücke's laboratory. His medical training must have made him aware of the requirements of scientific proof, and, although he was a poor mathematician, he kept up an interest in modern physics. But I do not think it likely that Jung ever regarded psychosis or neurosis as curable by methods only depending upon scientific detachment. Indeed, Jung took up the then neglected and undervalued speciality of psychiatry because Krafft-Ebing's *Textbook of Psychiatry* pointed out that so little had been established in this field that even psychiatric textbooks bore the stamp of subjectivity. Instead of being put off by this, as he would have been if he had been a pure scientist, Jung was immediately attracted to a branch of medicine which promised opportunities for him to use his own personality in the understanding and therapy of the mentally ill, as opposed to being the detached surgeon or specialist in internal medicine which he had originally planned to become. When he was only twenty-one years old, Jung gave a lecture to the Zofingia student fraternity with the title 'The Border Zones of Exact Science,' in which he postulated that critical examination of rational scientific claims leads into a realm which is immaterial or metaphysical.[2] The student was father to the man.

Jung never believed that the human problems with which he became concerned as a psychotherapist could be treated or understood in the same way as a problem in physics. This is entirely reasonable. I have elsewhere contrasted the special objective stance adopted by experimental psychologists with the way in which we interact with each other in ordinary social life.[3] Human relationships are based upon subjective assumptions of similarity and the capacity for empathy. We cannot understand others or ourselves if we look only at behaviour. Whereas Freud kept his patients at a distance by putting them on a couch and sitting behind them, Jung preferred to sit face-to-face with his patients and relate to them in a human, more ordinary fashion.

Jung displayed guru-like characteristics for reasons which can be traced to his own background and upbringing. I suggested earlier that potential gurus had often been rather solitary children. This was certainly true of Jung. Although he had a sister, who was born in 1884, he was an only child for the first nine years of his life. In his autobiography, he described playing solitary games and his dislike of being observed or interrupted whilst engaged in them. Albert Oeri, later the editor of the Basler *Nachrichten* and a member of the Swiss National Council, was brought by his parents to the Jung household when he and Jung were still very small boys in the hope that they would play together. To Albert's chagrin, the little Carl took no notice of him and went on playing with his own ninepins. Oeri, who had been brought up in a crowded nursery in which he was in constant association with other children, said that he had never encountered such an asocial monster.[4]

Jung wrote that he liked school because he at last found playmates; but also recorded that his efforts to fit in with his rustic schoolmates made it seem that they were alienating him from his true self. Throughout his life Jung remained a solitary person who only felt fully himself when he was alone. In the tower which he built at his country retreat at Bollingen on the upper lake of Zürich, he kept a 'retiring room' to which only he had access and in the last section of his autobiography he wrote:

> As a child I felt myself to be alone, and I am still, because I know things and must hint at things which others apparently know nothing of, and for the most part do not want to know.[5]

The other factor in Jung's background which influenced his becoming a guru rather than a mere psychiatrist was his religious background. Jung's father was a pastor in the Swiss Reformed Church. Two of his paternal uncles were also ministers. In addition, his mother was the daughter of a theologian, and five other members of her family were in the church. Jung found the atmosphere at home oppressive. He showed signs of rebelling against conventional Christianity very early in his life. In his autobiography, Jung recalled the first dream which he could remember, which he said occurred between the ages of three and four. This concerned his discovery of an underground chamber in which a huge phallus, some fifteen feet high, was poised upon a golden throne. This image haunted Jung throughout his youth, and signified to him that there was a subterranean god of a very different kind from the Lord Jesus with whom he was familiar. When Jung was eleven or twelve, he had a phantasy which was so shocking to him that, at first, he refused to let it complete itself. He was finally able to do so when he robustly concluded that God himself had put the phantasy into his mind for some purpose which he could not comprehend. Everyone who has read Jung's autobiography will recall his vision of God sitting on a throne above the cathedral of Basel and then letting drop an enormous turd which shatters the cathedral roof. Jung began to think that God might not be the all-loving deity which conventional Christianity postulated. Perhaps God had a terrible aspect as well. Jung's conventionally minded father refused to enter into discussions about religion with his more gifted son, and told him that he thought too much. According to the Reverend Paul Achilles Jung, who survived until 1896, the year in which Jung reached his majority, one ought not to think; one ought simply to believe.

By late adolescence, Jung had abandoned belief in the religion in which he had been reared. He read very widely, and was particularly influenced by the writings of Schopenhauer and even more so by those of Nietzsche. But, like Nietzsche and others who have been brought up in a strongly religious atmosphere, Jung found it difficult to live without a faith. The whole of his later work can be read as an attempt to discover a substitute for the religious faith which he had lost.

Jung shared with Freud a distaste for revealing anything personal. His autobiography contains very little about his relationships with others. His wife, for example, is hardly mentioned. Jung remains a solitary figure. Freud's psychoanalysis had as its ideal end-point of development a fully mature sexual relationship; whereas Jung's analytical psychology aimed at integration; a new balance of forces within the individual psyche, without reference to personal relationships. It is a point of view very much at odds with current psychological wisdom which tends to promote the idea that mature personal relationships are the only source of true happiness.

Jung's creative illness was prolonged and serious. It began in 1913 and lasted throughout the First World War. He himself concluded that he was 'menaced by a psychosis'. I myself believe that the illness was more than menacing. I think Jung passed through a psychotic episode, which had been foreshadowed by some of his early experiences. As often happens, this illness left traces behind which remained with him until the end of his life.

Jung's parents were not happy together. When Jung was three years old, his mother suffered some kind of breakdown which had required her admission to hospital for several months. Later in childhood, Jung records that his parents were sleeping apart, and that he shared a bedroom with his father.

From the door to my mother's room came frightening influences. At night mother was strange and mysterious. One night I saw coming from her door a faintly luminous, indefinite figure whose head detached itself from the neck and floated along in front of it, in the air, like a little moon. Immediately another head was produced and again detached itself. This process was repeated six or seven times. I had anxiety dreams of things that were now small, now large. For instance, I saw a tiny ball at a great distance; gradually it approached, growing steadily into a monstrous and suffocating object. Or I saw telegraph wires with birds sitting on them, and the wires grew thicker and thicker and my fear greater until the terror awoke me.[6]

These visual hallucinations and distortions closely resemble those described by schizophrenics. Elizabeth Farr, whose outstanding personal account of her schizophrenic illness is given in Ming T. Tsuang's book, *Schizophrenia: The Facts*[7], describes a variety of visual distortions. Space appeared to change, so that perspective became disordered and confusing. Her knees would appear to be too big, and would then shrink again, or her feet would seem to be so far away that she believed that her legs had grown longer. Sometimes the walls of a room would appear to expand and contract, as if the room itself was breathing.[8] Any psychiatrist who was told of the experiences listed above, and who also knew how isolated, vulnerable, and hypersensitive he was, would probably think that Jung was a likely candidate for schizophrenia in later life. The psychoanalyst

D. W. Winnicott, who was both a paediatrician and a specialist in child analysis, reviewed Jung's autobiography in the *International Journal of Psychoanalysis*. He described Jung as giving a picture of infantile schizophrenia and as being a recovered case of infantile psychosis.[9]

Jung's 'creative illness' or 'mid-life crisis' began with what he describes as being afflicted with a 'period of uncertainty' following the break with Freud. His last actual meeting with Freud had been at the Fourth International Psychoanalytic Congress, held in Munich on September 7th and 8th, 1913. Jung's period of uncertainty was succeeded by a 'sense of pressure' within himself which 'seemed to be moving outwards, as though there were something in the air. The atmosphere actually seemed to me darker than it had been. It was as though the sense of oppression no longer sprang exclusively from a psychic situation, but from concrete reality.' At this point, Jung began to confuse inner and outer in a way which is characteristic of psychosis. He was attributing an upheaval within his own mind to a disturbance in the external world. In October 1913, he describes being 'seized by an overpowering vision'.

I saw a monstrous flood covering all the northern and low-lying lands between the North Sea and the Alps. When it came up to Switzerland I saw that the mountains grew higher and higher to protect our country. I realized that a frightful catastrophe was in progress. I saw the mighty yellow waves, the floating rubble of civilisation, and the drowned bodies of countless thousands. Then the whole sea turned to blood. This vision lasted about one hour.[10]

The vision repeated itself a week later, with even more blood. Early in 1914, Jung repeatedly dreamed of a new ice age which destroyed all living things. Such visions and dreams of world destruction are frequent precursors of schizophrenic episodes. Eugen Bleuler, who was the chief physician at the Burghölzli hospital where Jung began his psychiatric career, wrote in his textbook on schizophrenia: 'Before the actual onset of the disease, the patients frequently complain about disturbing dreams which keep haunting them during their waking hours.'[11]

But Jung chose to ignore his former chief's teaching, and interpreted his visions and dreams as prophetic; anticipations of the First World War, which broke out a few months later. This interpretation may have convinced Jung that he was not suffering from a psychosis, but it obviously demands belief in precognition. It is also narcissistic, in that it presupposes special insight not granted to others; a presupposition which both Jung and his closest followers willingly accepted. I have already quoted his remark about knowing things of which other people know nothing. Jung seems to have believed that he was the vessel of a higher power which granted him insight into the future. Many of those who have not been able to make relationships on equal terms in childhood have phantasies of being 'special,' of being set above the common herd. Jung was much more gifted and better read than his contemporaries and of course realized this; but his belief that he was a chosen vessel is close to a grandiose delusion.

Jung's illness lasted until nearly the end of the First World War. Its intensity was such that his wife allowed Toni Wolff, Jung's mistress for nearly thirty years, to become a member of the household because she was the only person who could calm him down. Jung describes his illness as a voluntary confrontation with the unconscious, a scientific experiment. He then reverses this statement by saying that it was an experiment which was being conducted on him. He wrote: 'It is, of course, ironical that I, a psychiatrist, should at almost every step of my experiment have run into the same psychic material which is the stuff of psychosis and is found in the insane'.[12] I think it simpler and more accurate to say that Jung passed through a psychotic episode which demanded a great deal of patient support from both his wife and his mistress. Although I wrote earlier that I did not accept R. D. Laing's theory that psychosis is a path to higher wisdom, there are a few cases of rather acute episodes of psychotic illness from which the patient emerges changed and perhaps enriched, and this sequence of events appears to be particularly common in those who become gurus, because the revelation which enriches them forms the basis of their subsequent teaching. Jung certainly suffered from hallucinations and episodes of depersonalization. He withdrew from teaching at the university and found himself incapable of reading scientific literature. During these years, he wrote very little. At one point, he felt that his house became crowded with spirits which he concluded were the spirits of the dead. 'From that time on, the dead have become ever more distinct for me as the voices of the Unanswered, Unresolved, and Unredeemed.'[13] His response was to write the *Septem Sermones ad Mortuos*, which John Kerr describes as 'a thoroughly grandiose, almost paranoid tract that combines Gnostic terminology with the style of *Thus spake Zarathustra* to arrive at a deliberately obscure text ringing with the plaints of self-justification.'[14] I think that this extraordinary work owes more to Schopenhauer than to Nietzsche, and that Kerr's judgement is unduly harsh; but the obscurity of the piece is indisputable.

Jung himself said that the whole of his later work was based upon this long, stressful period. 'The years when I was pursuing my inner images were the most important in my life – in them everything essential was decided.'[15] Jung had been nearly overwhelmed, but his illness taught him that *pari passu* with the disintegration taking place within his mind, there was also a healing process which was striving to make sense of his experience and achieve a new integration. As John Kerr has perceived, Jung 'was able to observe his own dissolution with exquisite exactitude, and the observation itself became a kind of therapy'.[16] Jung's illness and subsequent illumination is an exceptionally fascinating example of the distress of chaos followed by the relief of a new order. It is interesting that, as early as 1898,[17] Jung quotes from Nietzsche's *Zarathustra*: 'I tell you, one must have chaos in one, to give birth to a dancing star.'[18] Twenty years later, this is what happened to Jung. He called his journey toward a new integration the 'individuation process'; a concept which may originally have been derived from his reading of Schopenhauer, in whose thought the *principium individuationis* plays an important part.

What he had discovered was that, although his conscious ego might be both threatened and helpless, it was possible to learn to listen to, and depend upon, an inner voice which manifested itself in dreams, phantasies, and other spontaneous derivatives of the unconscious. One of Jung's most fruitful ideas is that the psyche is self-regulating. His medical training had taught him that human physiology is a system of checks and balances which ensure that any tendency to go too far in one direction is compensated by an opposing swing in the other. These homeostatic mechanisms are dependent upon negative feedback. For example, fluctuations in blood sugar are reported to a central control which promptly sets in motion compensatory changes to restore the normal balance. Jung suggested that similar mechanisms occurred in mental illness. A person who becomes neurotic (or, in some instances, psychotic) is someone who has strayed from his own true path of development, perhaps because of intellectual arrogance, extreme extraversion or introversion, or perhaps from letting himself be overpersuaded or influenced by someone else. And just as there is a central control which governs human physiology, so there is also a central control which governs the individual's psyche. Neither control system is accessible to the conscious will; but there is a wisdom of the psyche as well as a wisdom of the body.

This seems to me to be an eminently sensible idea which finds confirmation in clinical practice. It can certainly be applied to cases which every psychiatrist has seen. For example, ambitious men who habitually overwork to the point of neglecting everything else which makes life worth living often break down in mid-life with a severe depression. This can be interpreted as the psyche's attempt at self-regulation. They are compelled by illness to slow down and reconsider their values. But formulating the idea of psychological self-regulation had a special meaning for Jung beyond the matter-of-fact exposition which I have just given. One of Jung's problems was his loss of religious faith. During his illness, he discovered that he had to submit to being guided by something within himself which was independent of his conscious intention. Could this be the psychological equivalent of God – a kind of 'God within' rather than 'God out there'?

If this was the case, then Jung could claim that he had discovered an answer to his own loss of faith; a psychological substitute for religion as well as a curative process. As I wrote elsewhere, the process of individuation could be described as 'a kind of Pilgrim's Progress without a creed, aiming not at heaven, but at integration and wholeness.'[19]

In 1910, Jung had written a letter to Freud in which he discussed the possibility of joining a new society, Knapp's *International Fraternity for Ethics and Culture*, called I.F. for short.

Religion can be replaced only by religion. Is there perchance a new saviour in the I.F.? What sort of new myth does it hand out for us to live by? Only the wise are ethical from sheer intellectual presumption, the rest of us need the eternal truth of myth.

You will see from this string of associations that the problem does not leave me simply apathetic and cold. The ethical problem of sexual freedom really is enormous and worth the sweat of all noble souls. But 2000 years of Christianity can only be replaced by something equivalent.[20]

This letter demonstrates how devastating his abandonment of conventional Christianity had been to him. Jung became a psychiatrist at the Burghölzli in 1900, nearly seven years before he first met Freud, and always claimed that he was critical of some of Freud's ideas from the beginning. However, A. A. Brill, who was an assistant at the Burghölzli when Jung was working there, reports that 'Jung was at that time the most ardent Freudian.'[21] Perhaps Freudian psychoanalysis, like conventional Christianity, was for Jung another light that failed, another faith that had to be abandoned, which left him bereaved and rudderless. It was only after his final parting with Freud that Jung was compelled to discover his own myth, even if he had to pass through a psychotic illness to do so.

When Jung became established as a world-famous figure, he specialized in treating a particular variety of patient. He described these people as suffering from the senselessness and aimlessness of their lives, rather than from any clinically definable neurosis. Most of them were successful, gifted, apparently well adapted, and middle-aged. Yet they had nothing to live by; no religious faith, no myth, not even a delusional system. Jung described these people as 'stuck', in that they had lost any sense of progress toward a goal. They lacked what a religious belief might have given them; faith, hope, love, and understanding, which Jung defined as the four highest achievements of human endeavour, but which he also claimed to be 'gifts of grace' which cannot be taught or learned, but which only come through experience.[22]

Among all my patients in the second half of life – that is to say, over thirty-five – there has not been one whose problem in the last resort was not that of finding a religious outlook on life. It is safe to say that every one of them fell ill because he had lost what

94

the living religions of every age have given to their followers, and none of them has really been healed who did not regain his religious outlook. This of course has nothing to do with a particular creed or membership of a church.[23]

One can argue that Jung may have attributed his own problem to these patients. However, most psychiatrists have some experience of people who are desperately in search of a meaning in life, but who are not psychiatrically ill in the conventional sense. In fact, this group of people often turn to gurus of far less integrity than Jung.

Although Jung thought that his personal experience of enlightenment was relevant to the cases described above, he did not believe that the spiritual journey which he called individuation should be undertaken by everyone. He considered that his message only applied to people in the second half of life; that younger people might well find that Freudian or Adlerian analysis was better suited to their needs. Jung's estimate of his own work was contradictory. On the one hand, he claimed that it was scientific, and could be verified by others. On the other hand, he called it a subjective confession.

The received wisdom has been that Jung differed from most gurus in that he did not try to force his conclusions on others, and resisted the setting up of institutions to promote his ideas for many years. However, Richard Noll, in his book *The Jung Cult*, prints a recently discovered document which appears to be a transcript of Jung's address inaugurating the first Jungian association, the Psychological Club in Zürich. Noll claims that this address was inaugurating a 'secret church' consisting of a few persons who had travelled the road of individuation, as sign-posted by Jung himself, which would develop, and was designed to develop, into a world-wide religious movement. I doubt this. I suppose that, given Jung's originality and charisma, it would be almost impossible that he should not collect around him a number of disciples who had accepted his views of the unconscious, who had been analysed by Jung himself or one of his close associates, and who wanted a forum in which Jung's ideas would constitute the principal focus of discussion. But this is not to imply that Jung wanted to found a new sect or a world-wide movement led by an élite group of the successfully individuated, as Noll suggests.

For literally tens of thousands, if not hundreds of thousands, of individuals in our culture, Jung and his ideas are the basis of a personal religion that either supplants their participation in traditional organized Judaeo-Christian religion or accompanies it. For this latter group especially, the Jungian experience, as it is promoted by its specialized caste of analysts, holds out the promise of mystery and the direct experience of the transcendent that they do not experience in any church or synagogue.[24]

Noll greatly exaggerates the number of Jungian adherents. There have never been very many 'Jungians' in the world; not nearly as many as there are 'Freudians'. Moreover, Noll gives the impression that Jungian followers constitute a single 'church' the world over, proffering the same teaching, and primarily motivated by the desire to obtain money from their analysands. Noll refers to 'a vast international network' of Jungian organizations, and calls Jungian analysis 'a capitalist enterprise.' In fact, there has been so much dissension that, in London alone, there were four incompatible groups all owing some allegiance to Jung. The idea of a universal Jungian church cannot really be sustained. Noll has constructed a conspiracy theory which does not bear examination.

Although Jung was greatly superior to most gurus in intellect, education, and integrity, he nevertheless shared with them a number of characteristics. He certainly thought of himself as a spiritual leader rather than as a psychiatrist treating neurotics. I first realized this on the only occasion on which I met him, on April 14, 1951. At that time, he was writing his controversial book, Answer to Job. 'What I'm writing now,' he told me, 'is pure poison. But I owe it to my people.' I was taken aback by this remark at the time, for I knew that no ordinary psychiatrist would talk like that of 'my people': that is the statement of a guru. Jung's discipleship might be small, but he had no doubts about his position. Marie-Louise von Franz, the most intelligent of the group of female disciples who surrounded Jung, records that he told her that Answer to Job was the only one of his books which he did not want to rewrite. It certainly propounds a strikingly unconventional view of the Deity. Jung was actually quite funny about conventional Christians. He told me that Archbishop William Temple had recently visited him, and that he had found him 'too much a Prince of the Church'. Jung asked Temple whether he thought the Virgin Birth was literally true, but Temple refused to face the question. 'Either Mary was a Virgin or Jesus was a civilian', was how Jung described Temple's dilemma.

Although Jung referred to his ideas as a subjective confession, and said that he did not want to force them on others, there is no doubt that he believed that he had privileged access to a realm beyond consciousness. When John Freeman interviewed Jung on television in October 1959, he asked him: 'Do you now believe in God?' Jung famously replied: 'Now? Difficult to answer. I *know*. I don't need to believe. I know.' When talking about dreams, Jung said to me: 'Every night you have the chance of the Eucharist'; and I have been told that the côterie of close disciples who knew him well waited hopefully each morning to hear if the great man had had another significant message from the unconscious.

Jung was not corrupt financially: since he had married a rich wife in 1903, he was not tempted to be so. But he was far from indifferent to wealthy supporters, and took pains to cultivate them. He made some of his rich American patients like Fowler McCormick and the Mellons into friends who put up money for various Jungian enterprises, including the valuable Bollingen series of books, named after his country retreat.

He did have affairs with at least two of his patients, Sabina Spielrein and Toni Wolff. The former is referred to, but not named, in his autobiography and in his correspondence with Freud. Although the seduction of patients is a professional misdemeanour, one has to remember that Spielrein was one of Jung's first analytical cases; that he certainly helped her; and that psychoanalytic rules were not yet codified. Although Toni Wolff had initially been one of Jung's patients, she did not become his mistress until long after her initial, successful treatment had ended and she had become an assistant and then a colleague. I do not think that Jung can be accused of exploiting his followers, either financially or sexually. Jung was a Victorian paterfamilias, but I know of no evidence that he used his dominant position to make unreasonable demands on his followers.

Jung was certainly élitist. He wrote: 'As a Swiss I am an inveterate democrat, yet I recognize that Nature is aristocratic, and, what is even more, esoteric. "*Quod licet Jovi, non licet bovi*" is an unpleasant but eternal truth.'[25] Jung passionately believed that the individual was the carrier of value, and that it was personal religious experience akin to his own which prevented the individual from dissolving in the crowd, or mindlessly adhering to some collective belief system like Communism.

Jung has sometimes been criticized for proposing that there is a 'collective unconscious'; a level of mind responsible for producing myths, visions, religious ideas and certain varieties of dream which are common to many cultures and to many periods of history. But this idea, in its simplest form, seems perfectly sensible. Man's anatomy and physiology have not greatly altered during the period of his existence on earth. It seems reasonable to assume that, although our knowledge and skills have greatly increased, the way the brain and mind function is basically the same as it always has been since *homo sapiens* first appeared. Myths, visions, religious ideas, and dreams are often expressive of fundamental psychological experiences which are common to all men. For example, the hero myths found in many cultures can be interpreted as myths about growing-up; its anxieties, tribulations, and rewards. We all have to pass from the state of being a helpless child to being an independent adult, capable of starting a new family. Hero myths tell a story of a child, often the youngest, embarking on a dangerous journey, facing perils, killing monsters, rescuing a beautiful maiden, and finally winning a bride and perhaps a throne. This is what Jung would call an 'archetypal' myth; a story found in different cultures all over the world which reflects basic aspects of the human condition. It seems perfectly understandable that there should be a substratum of mind, as common to all men as the structure of the brain, which produces the same kinds of myths about the human condition, and the same kinds of cosmogonies.

But Jung goes further than this, to a point where many cannot follow him. When Jung was an adolescent, he was, as I have indicated, deeply influenced by Schopenhauer, who himself owed a great deal to Kant. Schopenhauer realized that human perception of reality is limited by the construction of the human perceptual apparatus. We are bound to perceive objects in the external world as existing in space and time and as being governed by causal relations, and we cannot transcend the limitations which our concepts of space, time, and causality impose upon us. Schopenhauer concluded that we can never perceive objects as things in themselves; that we can only perceive their representations. If this is true, it follows that there must be an underlying reality in which things in themselves exist independently of human perception.

However, it follows that the underlying reality postulated must be one in which objects are not differentiated: in other words, a unity. For abolishing the categories of space, time, and causality necessarily makes it impossible to distinguish one object from another. Schopenhauer is resuscitating the medieval concept of the *unus mundus*; the notion that there is an ultimate unity outside the categories of time and space, and beyond the Cartesian separation of reality into mental and physical. Schopenhauer took over Plato's theory that Ideas, as ideal examples of Truth, Justice, Goodness and so on, existed as definable entities in some realm outside time.

Jung embraced this notion whole-heartedly. He equated archetypes with Platonic Ideas, and wrote:

> there are present in every psyche forms which are unconscious but nonetheless active – living dispositions, ideas in the Platonic sense, that pre-form and continually influence our thoughts and feelings and actions.[26]

That archetypes are present in every psyche is easy to accept, for the reasons given above. But many people will find more difficult to believe, as Plato, Schopenhauer, and Jung certainly did believe, that there is an objective order beyond the human psyche and the world of phenomena, including causality and time, in which Ideas or archetypes exist eternally. In his later writings, Jung more often refers to the collective unconscious as the objective psyche. In the *Septem Sermones ad Mortuos*, referred to earlier, Jung uses the Gnostic term *pleroma* to refer to an underlying 'nothing and everything' in which there are no opposites like good and evil, beautiful and ugly, time and space, or force and matter, because they are equally balanced. All opposites are a product of the Creation, the division of the world into distinct processes in space and time.

Since Heisenberg's Uncertainty Principle established that the position and velocity of particles could not simultaneously be determined because the act of observation influenced their behaviour, it has been impossible to show that atomic processes obey the laws of causality. Jung believed that the same was true in psychology, since the observer could not be separated from what he observed, and making the contents of the unconscious conscious altered the way in which each division of the mind functioned.

Jung thought that the physicist's investigation of matter and the psychologist's investigation of mind were different ways of approaching the same underlying reality. 'Heisenberg argued that ultimate reality is to be found not in electrons, mesons, and protons but in something that lies beyond them, in abstract symmetries that manifest themselves in the material world and could be taken as the scientific descendants of Plato's ideal forms.'[27] In Jung's view, this underlying reality was neither mind nor matter, but something which partook of both which he called 'psychoid'. Pauli, a world-renowned physicist who was also Jung's patient, thought that Jung's theories bridged the gap between subjective and objective which has plagued modern physics. He also postulated an underlying cosmic order distinct from the world of phenomena. David Bohm's 'implicate order' is another example of the same idea. The orders of matter, space, and time may all be explicate manifestations of an underlying implicate order.

Acceptance of the idea that there is a realm in which causality does not, or cannot be proved to, operate opens the door to other possibilities. Jung came to believe that there was an acausal principle which linked events having a similar meaning by their coincidence in time rather than sequentially. He called this principle *synchronicity*. Many people have been puzzled by what seem to be meaningful coincidences, but are content to assume that there are rational explanations for such things within the causal framework. For instance, a previously unfamiliar name seems to manifest itself with surprising frequency only because we have just become aware of it. Dreams and external events sometimes coincide: it would be surprising if they did not.

But Jung gives very few instances of synchronous happenings, and those which he does give are repeated several times in different places in his collected works. One favourite example is of a patient who had a dream in which she was given a golden scarab. Whilst she was recounting the dream, a rose-chafer beetle, which resembles a scarab, knocked against the window-pane and was caught by Jung as it flew in. Is this coincidence or a manifestation of synchrony between mind and the phenomenal world? Another is the story reported of Swedenborg, who, while he was in Gothenburg in 1756, had a vision of a great fire raging in Stockholm during the time it was actually taking place.[28] This latter example also demonstrates consistency in Jung's view of the world, since it first occurs in one of the lectures which he gave to the Zofingia student fraternity when he was still a medical student. Synchronicity entered Jung's vocabulary at a later date: at the time of this lecture, May 1897, Jung describes Swedenborg's vision as clairvoyant, adding that his audience must be content with this one example, since it would be a waste of time to cite additional cases. 'Anyone who has ever taken a look at the relevant literature can easily discover any number of cases substantiating this phenomenon.'[29] Can they? I doubt it.

I have already quoted from David Peat's book on synchronicity which is subtitled *The Bridge Between Matter and Mind*.[30] Although I am not wholly persuaded, Peat makes out a good case for supposing that synchronicity is compatible with the views of the universe advanced by modern physicists, and we are not justified in supposing that Jung's espousal of synchronicity is in any way comparable with the science fictions of Ouspensky or Gurdjieff.

Jung's interest in the occult goes back to before the time of his doctoral dissertation, *On the Psychology and Pathology of So-called Occult Phenomena*. In one of his lectures to the Zofingia student fraternity he affirmed his belief in spiritualism, more particularly in the materialization of mysterious hands which he claimed had been photographed. It is fair to say that, at that date, many intelligent philosophers and scientists were inclined to believe in spiritualism.

When I met him in 1951, he told me with evident relish that the inhabitants of the villages near Zürich still believed in magic and in local medicine men. For example, a schoolteacher became neurotic after his father's death. It turned out that, in a fit of pique, the teacher had driven a nail into the father's favourite apple tree. The father made no comment, but soon became ill and died. Two cows were found with their horns locked together and their necks through the same halter in a way so unnatural that no one could make out how they could have got like that. Was it witchcraft? 'One doesn't talk about these things,' said Jung.

Jung had more than a passing interest in astrology. In a letter to Freud dated 12 June, 1911, he described his evenings as being taken up with horoscopic calculations. 'I dare say that we shall one day discover in astrology a good deal of knowledge that has been intuitively projected into the heavens.'[31] In a letter written in 1970, the art historian Edgar Wind recalls a meeting with Jung.

The conversation with Jung (which took place in the middle thirties in London) was confined to one subject – astrology. He explained that he had calculated his own horoscope and, by doing so, had learned a great deal about himself; and that he often recommended it to his patients, who likewise learned a great deal about themselves by that method. I then asked him whether he meant that astrology (as the official practitioners assert) is a science that enables you to predict future events, or merely that a horoscope can be used as a schematic substratum – just as coffee grounds or a pack of cards is used by prophetic gypsies, or a crystal by a crystal-gazer – to arouse the imagination and project into the schema certain images that unconsciously occupy your mind. He burst out laughing and said that of course he meant the second, but that if he told that to his patients it would not work. I replied that, in view of the fact that I was not his patient, he should perhaps not use with me the same mystifying language that he might find appropriate in the consulting room. But he did not agree with that at all. What was good for his patients and for himself was good for everybody, and if I declined to calculate my own horoscope, this merely showed that I had a resistance to learning to know myself a little better.[32]

Jung thought that there were long-lasting transformations of the collective psyche which corresponded with the ancient idea of the Platonic year in which the earth's axis revolves round an imaginary point in the course of some 25,000 years. At intervals of approximately 2,100 years there is a shift in the vernal equinox. Adopting the prophetic role which he had formerly repudiated, he considered it his duty to warn that vast changes were imminent, although he realized that most scientists and psychologists would dismiss these ideas as rubbish.

It is not presumption that drives me, but my conscience as a psychiatrist that bids me fulfil my duty and prepare those few who will hear me for coming events which are in accord with the end of an era. As we know from ancient Egyptian history, they are manifestations of psychic changes which always appear at the end of one Platonic month and at the beginning of another. Apparently they are changes in the constellation of psychic dominants, of the archetypes or 'gods' as they used to be called, which bring about, or accompany, long-lasting transformations of the collective psyche. This transformation started in the historical era and left its traces first in the passing of the aeon of Taurus into that of Aries, and then of Aries into Pisces, whose beginning coincides with the rise of Christianity. We are now nearing that great change which may be expected when the spring-point enters Aquarius.[33]

Jung certainly believed that his superior insight and special grasp of unconscious processes justified his assumption of the prophetic mantle. 'It is important to have a secret, a premonition of things unknown. It fills life with something impersonal, a *numinosum*. A man who has never experienced that has missed something important.'[34]

Jung's loss of faith, first in orthodox Christianity, later in Freudian psychoanalysis, led to his discovery of God in the unconscious. Naturally enough, he believed that his variety of analysis could be the answer for others who found themselves distressed because of a similar loss of faith. But, to my mind, he failed to consider other solutions. Jung became angry when Sabina Spielrein suggested that the phantasies with which he was wrestling might be something to do with art. Because he rated religion as being of far greater significance than art, Jung had to interpret the healing factor which he perceived as active within his own psyche as a religious phenomenon. Yet the mandalas which he found himself painting, which he interpreted as symbols of 'wholeness', could equally well have been understood as aesthetic, rather than religious, ways of ordering the chaos of conflicting emotions which beset him.

In another book, I compared Jung's loss of faith with Nietzsche's.[35] Nietzsche agreed with Jung in thinking that it was necessary to depend upon something other than the ego; but Nietzsche used the language of aesthetics to describe his search for meaning and order. Although Nietzsche eventually succumbed to general paresis, I think that his perception of the problem which faced both Jung and himself was equally convincing. Both men recognized that conscious striving is not enough; that the processes which make coherent sense out of existence proceed unconsciously and cannot be willed, although the right conscious attitude may promote their progress. But Nietzsche's vision is the wider one. He realized that there were a number of different ideals to which men could devote themselves which could make life worthwhile, including music and art. As Roger Scruton wrote: 'If proof is needed of the ease with which the aesthetic may replace the religious as an object of philosophical interest, it is to be found in the thought and the personality of Nietzsche.'[36] Jung continued to place religion in a separate, superior category.

Jung, like others who become gurus, was originally an isolated child. There is a sense in which he remained isolated, as he himself recognized. Indeed, one critic of his autobiography referred to his 'insane self-absorption'. I don't know of any other analyst – except for Jung's close followers – who writes so little about personal relationships, so much about self-development. His narcissistic needs may have made him unscrupulous sexually, but he behaved no worse than many other men who are gifted with great energy and drive. He was not a confidence trickster or manipulative. Some of his beliefs bordered on delusion; but his period of mental illness opened doors of perception which are closed to normal people. As compared with the beliefs of Gurdjieff and Steiner, the views of the universe propounded by Jung seem only mildly eccentric. Yet he shared with them a conviction that he was right, that he *knew*, which disdained evidence and which is based on subjective revelation following breakdown rather than upon observation and proof.

Jung was an impressive figure even in old age; tall, powerful, both humorous and serious, and a far more fluent talker than writer. He was highly intelligent and immensely well read. Those who find themselves frustratingly confused by Jung's writings should turn to the verbatim reports of his seminars which reveal him as an accomplished off-the-cuff speaker both in German and in English. His charisma was based upon his certainty that he was right, but was reinforced by his verbal fluency and by his ability to quote support for his doctrines from innumerable obscure sources. Jung's contributions to psychology and psychotherapy have been underestimated, because of the revelatory, unproveable basis upon which they rest, and the general perception that he is a difficult writer preoccupied with esoteric subjects. Although conventionally-minded sceptics like myself are likely to regard some of Jung's beliefs as eccentric, this is not a reason for dismissing everything which he wrote. His conception of the psyche as a self-regulating system is illuminating. His typology of introvert and extravert has been adopted by experimental psychologists. He made original contributions to psychotherapy which are important and lasting. Because of his own experience, he drew attention to a phenomenon which has not received the investigation it deserves: the need which those who have lost their faith feel for something to replace it, and the dangers which threaten us all when whole populations worship dictators like Stalin and Mao rather than a god beyond the skies. Experimental psychologists, for the most part, do not feel the need to believe in anything other than science; but experimental psychologists are only a tiny fraction of mankind.

Jung was a guru who saw the light, who generalized from his own experience, who abandoned the scientific tradition in which he had been trained, and who knew that he was right. In spite of this, he made valuable contributions to psychology and to our perception of human nature.

VI

SIGMUND FREUD

SIGMUND FREUD

THROUGHOUT HIS LONG life, Freud claimed to be a scientist. He would have indignantly repudiated the title of guru, and dismissed any suggestion that he was promulgating a faith. Yet psychoanalysis is partly based on personal revelation and is neither a science nor merely a method of treatment. Ernest Gellner's brilliant book *The Psychoanalytic Movement* is an enquiry into how psychoanalysis so quickly became 'the dominant idiom for the discussion of the human personality and of human relations.'[1] He calls psychoanalysis 'a theory, a technique, an organization, a language, an ethos, an ethic, a climate.'[2] Freud was far more of a guru than his followers have acknowledged.

It is true that, in German speaking countries, the word 'science' has different overtones from those to which we are accustomed in England. *Naturwissenschaft* is what we call science: *Geistwissenschaft* refers to the humanities. But the same word *Wissenschafter* is used for both scholar and scientist, which somewhat blurs the distinction. Freud certainly began his professional career as a scientist in the English sense, for he carried out anatomical and physiological research in the laboratories of Ernst Brücke, who was a notoriously hard-headed determinist. Freud remained a determinist, believing that all psychological phenomena are rigidly determined by the principle of cause and effect. If he could have afforded to do so, Freud would have preferred to spend his life in scientific research; but his wish to get married compelled him to qualify in medicine and embark upon medical practice as a way of making a living. Freud cannot be accused of not understanding the requirements of science, although he himself abandoned them.

It can be argued that Freud spent most of his life in work which is as difficult to quantify or replicate as is philosophy. But he insisted on calling psychoanalysis a science, in spite of the fact that very few of the hypotheses of psychoanalysis can be subjected to scientific scrutiny and proved or disproved. Observations made during the course of psychoanalytic treatment are the basis for most psychoanalytic theories; but each psychoanalytic session is unique and cannot be replicated. Moreover, observations made during the course of psychoanalytic treatment are inevitably contaminated with the subjective prejudice of the observer. This is why philosophers and scientists have generally rejected psychoanalysis as scientifically unsound. If Freud had been content to maintain that psychoanalysis was a hermeneutic system, a historical way of interpreting human behaviour in terms of past events and influences, he might have kept the respect of scientists.

However, the fact that Freud was not the scientist which he claimed to be does not diminish his importance. He is rightly linked with Marx and Darwin as being one of the three original thinkers who have most altered man's view of himself in the twentieth century. Even if every theory which Freud advanced could be proved wrong, it would still be the case that Freud caused a revolution in the way we think. Freud did not invent the concept of the unconscious, but he applied it clinically and made it operational. His reductive approach to the mind tended to interpret highly complex behaviour in terms of simple, biological origins. He was an expert at undermining pretensions, and at reducing all human striving to the lowest common denominator. The founder of psychoanalysis had a low opinion of the majority of human beings. As he remarked in one of his letters to Fliess, he became a therapist against his will, and was not inspired by any altruistic desire to relieve suffering. But the fact that he remained detached and impersonal when treating patients contributed to his insights, especially to his discovery of transference. Freud was a remarkably perceptive observer whose detailed accounts of mental states like melancholia and obsessional neurosis are still illuminating. Many of his original papers are classics, which should be read and re-read because of the excellence of Freud's clinical descriptions. It is psychoanalytic causal explanations in terms of infantile experience and phantasy which make us incredulous, not Freud's portrayals of psychiatric phenomena.

It is still insufficiently appreciated that some of the most fundamental hypotheses of psychoanalysis had nothing to do with the objective observation of clinical cases. As with the revelations of the gurus whom we have already examined, they had a purely subjective origin, and followed upon a period of mental and physical distress; Freud's 'creative illness'. The Oedipus complex and the theory of dreams were the product of Freud's own self-analysis. As Ellenberger points out:

> Over a period of about six years (1894 to 1899) four events are inextricably intermingled in Freud's life: his intimate relationship with Wilhelm Fliess, his neurotic disturbances, his self-analysis, and his elaboration of the basic principles of psychoanalysis.[3]

During these years, Freud broke with Josef Breuer, his first collaborator. He also wrote, and then abandoned, his *Project for a Scientific Psychology*, which was his attempt to link psychological and neurological mechanisms. He suffered from a recurrent cardiac arrhythmia, shortness of breath, and disturbing doubts alternating with the conviction that he was on the brink of making great discoveries. He brooded constantly on the problems of the neuroses. His letters to Fliess reveal a recurrent state of mental torment. His distress was increased by the death of his father in October 1896.

The publication of *The Interpretation of Dreams* in November 1899, the book which more than any other enshrines Freud's 'revelation', can be taken to mark the end of his creative illness. He was convinced that he had indeed discovered a new theory of the mind. As Peter Gay puts it: 'By the time he published *The Interpretation of Dreams* at the end of 1899, the principles of psychoanalysis were in place.'[4] But these principles were based more upon Freud's own subjective experience and his own dreams than upon clinical observation. He himself recorded the subjective origin of his dream theory. While staying at the Schloss Bellevue outside Vienna in July 1895, Freud dreamed his famous dream of 'Irma's injection.' The details of this famous dream, which has provoked a vast literature, can be found in *The Interpretation of Dreams*. In this context, it is enough to say that Freud interpreted the dream as an attempt to absolve him from mishandling the treatment of a patient, and therefore concluded that the dream represented the fulfilment of a wish. When he stayed again at the Schloss Bellevue in 1900, he wrote to his friend Fliess:

Do you suppose that someday one will read on a marble tablet
on this house:
Here, on July 24, 1895,
the secret of the dream
revealed itself to Dr. Sigm. Freud.[5]

Freud's creative illness was followed by the conviction that he had
indeed discovered a new theory of the mind. He continued to believe
that *The Interpretation of Dreams* contained the most valuable of all
his insights. It was because so many of his ideas originated from his
self-analysis that Freud was certain that they were valid. For example,
he wrote to Fliess:

A single idea of general value dawned on me. I have found, in
my own case too, [the phenomenon of] being in love with my
mother and jealous of my father, and I now consider it a universal
event in early childhood.[6]

This is how the Oedipus complex became established as a corner-
stone of psychoanalytic theory!

We have already observed that one of the characteristics of gurus
is that they generalize from their own experience. Freud is a prime
example. As Breuer wrote to Auguste Forel:

Freud is a man given to absolute and exclusive formulations:
this is a psychical need which, in my opinion, leads to excessive
generalization.[7]

A good example of this is Freud's theory of dreams. Freud stated
that, with very few exceptions, dreams were disguised, hallucinatory
fulfilments of repressed sexual wishes of an infantile kind. In spite of
a good deal of evidence to the contrary, Freud tenaciously held to
this theory, providing many extremely ingenious interpretations of
dreams to support it. There is ample reason to suppose that dreams
are of many different varieties, but once Freud had formulated a
theory, he was so convinced that he was right that no criticism by
others was able to shake him. Again, we encounter a belief system
rather than a scientific theory which can be proved or disproved.

Freud originally thought that hysteria was caused by premature sexual experience in the early years of childhood, and that this was the result of seduction by a parent or other adult. In his paper *The Aetiology of Hysteria,* he wrote that, on the basis of eighteen cases,

Whatever case and whatever symptom we take as our point of departure, *in the end we infallibly come to the field of sexual experience.*[8]

This was the last time Freud attempted to give any figures concerning aetiology, and, even in this instance, there were no controls. There is also no evidence that the analysis of any of these cases was completed or that any of the patients were actually cured. Freud went on to say:

I therefore put forward the thesis that at the bottom of every case of hysteria there are *one or more occurrences of premature sexual experience,* occurrences which belong to the earliest years of childhood, but which can be reproduced through the work of psychoanalysis in spite of the intervening decades. I believe that this is an important finding, the discovery of a *caput Nili* in neuropathology.[9]

He believed that the repression of such incidents prevented the adult from achieving a normal sex life, but that psychoanalysis could bring the traumatic events back to consciousness, and, by abreacting the emotions connected with them, free the patient of their malign effects.

There are in fact a variety of reasons why patients develop hysterical symptoms. One such reason is the necessity of escaping from an intolerable situation. Soldiers exposed to long periods of stress in the trenches during the First World War sometimes developed paralyses, blindness, or other symptoms for which no organic cause could be discovered, but which had the result of temporarily removing them from the front line. Sexual trauma is not the only kind of trauma to give rise to hysterical symptoms; but Freud gave sexuality so central a place in psychoanalytic theory that he paid scant attention to other factors. It was Freud's insistence that sexuality was the causal factor in *every* case of hysteria that brought an end to Josef Breuer's collaboration with him.

Freud came to believe that his first theories were wrong; that not all cases of hysteria could be explained by actual sexual seduction in early childhood. Although he recognized that such seductions undoubtedly occurred, and might cause lasting damage, he could not believe that they happened quite as frequently as his growing practice suggested. Moreover, he had observed that his brother and sisters exhibited some hysterical symptoms. If actual seduction was the cause, Freud would have had to incriminate his own father, who, he was sure, could not have behaved in such a fashion. It took him a long time and a great deal of dedicated self-analysis before he could construct alternative theories which satisfied him. As his own childhood memories emerged, he became gradually more aware of his own early sexual phantasies. This led him to conclude that neurotic symptoms were more closely related to phantasies than to actual events.

Freud's original aim was to establish psychoanalysis as a method of treatment comparable with the medical treatment of disease. He believed that he had discovered the cause of neurotic symptoms, and also a technique for getting rid of them. After abandoning the seduction theory, he concluded that what was subjected to repression were instinctual impulses manifesting themselves as phantasies. If a patient could be helped to overcome the blocks imposed by repression, and recall his or her earliest infantile sexual impulses, these could be brought into consciousness and abreacted, thus opening the previously impeded path toward sexual maturity. If this goal was reached, neurosis must disappear; since, according to Freud, all neuroses were the indirect expression of repressed infantile sexual impulses and mature sexual satisfaction was incompatible with neurosis.

If Freud's original model had been true, psychoanalysis could have been taught and learned like any other medical or surgical technique, and the analyst could have remained a detached, skilled practitioner who simply observed his patient's behaviour and interpreted his verbal communications. There were three main reasons why this hope remained unfulfilled. First, to Freud's initial distress, he encountered the phenomena of transference. Although Freud tried to maintain his preferred role of being no more than a 'mountain guide', he found that, inevitably, his patients put him in the position of a father-figure, an idealized lover, or even a saviour. What his patients wanted was far more than the abolition of their neurotic symptoms: they wanted his understanding, his appreciation of them as individuals, his concern, even his love.

Second, as Freud developed psychoanalytic theory, he spread its net wider and wider, until it included art, literature, religion, humour, and anthropology. In other words, psychoanalysis became a generalized psychology which purported to explain the normal human being as well as the neurotic, and which could be applied to the whole of human culture.

Third, the type of patient seeking psychoanalytic treatment changed. Many of Freud's early patients were hysterics of a type rarely encountered today. Others were obsessionals with clear-cut symptoms in the shape of compulsive rituals or thoughts. As psychoanalysis became established, the boundary between psychological health and illness became blurred, so that more and more patients consulted psychoanalysts about what have been called 'problems in living'; difficulties in relationships, or a generalized dissatisfaction with life. Some analysts believed that, if men and women were to be able to reach their full potential, everyone should be analysed. For many who volunteered to lie on the couch, psychoanalysis was no longer a technique of abolishing neurotic symptoms. It had become a way of making sense out of life and giving it meaning.

In the early days there was no question in Freud's mind of psychoanalysis becoming a substitute for religion, since he himself rejected religious belief as a disguised infantile longing for a father's protection, and interpreted religious observances as ritual ways of defending the self against the incursion of unacceptable instinctive forces. In Freud's view, religion was no more than a universal obsessional neurosis. The last sentence of his book *The Future of an Illusion* is:

No, our science is no illusion. But an illusion it would be to suppose that what science cannot give us we can get elsewhere.[10]

However, Freud's belief in psychoanalysis went far beyond any scientific evidence which might support it. In May 1913 he wrote to his disciple Ferenczi, 'We possess the truth; I am as sure of it as fifteen years ago'[11] (when he was writing *The Interpretation of Dreams*).

Although Freud continued to proclaim that psychoanalysis was a science, psychoanalysis became a movement which more closely resembled a secular religion than a set of scientific theories. It may have been inevitable, though regrettable, that a theory which apparently comprehended so much of that which constitutes human life should itself become a way of life, and, since Freud was its originator, that he should be regarded as someone who knew and taught how life should be lived; a guru rather than merely a physician. But Freud was certainly not averse to adopting this role.

If we compare Freud with the other gurus whom we have considered, we can say that he was less isolated in childhood and adolescence than some. But he confessed that he was bored by most of his contemporaries, and concentrated on one or two intimates. One such was Eduard Silberstein, a young Romanian whom Freud met when in his early teens. They learned Spanish together, and formed a kind of secret society for two with its own private terms of reference. Freud's friendship with Silberstein is the nearest he came to a relationship on equal terms. However, as Phyllis Grosskurth points out, 'it is clear that for Freud letters were more important than actual encounters.'[12] Freud suggested that a weekly exchange of letters describing each other's activities would be more revealing than meeting. When Silberstein admitted his infatuation with a girl whom Freud considered his inferior, Freud exhibited considerable jealousy. Silberstein later married a wife who became so severely depressed that he sent her to Freud for treatment. Whether Freud actually saw her or not is unclear; but she committed suicide on May 14, 1891 by throwing herself down the stairwell of the building in which Freud practised.

Another intimate was Wilhelm Fliess, the recipient of the famous series of letters from Freud which have thrown so much light upon the history of psychoanalysis. Although Fliess was a little younger than Freud, Freud looked up to him, idealized him, and was sometimes embarrassingly sycophantic. As Fliess practised as a surgeon in Berlin and Freud lived in Vienna, their relationship was chiefly epistolary. Freud's dependency on Fliess gradually diminished until their friendship came to an end by the beginning of 1902. Freud's masochistic submission, in this example, can be seen as the reverse of the dominance which he later established over his pupils and disciples. Like other gurus, Freud found it difficult to achieve relationships on equal terms. It is interesting and relevant that *An Autobiographical Study* concentrates almost exclusively on the development of psychoanalysis, and tells us hardly anything about his personal life or relations with other people.

Freud also resembled other gurus in being intolerant of criticism. He treated disagreement as personal hostility. He remained the dominant figure in the Vienna Psychoanalytic Society, and maintained his ascendancy by keeping a distance between himself and the other members. Even his earliest and most faithful adherents could claim Freud only as a Master, not as a friend.

Although Freud revised his ideas on a number of occasions throughout his life, the revisions were always brought about by new insights of his own rather than as a consequence of criticism by others. It has often been remarked that the squabbles about psychoanalytic theory which resulted in so many members of Freud's early circle resigning or being expelled as heretics seemed like doctrinal disputes within a Church rather than scientific disagreements. The latter can certainly be bitter; but seldom involve the character assassination and pejorative language which Freud used to describe those adherents who later disputed his theories. Freud's dogmatism and intolerance of disagreement led to the departure of many colleagues, including Adler, Stekel, Jung, and eventually Rank and Ferenczi, from the psychoanalytic movement. When his associates remained faithful disciples, Freud gave them his approval; but when they disagreed, he abused them, or accused them of being mentally ill. Adler was described by Freud as paranoiac; Stekel as unbearable and a louse; Jung as brutal and sanctimonious. Psychoanalysis became more and more like a religious cult, and Freud himself applied the term *heretics* to defectors.

Although Freud dismissed religion as an illusion, his conviction that he was right was a matter of faith rather than of reason. As Richard Webster aptly observes:

What is remarkable about Freud's leadership of the psychoanalytic movement is that although he quite clearly did not believe in any kind of supernatural creator, he adopted almost without exception the strategies of those who did. In effect he treated his own theories as if they were a personal revelation granted to him by God and demanded that others should accord to them the reverence which the sacred word usually commands.[13]

As Freud himself might have remarked, but did not do so in his own case, this insistence that disciples accept a guru's message without criticism argues that the guru himself has secret doubts. We have already observed that gurus need the reassurance which disciples provide, just as disciples need the guru as leader.

Freud was certainly deeply disturbed by the defection of Jung. However, he was somewhat mollified by the suggestion, advanced by Ernest Jones and Sandor Ferenczi, that a secret committee of true believers should be formed which would preserve and protect both Freud and his theories. The committee consisted of Karl Abraham, Max Eitingon, Ernest Jones, Hanns Sachs, Sandor Ferenczi, and Otto Rank, who were selected as especially dependable, although as noted earlier, the last two eventually defected.

Like other gurus, Freud possessed considerable charisma, based upon his certainty that he was right. His ideas began to spread throughout the western world, partly because he was a gifted writer and speaker. Freud's literary style was commented upon favourably while he was still at school. In 1930, he was awarded the Goethe prize for literature. Even in translation, Freud's writings are a pleasure to read. He is persuasive because he is at pains to disarm possible critics, and because he presents his conclusions as the only sensible deductions from the facts. The reader is lulled into accepting Freud's conclusions because his literary skill has made them appear more reasonable than they are.

He was equally persuasive as a speaker. Freud was never a demagogue, but he was a fluent lecturer who could hold forth coherently without notes for as long as four hours to an audience who listened enthralled. He did not harangue, but spoke slowly, clearly, and energetically. Often, he would interrupt his discourse to invite questions. His *Introductory Lectures*, delivered in three series at the University of Vienna, and subsequently published, were among the most commercially successful of his writings. His biographer, Peter Gay, admired his persuasive skills and wrote:

The very sequence of the lectures was a cunning effort at seduction: by beginning with slips, Freud introduced his audience to psychoanalytic ideas through ordinary, often amusing, mundane events; moving on to dreams, another mental experience familiar to all, he departed from the solid ground of common sense, slowly, deliberately.[14]

As we have seen, Freud exhibited a number of the typical features of gurus, but virtually none of their corrupt or disreputable characteristics. He charged high fees to those who could afford them, but was also generous to those in need. He himself lived simply; and apart from his obsessional accumulation of antique statuettes, showed no evidence of extravagant tastes or of personal concern with accumulating money. It may have been different where funding the movement was concerned. Frederick Crews has disinterred a disagreeable story of Freud suggesting to a colleague that he should proceed with his aim of divorcing his wife and marrying an heiress in order to get hold of some of her money for the 'Psychoanalytic Funds'.[15] But the tone of Freud's reported letter about this is ironic and facetious, and it would be unwise to read much into it.

Freud was dogmatically sure of his theories; but, unlike some of the gurus whom we have considered, exhibited no features of psychotic illness like delusions or hallucinations. He may sometimes have over-emphasized the antisemitism which had delayed his professional promotion, and which, in his view, also posed a threat to psychoanalysis; but it could not possibly be alleged that he was seriously paranoid. For antisemitism in Vienna was an ever-present reality. It markedly increased during the latter years of the nineteenth century. A stock market crash, for which the Jews were blamed, occurred in 1873, the year in which Freud went to university. Karl Lueger, who became Mayor of Vienna in 1897, had made antisemitism a feature of his election campaign. When Hitler marched into Austria in March 1938, the Viennese Nazis were amongst the most virulent of his antisemitic followers.

Freud was not above enlisting the help of former patients to gain advancement, but this hardly amounts to corruption. Frau Elise Gomperz and the Baroness Marie von Ferstel both approached the Minister of Education on Freud's behalf, asking that he should be given the position of associate professor, for which he had been repeatedly rejected over several years. The Baroness presented the Minister with a painting for the new gallery he was intending to establish, which may have been a token of gratitude.[16]

Freud may or may not have had an affair with his sister-in-law, but there is no evidence, so far as I know, that he abused his position by seducing either patients or psychoanalytic colleagues. He was certainly attracted by Lou Andreas Salomé – who wasn't? – but he did not meet her until 1911, when she was fifty and he was fifty-five. Her picture adorned his study wall, and he conducted a long correspondence with her. Judging by what we know of Freud's character, it is unlikely that he was sexually active outside marriage. He was busy with patients during the day, and then wrote late into the night.

Although many of Freud's ideas were unsound, I think his influence upon the way we think about ourselves has, on the whole, been beneficial. Psychoanalysis has increased tolerance of unconventional behaviour and has banished some forms of prudery. Freud's technique of listening to distressed people over long periods rather than giving them orders or advice has formed the foundation of most modern forms of psychotherapy, with benefit both to patients and practitioners. But the fact that Freud became elevated into a guru and that psychoanalysis became a way of life has had a number of undesirable consequences from which we have not fully recovered.

In the 1930s and well into the 1950s, psychoanalysts considered themselves, by virtue of their training, to have acquired a unique insight into human nature from which those who had not been analysed must always be excluded. Psychoanalytic training offered membership of an élite circle claiming superior knowledge and status. Those who questioned psychoanalytic theory or practice were said to be insufficiently analysed. As an inevitable consequence of faith combined with intolerance, psychoanalytic societies and institutes, on both sides of the Atlantic, became divided into splinter groups and warring factions, each claiming possession of 'the truth', exactly as happens in religious movements. Freud was more of a messianic figure than many people realize; but some of his disciples became deluded fanatics.

Many psychoanalysts, convinced of their own superior wisdom

and insight, became as intolerant as their Master toward any who disagreed with them, including their own colleagues. The history of the internal quarrels in the British Psycho-Analytical Society between orthodox Freudians and the adherents of Melanie Klein is both absurd and intensely depressing. Here were supposedly adult, intelligent people who all professed a special understanding of human nature and considered themselves qualified to help others resolve their emotional problems, vilifying each other and tearing the Society in pieces, because of disputes about psycho-analytic doctrine which seem as ridiculous to the non-believer as do the disputes about ὁμοούσια (homoousia) and ὁμοίουσια (homoiousia), the Arian controversy which divided the Christian church in the fourth century.

One of the regrettable aspects of becoming a psychoanalyst was, and maybe still is, a tendency to become more and more isolated from the ordinary world. Janet Malcolm, describing a New York émigrée analyst, wrote:

Her entire life was taken up with psychoanalytic concerns: during the day she saw patients, at night she went to meetings at the Institute, and when she and her husband went out to dinner or entertained at home it was always with analysts. Other people fall away, she explained. There is less and less to talk about with people on the 'outside' who don't look at things the way analysts do.[17]

This is a danger affecting all esoteric groups. Just as disciples reinforce a guru's belief in himself and his mission, so disciples reinforce each other's beliefs and allegiance. Esoteric groups become mutual reassurance systems, confirming each disciple's conviction that he or she has special insights as to how life should be lived which are denied to the ordinary person.

Since psychoanalysis became a faith rather than a form of medical treatment, it was indiscriminately applied by its practitioners to all kinds of psychiatric cases, whether they showed benefit or not. One does not expose 'the truth' to the dangers of critical evaluation. The length of time required for 'complete analysis' became more and more extended. Obsessional patients, if they have the money, are notoriously liable to continue with analysis for ever, since they are often in search of a perfection which is unattainable. Since such patients provide analysts with a long-term regular income, it is unsurprising that their analyses may go on for ten years or more with minimum benefit. Other psychoanalysts have specialized in treating psychotic patients whom Freud himself would have refused to take on for treatment. As early as 1904, Freud specifically advised that analysts should only take on patients who exhibited some degree of normality from which morbid manifestations could be differentiated. This is not the case in the major psychoses. Although it is certainly true that patients suffering from schizophrenia and manic-depressive illness benefit from less doctrinaire forms of psychotherapy combined with medication, the long-term attempts of psychoanalysts to cure psychotics by Freudian psychoanalysis alone have proved so unsuccessful that some psychiatrists consider such attempts malpractice. These abuses are a direct result of psychoanalysis having been elevated into a faith, rather than remaining a treatment for illness which can be criticized, modified, or replaced by something better.

Psychoanalysis was acclaimed in the United States with particular enthusiasm. Its pre-eminence as an article of psychiatric faith was greatly increased by the influx of refugees from Central Europe who fled the Nazis. For a time, it became difficult for an aspiring psychiatrist to attain a leading position unless he had been trained as a psychoanalyst and had been accepted by one of the recognized psychoanalytic organizations. Now that psychoanalysis has been largely discarded in favour of biological psychiatry, which takes the view that mental illness depends upon physical malfunction of the brain, exactly the opposite state of affairs prevails. Freudian psychoanalysis has been so discredited that the value of psychotherapy of any kind tends to be underestimated. The prescription of drugs is easily learned, but it can never wholly take the place of psychotherapy. In the training of psychiatrists, the wheat has been thrown out with the chaff, the baby with the bath-water. This is another unfortunate consequence of psychoanalysis having become a belief system rather than remaining a heuristic discipline.

It was Freud who taught us how to listen; and, as I have already observed, his technique of giving undivided attention to the problems of distressed people over long periods of time has had a strikingly beneficial effect upon many forms of psychotherapy which do not accept the doctrines of psychoanalysis in their original form. People who are mentally ill or who are suffering from severe emotional stress are in need of understanding and acceptance, whether or not they require medication. Psychotherapists learn to listen without passing judgement; to accept without issuing orders or proffering direct advice; to be both objective and compassionate. Some other gurus who were not psychoanalysts seem to have adopted this attitude to their followers when the latter needed help, as we noted in the example of Gurdjieff. The story of the rise and fall of psychoanalysis has much to teach us about those who need gurus.

Many of those who have been psychoanalytic patients do not lose all their symptoms or accept the psychoanalytic interpretation of those symptoms. Yet a number will persist with analysis in spite of not being 'cured'. I think this is because the psychoanalytic procedure provides valuable experiences which are not easily available in ordinary social life. First, simply talking about personal problems with the minimum of interruption objectifies those problems and, in doing so, may make them more easily soluble. Nearly everyone who has been in analysis gains some increase in self-understanding, because talking clarifies the issues. It could be argued that keeping a detailed diary might have the same effect; and I certainly support the idea that diaries can increase insight. But keeping a diary does not give a distressed patient the sense of being accepted as a person which a favourable experience of analysis brings. Many of those who seek analysis feel that they have never been accepted or valued for what they are. The discovery that another human being is prepared to listen, to get to know one intimately and still not reject one, is a revelation to some people.

What Freud believed he was providing is very different from what he actually provided. He thought that he had found both an explanation of neurosis and a way of curing it. But only one of the four cases which he treated personally and described in detail could be said to be cured, and we have no long-term follow-up of this patient (the 'Rat Man').[18] What he did provide was tolerant, continuing care over a long period, which in itself is therapeutic. The so-called 'Wolf Man' exemplifies this conclusion. He was first seen by Freud in 1910 and treated by him until July 1914. He returned to treatment with Freud from November 1919 until February 1920, and was later treated by at least four other psychoanalysts. A series of interviews with him when he was in his eighties revealed that he actually rejected the causal interpretations which Freud made about the origin of his disorder, rightly calling them far-fetched. What he valued was Freud's personal care of him. The 'Wolf-Man's' considerable improvement after his first period of treatment with Freud had nothing to do with Freud's reconstruction of his supposed infantile sexuality, but depended upon his finding in Freud an understanding father-figure upon whom he could rely.

The last of Freud's *New Introductory Lectures on Psycho-Analysis* is given the title 'The Question of a Weltanschauung.' It is an enthralling piece of writing which strives to persuade us that psychoanalysis is a specialist branch of science which accepts the scientific view of the universe and which is therefore quite unsuited to construct a *Weltanschauung* of its own. Freud rightly affirms that science

> asserts that there are no sources of knowledge of the universe other than the intellectual working-over of carefully scrutinized observations – in other words, what we call research – and alongside of it no knowledge derived from revelation, intuition or divination.[19]

But as we have seen, revelation played a vital part in Freud's original formulations. Freud then claims that psychoanalysis has extended scientific research to the mental field; a claim which cannot be substantiated. He goes on to point out that Marxism, having begun as a social science, developed into a *Weltanschauung*.

> Any critical examination of Marxist theory is forbidden, doubts of its correctness are punished in the same way as heresy was once punished by the Catholic Church. The writings of Marx have taken the place of the Bible and the Koran as a source of revelation, though they would seem to be no more free from contradictions and obscurities than those older sacred books.[20]

If we substitute the word 'psychoanalysis' for 'Marxist theory' in the first sentence of this passage, and the name 'Freud' for that of 'Marx' in the second sentence, we have an exact description of what happened to psychoanalysis, especially in its early days; but Freud was unable to see this.

Freud ostensibly rejected the role of guru, but in fact exemplified it. As is the case with other gurus, his legacy is mixed. Freud was both inventive and ingenious. Although the light which he shed on the human mind is not so bright as his disciples claimed, it has nevertheless illumined some dark corners of human behaviour, increased tolerance, contributed to the technique of psychotherapy, and revolutionized the way we think about our own behaviour. Twentieth-century man in greatly indebted to Freud.

VII

THE JESUIT AND JESUS

IGNATIUS OF LOYOLA

IGNATIUS OF LOYOLA, founder of the Society of Jesus, is regarded by the Roman Catholic Church as one of the greatest saints who ever lived. What is particularly interesting about him in the context of this book is the nature of his creative illness and the revelation which followed it, which transformed him from a hidalgo into a spiritual teacher. Although Rudolf Steiner claimed that 'The Mystery of Golgotha' was central to his view of the universe, he could not be described as an orthodox Christian. In contrast, Ignatius was able to incorporate his own conversion and revelation into the framework of Catholic doctrine although his teaching was initially regarded with some suspicion by the Inquisition. Many of the experiences which he described and which he continued to have throughout his life would certainly be interpreted as evidence of mental illness by psychiatrists if they were reported by someone who was socially incompetent; but Ignatius was one of the most effective leaders whom the Church has ever produced. Today, the Society of Jesus is the largest male religious order in the world, with twenty-six thousand members.[1]

Iñigo de Loyola was an aristocrat, the scion of an ancient Basque family which was settled in the province of Guipúzcoa and which can be traced back to the thirteenth century. He was probably born in 1491 – the exact date is uncertain – in the castle of the Loyolas; it is likely that his mother, who had already borne nine other children, died shortly after his birth. In 1492, Granada was reconquered and the Moors finally expelled from Spain. After his father died in 1507, Iñigo was sent to live in the household of Velázquez de Cuéllar, a nobleman who was Treasurer-General of Castile and attached to the court of Queen Isabella. The adolescent boy was trained as a courtier and a soldier. He is reported as becoming ambitious, vain, and courageous: a swordsman eager for military glory; a gallant who had various affairs with women; a dueller and a gambler.

In 1517, Velázquez de Cuéllar died. His widow María de Velasco found a position for Iñigo de Loyola in the household of the Duke of Nájera, who had been appointed Viceroy of Navarre, a frontier province much fought over because of its position on the borders of France. It had been annexed by King Ferdinand in 1512, who built the citadel of Pamplona, which became the key city to the conquest of the province. When Francis I of France invaded, Iñigo was instructed to march to the city's defence. Although its magistrates had agreed to yield the city, its citadel remained intact, and Iñigo persuaded the garrison to defend it, in the hope that reinforcements would eventually arrive. On May 23 or 24, 1521, Iñigo was seriously wounded. A cannon ball passed between his legs, fracturing his right leg severely, and leaving gaping flesh wounds in his left. After a six-hour artillery battle, the citadel fell to the French. The French doctors did what they could to treat Iñigo, and, after a delay of some nine days, he was transported on a litter to his sister's residence at Anzuola. From there he reached the castle of the Loyolas soon after the middle of June.

Although the French doctors had treated him with great kindness, the Spanish surgeons concluded that the bones in his right leg must be broken again and reset if they were ever to mend satisfactorily. He bore this extremely painful operation with great fortitude, but became so severely ill afterwards that his life was in danger and he was advised to make his final confession. Following his prayers to St. Peter, a sudden change for the better occurred, and he was soon considered to be out of danger. Although the bones of his leg reunited, an unsightly bony protuberance remained which prevented him from wearing the elegant boots of the hidalgo. He begged the surgeons to remove this, although he knew that the pain of having it sawn off would be worse than any which he had yet endured. His biographers point to this demand for an operation for cosmetic reasons as evidence of his continuing masculine pride, but also pay tribute to the silent courage with which he endured this third operation and the painful traction which followed it. Unable to walk, Iñigo had to spend many weeks in bed. It was not until February 1522 that his legs were sufficiently healed to permit him to leave his ancestral home, and even then he was left with a limp and some degree of deformity.

Any man who has based his self-esteem upon physical courage, skill, and endurance, whether or not combined with sexual prowess and leadership, will understand the depressing and disturbing effect such a disabling injury must have. Psychiatrists are accustomed to seeing the devastating results which illness, injury, and early retirement have upon the lives of athletes. Some never emerge from the inevitable depression, and end up as alcoholics. Others find jobs as journalists, commentators, or men of business. It takes time, determination, and considerable strength of character to achieve this complete change in identity. Iñigo de Loyola's transformation into Ignatius, the founder of the Society of Jesus, began with his enforced immobility and consequent depression: a creative illness imposed upon him by external misfortune rather than originating spontaneously from within.

He spent much of his prolonged convalescence in reverie. One recurrent fantasy, resembling those of Don Quixote, was of serving a lady of noble birth for whom he would perform feats of arms, winning both her love and also glory for himself. But he also read what books were available to him; amongst them, the *Life of Christ* in four volumes by the Carthusian monk Ludolph of Saxony, and *Lives of the Saints* by the Italian Dominican, Jacopo de Voragine.[2] These writings gradually exerted a profound effect upon him. He became fascinated by the lives of certain saints; especially by St. Honofrio, an ascetic solitary who lived in the desert for seventy years; by St. Dominic, and by St. Francis, who, like himself, had spent his early life in worldly pursuits, but who, after an illness, became changed into a saintly prophet. According to his own account, he began to have fantasies of becoming like St. Francis or St. Dominic which alternated with his conventional, knightly and sensual day-dreams. He gradually became convinced that his worldly fantasies came from the devil but that his spiritual fantasies came from God. Towards the end of this long period of immobility and contemplation, Iñigo had a vision of the Virgin Mary with the child Jesus which filled him with joy and put an end to his fantasies of earthly love. From this time on he recorded that he was never again troubled with fleshly temptations. The vision led to his abandoning his identity of a dashing hidalgo in favour of ascetic sainthood and he conceived the wish to make a pilgrimage to Jerusalem.

When he was finally able to walk again, he took the first steps on his pilgrimage by going to the monastery of Montserrat, which is high on a mountain about thirty miles from Barcelona. Here he abandoned the sword, clothes and other trappings of his former life as a gentleman in favour of the sackcloth robe and hemp girdle of the pilgrim. He also parted company with his family, and did not communicate with them for the next ten years. Perhaps he believed that family ties were a hindrance to his attachment to God. As we know, Jesus had set a precedent. Iñigo made his confession to a French priest named Jean Chanon, and after three days made his way to Manresa, a small town below Montserrat, where he remained from March 1522 until February 1523.

During the first few months his mental state was one of constant happiness, but his mood then changed and he entered upon a period of severe depression which continued from July to October 1522. There can be little doubt that Iñigo was temperamentally manic-depressive and therefore liable to extreme alternations of mood; but it is likely that this period of depression was partly precipitated by the savage penances which he inflicted upon himself for what he considered to be the sins of his former life. He spent much of his time in solitude on an overhanging rock by the river Cardoner. He imposed such severe fasts upon himself that his health deteriorated. These months of depression constituted a 'dark night of the soul' in which he felt alienated from God, and was recurrently tempted by suicide, in spite of spending many hours of every day in prayer. He suffered from sleeplessness and was tormented by 'scruples': that is, he felt compelled repetitively to search his conscience in case there was some sin which he had minimized or failed to confess. He starved himself for a whole week in the hope that God might take pity on his misery. During this period he developed gall-stones which intermittently caused him the torments of biliary colic for the rest of his life. Because he had formerly taken pride in his appearance, and in emulation of St. Honofrio, he allowed his nails and hair to grow untrimmed. At one point in the autumn of 1522, he was discovered unconscious at a shrine and had to be nursed by friends through a severe fever, which recurred during the winter.

However, shortly before this fever attacked him, he experienced a series of spiritual illuminations which seemed to have marked the end of his scruples and his period of depression. These experiences brought him a deep serenity and peace which never subsequently left him. As he himself related, he thought he saw the Holy Trinity under the figure of three keys; a visionary experience which brought him such consolation and joy that he could not restrain his tears. On another occasion he had a vision of something white from which he believed that God had created light. He felt that 'he saw in a distinct manner the plan of divine wisdom in the creation of the world'.[3] At another time, during Mass, he saw something like white rays emanating from above which seemed to him to be related to the presence of Christ in the sacrament. When praying, he saw on many occasions a white body which he believed to signify the humanity of Christ.

How far these visionary experiences may be related to the peculiar physiological states which his fasting induced is a matter for conjecture. One vision which recurred over a period of fifteen years had the form of a serpent which was beautiful, brightly coloured, and covered with objects that shone like eyes. At first, he was comforted by this vision, but at a later time decided that it was sent by the devil. Jung discusses the archetypal significance of Ignatius's vision in his essay *On the Nature of the Psyche*.[4] There is no doubt that such visions occur in manic-depressive illness. Martin Luther, whose periods of depression were as severe as those of Iñigo de Loyola and probably more frequently recurrent, also had episodes of exaltation in which he had religious visions. Although Iñigo found it hard to describe these visions, they had such a profound effect upon him that he felt impelled to share his insights with others. The person who finally emerged from the rocks of Manresa had abandoned his former way of life, tamed his sensuality, conquered his desire for wealth and worldly eminence, and had adopted entirely new goals.

The convert hidalgo anxious only to outstrip the saints in their penances was now dedicated to the service of others. He wanted now not just to visit Jerusalem, but to work for the conversion of the Muslims.[5]

From his experience of this profound change in direction emerged the famous *Spiritual Exercises*, which, according to Catholic scholars, is an original and highly influential book of profound significance. The *Spiritual Exercises* is a practical manual designed to aid the believer's spiritual progress toward the goal of salvation. It is also designed to help the individual discover his own place in God's plan of history. Ignatius believed that, in some time in the future, God's kingdom would be established and that his supremacy would at last be recognized by all his creatures. Ronald Knox calls the *Exercises* 'a weapon of unexampled power for their own purpose. That purpose was to convert the soul, as by a kind of treatment, from worldliness and selfishness till it reached a state of unhesitating obedience to God's will and to Christ's cause.'[6] Loyola's fundamental conviction was that 'Man is created to praise, reverence, and serve God our Lord, and by this means to save his soul.'[7] Anything which obstructs this aim is to be discarded; anything which furthers it is to be cultivated. Ignatius demanded that the believer should meditate on the person of Christ as a model which he should imitate, and as an ideal to which he should submit himself. By constantly meditating on the person of Christ, using all five senses, the image of the Saviour becomes more and more vividly real until Christ partially replaces the ego of the person engaged in meditation. The object is complete submission to God's will and the abolition of all self-seeking.

This technique of imaginative contemplation is somewhat analogous to Rudolf Steiner's concentrated 'thinking' which supposedly leads to spiritual perception. However, it more closely parallels Jung's technique of 'active imagination' in which the subject deliberately enters a state of reverie during which figures derived from the unconscious are addressed and listened to as if they were persons in the external world. All three procedures are designed to enhance the reality and significance of the inner imaginative world of the subject.

Over four hundred years after its final revision in 1541, the *Spiritual Exercises* continues to engage the interest of scholars and students. In 1939, Jung gave a series of lectures on the book at the Swiss Technological Institute in Zürich, since he perceived parallels between his own concept of the individuation process and Loyola's ideas of spiritual development.

Ignatius de Loyola, as he now became, exhibited a number of the guru-like characteristics described earlier. He did claim to have been granted special spiritual insight through his visions, although he was careful not to claim too much when being questioned. At first, the leaders of the Church were suspicious of his message. He was investigated by the Inquisition in 1526 and actually imprisoned for forty-two days in 1527. Various other enquiries followed. It was determined that nothing in his teaching was heretical, but he was nevertheless forbidden to teach without studying theology and obtaining a degree from a University; a typical response of the Establishment toward a threatening newcomer.

Compared with other gurus, Ignatius was not isolated in childhood, although he had lost his mother. His wet-nurse had children who became his playmates. There is no reason to think that his conviction that his message applied to everyone derived from ignorance of the psychology of others, as it seems to in the case of some gurus. But he did of course believe that the Christian faith was absolute and universal truth, and no doubt thought that his version of it had particular merits. Dr. Meissner's psychoanalytic biography stresses his narcissism; his pride and vanity before he was wounded; his aggressiveness and self-assertion; his need to excel. These deep-rooted character traits were profoundly modified by his traumatic experience, but they did not disappear. Iñigo de Loyola, the dashing military commander, became Ignatius, the first General of the Society of Jesus, a spiritual hero specially selected by God to preach, teach, and lead.

As with other spiritual leaders, Ignatius's new insight followed a period of physical illness and then a period of severe depression. What is so interesting and unusual is that this change of direction came about largely through his own reading and strenuous efforts to alter himself. It is a very deliberate self-conversion, marked by conscious struggle rather than by unconscious serendipity. The *Spiritual Exercises* are a frontal attack on the worldly desires of the hidalgo. Ambition must be conquered by humility, the desire for wealth by embracing extreme poverty, the lusts of the flesh by scourging and starving the body. The aggression of the soldier has not disappeared; it has become redirected against a new enemy, the sinful former self.

There can be no doubt about Ignatius's charisma. His skills as a preacher were said to be limited; but in private conversation or in small groups, his sincerity, directness, and complete conviction were extremely persuasive. He was undoubtedly attractive to women: many women of every rank sought his spiritual guidance, and he seems to have been particularly dedicated to their welfare. His self-control, certainty, and preoccupation with obedience made him seem forbidding to some who encountered him. Perhaps 'formidable' would be the best single adjective to apply to him. By the time the Society of Jesus was established in Rome at the house of La Strada, near the church of Santa Maria, his followers regarded him as a saint whose word was law and whose every utterance was inspired.[8]

Ignatius demanded of himself complete submission to what he conceived to be the will of God, involving the abandonment of all fleshly temptations and worldly ambitions. But his insistence on obedience went much further, in that he demanded unquestioning submission to the orders of religious superiors, affirming that the authority of such superiors came directly from God and must therefore reflect the will of God. When one recalls the behaviour of certain Popes, it is hard to understand how anyone could believe this. Moreover, although even agnostics can easily appreciate that embracing poverty and chastity can be seen as promoting the life of the spirit, modern Protestants find it much harder to abandon the ideals of self-reliance, self-determination, and independence of mind which western education instils as virtues. Advances in knowledge in any sphere of human endeavour must depend upon being able to criticize accepted authorities.

However, Ignatius's demand for total obedience enshrines and underlines one feature of the attraction which gurus have for those who follow them. For some people, complete submission to a higher power is seductive, in that it involves abrogating responsibility, doubt, and anxiety. Stanley Milgram's famous experiments, described in his book *Obedience to Authority*, demonstrate how easy it is to persuade normal people to inflict pain on others because an authority tells them to do so.[9] I myself believe that the tendency toward obedience is one of the most sinister of human traits.[10] But Jesuits think otherwise. William James, in *The Varieties of Religious Experience*, quotes Alfonso Rodriguez S. J. as writing:

One of the great consolations of the monastic life is the assurance we have that in obeying we can commit no fault. The Superior may commit a fault in commanding you to do this thing or that, but you are certain that you commit no fault so long as you obey, because God will only ask you if you have duly performed what orders you received, and if you can furnish a clear account in that respect, you are absolved entirely.[11]

Many victims of the Inquisition must have regretted that obedience to superiors has been so lauded in the Roman Catholic Church. 'I was only obeying orders and doing my duty' is the commonest excuse offered by torturers, concentration camp guards, and others who commit appalling cruelties.

There is no reason to think that Ignatius was in any way corrupted by the power which he exercised. The *Spiritual Exercises* demand a great deal from those who practise them; but Ignatius demanded more of himself than he did of any of his followers. He could be authoritarian and even harsh; but he could also be sensitive to the spiritual needs of others, and particularly comforting to those who were depressed or in other ways distressed, perhaps because of his own experience of depression. He is reported as being expert at bringing comfort to the inmates of hospitals and prisons. Here again, his own experience of being confined as a patient for a long period may have fuelled his understanding and capacity for empathy. He was an able organizer and administrator who established the Society of Jesus as a stable religious institution which was, at the same time, a missionary organization dedicated to extending God's kingdom throughout the world.

I suggested earlier that Ignatius's temperament was that of someone liable to manic-depressive illness, and that he experienced depression of psychotic intensity during the period in Manresa. The severity of this illness may have been partially induced by the physical deprivations which he inflicted upon himself at the time, but which he subsequently deplored as excessive. When, for example, the level of blood sugar drops to a low point, strange things happen to the brain, and therefore to the mind. Although his temperament may subsequently have caused him to have mood-swings of more than usual intensity, we do not know whether the hallucinatory visions and voices which intermittently recurred throughout his life were related, as they sometimes are, to periods of exalted mood or hypomania. What we do know is that these visions and voices, which psychiatrists might deem psychotic in a socially maladapted person, seem only to have enriched and strengthened the already powerful personality of Ignatius.

In addition, Ignatius described recurrent ecstatic states of the kind which have often been described by a variety of people ranging from Luther to Wordsworth. We shall return to these mystical experiences of illumination and union in a later chapter. Since such experiences happen to agnostics as well as to believers, they need not necessarily be interpreted in religious terms; but Ignatius of course does so interpret them, and indeed has his own special term for them, calling them 'consolations', which indeed they are. The ecstatic experience, during the short time it lasts, seems like the solution to all problems: *Eureka* to life. In the case of Ignatius, such experiences were often accompanied by floods of tears, but these were tears of joy which frequently occur in the ecstasies of both believers and agnostics. Ecstasies 'come to' the person concerned: that is, they cannot be attained by the exercise of the will alone, although there can be little doubt that prolonged prayer and meditation promote the likelihood of their occurrence. According to a contemporary, Ignatius said that 'as far as he could judge, it would not be possible for him to live without consolation, that is, without experiencing in himself something that was not and could not be a part of himself, but depended entirely on God'.[12] Ignatius was well aware that these precious 'consolations' were beyond the reach of the will, for he wrote:

> It belongs to God alone to give consolation without previous cause, for it belongs to the Creator to enter into the soul, to leave it, and to act upon it, drawing it wholly to the love of His Divine Majesty. I say without previous cause, that is, without any previous perception or knowledge of any object from which such consolation might come to the soul through its own acts of intellect and will.[13]

William James includes a number of examples of ecstatic mystical experiences in *The Varieties of Religious Experience*. He includes a quotation from Bartoli-Michel's life of Ignatius, in which the author claims that Ignatius told one of his confessors that 'a single hour of meditation at Manresa had taught him more truths about heavenly things than all the teachings of all the doctors put together could have taught him'.[14]

There is no doubt that Ignatius went through a profound physical and mental illness which might have destroyed someone less robust. He emerged from it with a burning faith which made sense of life for him and which inspired him as a teacher and founder of a world-wide movement. Ignatius was an effective leader, a superb organizer, and a skilled diplomat. Christians will no doubt consider that Ignatius found the truth, and that the truth made him whole. Those who are not Christians will think that the illness and recovery of Ignatius is an example of a pattern we have already encountered in other gurus. Because the faith of Ignatius was contained within the Christian tradition and enriched that tradition, agnostics may be puzzled or envious, but are unlikely to dismiss it in the way they might dismiss the beliefs of Steiner or Gurdjieff. But the pattern of mental distress followed by an irrational solution is characteristic of gurus, whether they are mad or sane, good or evil. Agnostic sceptics do not always realize how deeply irrational normal people can be.

Let us turn from the study of Ignatius to a brief consideration of his Lord and Master, Jesus Christ. Those of us who were brought up as believing Christians find it difficult to look at Jesus objectively. However, there are a number of books which help us to do so, including excellent recent accounts by Humphrey Carpenter, E. P. Sanders, Geza Vermes, and A. N. Wilson. Perceiving Jesus as one example amongst many gurus actually emphasizes his unique qualities; but those who regard him as their saviour may think this approach irreverent. It is important to remember that Jesus was not a Christian.

David Koresh's apocalyptic vision, based on The Book of Revelation, was briefly described earlier. In order to understand Jesus, we must know something about pre-Christian apocalyptic beliefs. In *Cosmos, Chaos, and the World to Come*, Norman Cohn has assigned the origin of apocalyptic faith to Zoroaster, who, it is now supposed by scholars of the period, probably lived some time between 1500 and 1200 B.C.[15] Before Zoroaster appeared, the ancient Egyptians, the Mesopotamians, and the early Indo-Aryan inhabitants of the Indus valley all believed that the world had been created by the gods once and for ever and that it would not change. The world was recognized to be a turbulent place, in which order was perpetually threatened by disruption, and cosmos by chaos. 'Combat myths' which tell how a god or gods have defended the ordered world against the assaults of chaotic forces were already established in the third millennium. Some of these myths resembled modern science fiction 'horror movies', in which dreadful monsters threaten to overwhelm mankind. One example was the Sumerian monster *Labbu*, a sea dragon three hundred miles long and thirty miles high, which came ashore from time to time to wreak havoc. But the demonic forces of evil were always defeated by the gods, although devastation by flood, plague, or drought might temporarily disrupt the established order. These early civilizations did not believe that the world could ever be greatly changed, let alone made perfect. Peace was only attainable in heaven, where those who had fulfilled their proper functions on earth were assured of a blissful life after death.

Then came Zoroaster, who proclaimed that there had originally been only one god, Ahura Mazda. Zoroaster began as a priest of the traditional religion of the Iranians. Then, in a way characteristic of some other later gurus, he embarked on a period of wandering amidst visionaries and seers, which culminated in a new revelation.

> At some point he had illuminations, or hallucinations, in which he saw and heard the great god Ahura Mazda – Lord Wisdom – surrounded by six other radiant figures. From that time onward he felt himself to be the divinely preordained prophet of a religious faith that differed greatly from the traditional faith.[16]

Ahura Mazda was responsible for all that is good in the universe, including its all-embracing order, known as *asha*. Opposed to Ahura Mazda was Angra Mainyu, (later Ahriman), the spirit of destruction, who supported the principle of *druj*, which included both falsehood and disorder. The struggle between these two principles constituted the past, present, and future history of the world. However, the Zoroastrian view, as opposed to earlier beliefs, was that this struggle would not go on for eternity, but would be finally resolved at some definite point in the future. Following this resolution, peace and order would prevail throughout the world, and chaos be abolished for ever. Instead of waiting for heaven, the new order would be established on earth. The righteous dead would come back to earth with new bodies; and all mankind would form a single community of Zoroastrians, united in the worship of Ahura Mazda. This eagerly awaited transformation was called 'the making wonderful': it is the earliest known example of 'millenarian' prophecy. Zoroaster himself probably believed that 'the making wonderful' was imminent; but as the centuries passed, the prophecy became modified, and the date of the final struggle postponed. This did not mean that the new myth lacked influence. As Norman Cohn points out, the idea that a final resolution of conflict between the forces of good and evil is possible on earth is revolutionary rather than conservative, and appealed particularly to the poor and weak who felt themselves defenceless against the predatory authorities and powerful enemies who habitually exploited them. Echoes of this belief are recognizable in Marxism.

There can be little doubt that Jesus believed in a conflict between the forces of good and evil which would finally be resolved and permit the establishment of God's kingdom upon earth 'as it is in heaven'. The temptation of Jesus in the wilderness, which takes place after his baptism by John the Baptist, is a portrayal of the struggle between good and evil, a trial of strength from which Jesus emerges proclaiming his message 'Repent; for the Kingdom of Heaven is upon you.'[17] No one can survive for forty days without food and water; and it is possible that the number forty is a reference to the forty years which the Israelites spent in the desert after the exodus from Egypt. It is appropriate to view the sojourn in the wilderness as another example of a period of 'creative illness': a time of inner chaos and struggle deliberately induced by a retreat into solitude, through which conflict was resolved and from which a new vision was born.

There have been many arguments as to what Jesus really meant by announcing the coming of the kingdom of God, and about how soon he expected it. Jesus himself said that it was imminent, although he did not know exactly when it would take place. But entering into the kingdom required both urgent repentance and watchful alertness. The Son of Man will come when he is least expected, and, according to Luke, Jesus said that some of those then listening to his teaching would not die before they had seen the kingdom. The idea that the kingdom of God represented an inner spiritual change within the hearts of men rather than an external, expected event is difficult to sustain, although it is easy to appreciate that Christian believers would prefer such an interpretation to admitting that Jesus was wrong in his prophecy. It seems inescapable that Jesus did share the apocalyptic view that God's final conquest of evil was at hand and that God's kingdom would be established upon earth in the near future. As E. P. Sanders writes in his chapter *The Coming of the Kingdom*, 'We may be quite confident that Jesus had an *eschatological* message'.[18]

Jesus also predicted that the coming of the kingdom would be preceded by a time of troubles: false prophets, famines, wars, and earthquakes.

> As soon as the distress of those days has passed, the sun will be darkened, the moon will not give her light, the stars will fall from the sky, the celestial powers will be shaken. Then will appear in heaven the sign that heralds the Son of Man. All the peoples of the world will make lamentation, and they will see the Son of Man coming on the clouds of heaven with great glory. With a trumpet blast he will send out his angels, and they will gather his chosen from the four winds, from the farthest bounds of heaven on every side.[19]

After the crucifixion and the reports of the resurrection, the disciples were convinced that Jesus would soon return and establish the kingdom which he had predicted. It may have been the disappointment of these early hopes which prompted the need for coherent accounts of Jesus's life and teachings. If his return was considered imminent, a historical account would not be needed. The gospels were probably composed anonymously between the years 70 and 90 A.D., although some scholars believe Mark to be earlier.[20] They were not attributed to Matthew, Mark, Luke, and John until about 180 A.D.

If we can disentangle ourselves from the toils of centuries of Christian speculation, we can see that Jesus resembles other gurus in undergoing a period of inner conflict which is resolved by a new and special spiritual insight which he believed to come direct from God his father. As E. P. Sanders points out, Jesus was a charismatic and autonomous prophet whose authority came from his own conviction of personal intimacy with God.

However, according to the account in the synoptic gospels, Jesus at first submitted to baptism by John the Baptist, and there is some doubt as to whether he himself assumed the role of Messiah, or what that title meant to him. When Jesus and his disciples were on their way to the villages around Caesarea, after the miracle of the loaves and fishes and the restoration of sight to the blind man of Bethsaida, he asked them ' "Who do men say I am?" They answered, "Some say John the Baptist, others Elijah, others one of the prophets." "And you," he asked, "who do you say I am?" Peter replied: "You are the Messiah." '[21] Jesus does not deny this, but tells the disciples to keep it to themselves. Later, he warns the disciples to beware of impostors claiming to be messiahs or prophets. At his trial, the High Priest Caiaphas asks Jesus the question: 'Are you the Messiah, the Son of the Blessed One?' According to Mark, Jesus replied, 'I am; and you will see the Son of Man seated at the right hand of God and coming with the clouds of heaven.'[22] According to Luke, Jesus said that if he told them, they would not believe him. According to Matthew, he threw the question back. Most scholars do not believe that Jesus was making political claims in the sense of being the Davidic Messiah who would restore the fortunes of Israel, conquer their enemies, abolish foreign domination, restore the Temple of Yahweh, and reign in Jerusalem, although such were the conventional hopes of the Jews. E. P. Sanders thinks that it is probable that Jesus did not think of himself as the Messiah, but that he was making an even higher claim for himself as being God's viceroy.

Humphrey Carpenter, in his excellent short book *Jesus*,[23] explores the question of who Jesus thought he was. If we conclude that he did really believe that he was God's deputy and that he would return to earth in the clouds of heaven and rule in glory, Jesus, in this respect, if in no other, is closely similar to other gurus whom we judge to be expressing delusions of grandeur. According to Mark, the family of Jesus attempted to take charge of him because people were saying that he was out of his mind. When they tried to speak to him, he repudiated them, saying, 'Who is my mother? Who are my brothers? And looking round at those who were sitting in the circle about him he said, "Here are my mother and my brothers. Whoever does the will of God is my brother, my sister, my mother." '[24] Jesus was not the champion of family life which his present day followers would have us believe. It will be recalled that he had told his disciples that brother would betray brother, that the father would betray his child, and that children would turn against their parents and send them to their death because of allegiance to himself. 'Jesus's underlying message is that every man devoting himself to a whole-hearted search for God's Kingdom is essentially alone.'[25] As I suggested earlier, gurus often seem indifferent to family ties.

It is difficult for us to project ourselves backward in time and imagine what beliefs we might have held in the first century A.D. What is certain is that each one of us would have professed beliefs that would be called delusional in the light of modern knowledge. Assessing the mental state of Jesus is a futile exercise for three reasons. First, we cannot become time travellers: second, the Gospels are scrappy, contradictory, and written long after the events depicted: third, whether we regard a belief as evidence of mental illness depends upon the social context. In twentieth-century England, an individual announcing that he was the son of God and would return after death in glory on the clouds of heaven would probably attract psychiatric attention; but earlier generations might have regarded such claims as unsurprising.

From the evidence available, it seems quite probable that Jesus went through some kind of crisis, represented by the temptation in the wilderness; that he emerged with a new call to repentance, because he had become convinced that the reign of God upon earth was about to be established; that he believed that his own death would act as an atonement for the sins of Israel; and that he regarded himself as a divine being who would sit at God's right hand and judge mankind. Even if many Christian theologians are disconcerted by the idea that Jesus prophesied an apocalyptic end to the world which did not happen, this in no way detracts from the value of what Jesus taught. He was a man of his time as we are men and women of our time. Escape from the limitations of one's own era is always incomplete, even in the case of highly creative individuals.

What is so remarkable about the teaching of Jesus is his emphasis on the inner man. Compliance with Judaic Law is to be encouraged, but outward obedience is not enough. The inner man must also be purged of evil thoughts and desires so that a person becomes truly able to learn to love his enemies and treat all men as he himself would like to be treated. It is surely this emphasis upon real change within which elevates the teaching of Jesus so much above mere prescriptions for behaviour. The parable about the Pharisee and the tax-gatherer emphasizes the point that outward conformity and virtuous practice count for little if the person practising these virtues is self-righteous.

> Two men went up to the temple to pray, one a Pharisee and the other a tax-gatherer. The Pharisee stood up and prayed thus. 'I thank thee, O God, that I am not like the rest of men, greedy, dishonest, adulterous; or, for that matter, like this tax-gatherer. I fast twice a week; I pay tithes on all that I get.' But the other kept his distance and would not even raise his eyes to heaven, but beat upon his breast, saying, 'O God, have mercy on me, sinner that I am'. It was this man, I tell you, and not the other, who went home acquitted of his sins. For everyone who exalts himself will be humbled; and whoever humbles himself will be exalted.[26]

Jesus also suggests that going to the temple to pray is often hypocritical.

> But when you pray, go into a room by yourself, shut the door, and pray to your Father who is there in the secret place; and your Father who sees what is in secret will reward you.[27]

Jesus resembled other gurus in believing that God had granted him a special revelation. However, his message was not at first generalized to apply to all mankind. Norman Cohn insists that the Gentiles were of little concern to Jesus, and that his apocalyptic message was addressed to Jews alone.[28] It was only after stories of the resurrection began to circulate that the early Christian Church came into existence and that Christianity gradually became established as a world religion.

We may be sure that Jesus believed in his new revelation with complete conviction. Humphrey Carpenter thinks that the moral teaching of Jesus could not alone have accounted for the attention afforded him, and believes that his miracles were responsible. To my mind, this underestimates Jesus's charisma. We have rather little evidence of the impact which he made upon others, but all we do know suggests that this was remarkable. When Jesus summons Simon called Peter and his brother Andrew to follow him and become fishers of men, they leave their nets, their boat, and their father without hesitation. After the Sermon on the Mount, Matthew tells us that 'the people were astounded at his teaching; unlike their own teachers he taught with a note of authority'.[29] Authority is an important attribute of gurus, underpinning, but not identical with, charisma. The conventional teachers or scribes were experts in interpreting the scriptures and used many quotations from them; whereas Jesus spoke directly from his own conviction. The authority displayed by Jesus seems to have depended upon his certainty that he was the messenger of God combined with his compassion for the poor, the weak, the ill, and for sinners. Like other gurus, Jesus was élitist in the sense of believing that he was specially selected by God. But, since he mixed with all kinds of people, it would be wrong to describe him as anti-democratic. Such a term is meaningless in the context of the time. Sheer goodness is rare, and when one encounters someone who genuinely cares little for himself, but much for others, and who rates the rich and powerful below the poor and weak, the impression can be overwhelming as well as revolutionary. When Jesus hung on the cross in agony and finally died, the centurion in charge is reported as saying, 'Truly this man was a son of God'.[30] This is dismissed by Geza Vermes as 'an anachronistic ecclesiastical confession formula'[31]: naïvely, I had hoped that it was recognition of simple goodness.

So far as we know, no one could have been less corrupted by power or less prone to sexual temptation. Jesus regarded the possession of wealth as a hindrance to salvation, and would have none of it. He accepted the ministrations of the woman who washed his feet with her tears, and who anointed them with myrrh; but we get no hint of his using his spiritual authority to exploit others. Since Jesus was convinced that God his father had spoken to him directly, he had no reason to invent a background of mystery or claim other esoteric sources of wisdom.

Disciples sometimes exalt a guru's status far above his own expectations. Jesus himself could not possibly have known that his teaching would initiate a world religion; and many of his disciples, along with the Judaic and Roman authorities, must have believed that crucifixion had put an end to Jesus for ever. When Jesus (if he really did so) cried out on the cross: 'My God, my God, why hast thou forsaken me?'[32] we may wonder whether, at this moment, he was recalling the first line of Psalm 22, or whether he himself doubted his own claim to being God's special emissary.

Few subsequent gurus seem to have matched the simplicity and directness of Jesus's message; but it must be remembered that we have very little information. If the world had possessed a detailed biographical account of Jesus, an authentic picture of what he was like as a man, it is quite possible that Christianity would not have been established as a world religion. I am not suggesting that Jesus would have been shown up as dishonest or inauthentic; but simply indicating that a person is more easily made into a mythical figure if the outlines of his personality are blurred. Myths are largely constructed from our own projections; and the imagination cannot flourish where the exact facts are known.

The Gospel stories, however much they may contradict each other, are so intimately a part of the culture in which we live that, even if we regard them as more myth than history, we cannot escape their emotional impact. The babe in the manger touches the hearts of most of us, although the New Testament nowhere states that Jesus was born in a stable. The Sermon on the Mount, the Last Supper, the betrayal by Judas, and the Crucifixion itself are so familiar and so moving that we can never look at them objectively. Great music underlines and enhances our emotional response. Handel's *Messiah* and Bach's settings of the Passions are among the wonders of Western civilization which can move agnostics to tears as well as believers.

I referred earlier to the attractions of simplicity. In his famous book *Orpheus: A History of Religions*, Salomon Reinach wrote that the Gospels contain many contradictory statements.

But, as a whole, the teaching of benevolence, patience, justice, chastity and other virtues is the more conspicuous, in harmony with the beauty, now idyllic, now tragic of the legend. It is true that Christian morality is no more original than is any other morality, religious or secular; it is that of the contemporary Jewish schoolmen, of a Hillel or a Gamaliel; but in the Gospels it appears divested of all scholasticism and ritualistic pedantry, robust and simple as befits a doctrine setting forth to conquer the world.[33]

VIII

SANITY
AND INSANITY

PAUL BRUNTON

READERS OF THIS BOOK who are not professionally involved in psychiatry are likely to conclude that, although they exhibit considerable variations in personality, the majority of gurus are madmen. What other explanation can there be to account for someone who alleges that he has special powers of clairvoyant perception, or who claims that he himself is God, or who advances absurd theories about the universe which command neither scientific support nor general acceptance?

We have seen that some gurus, including Jim Jones and Bhagwan Shree Rajneesh, manifested obvious mental deterioration toward the end of their missions. Jones dosed himself with large quantities of amphetamines and anti-depressants; Rajneesh used valium and nitrous oxide. It is reasonable to conclude that their deterioration was due to the toxic effects of these substances on the brain. Ignatius, because he starved himself, may have suffered some temporary impairment of brain function during the Manresa period which contributed to his visions and hallucinations, but any such effects were clearly transient. The brain of Ignatius functioned with exemplary efficiency and vigour during the rest of his life. Although much remains to be discovered about the various forms of dementia, and the types of mental illness due to brain damage by drugs, alcohol, tumours, or infections, these illnesses can be regarded as comparable with other bodily diseases. They are simply diseases in which the brain is the organ most affected, rather than the heart, liver, lungs, or kidneys. Moreover, although the severity of the brain disease or damage varies, modern methods of examining the brain, together with psychological tests, can generally establish a definite diagnosis. A patient either has brain damage or he has not. There may be disagreements about the cause of a particular deficit, but the fact of cerebral impairment will not usually be in doubt. We are justified in assuming that mental illness due to brain damage or disease plays little part in the guru phenomenon. The mental disturbances displayed by gurus are more closely related to manic-depressive illness or to schizophrenia; the two main categories of psychotic illness in which no definite cerebral pathology has yet been demonstrated, although both varieties of mental illness are strongly influenced by genetic factors.

However, mental illness or 'madness' is usually associated with 'breakdown', with the inability to cope with life in our society, whereas many gurus are effective social leaders, proselytizers, and orators. Even if gurus are deemed to be mentally abnormal, they do not usually become psychiatric patients or end their days in mental hospitals. The phenomenon of the guru raises difficult problems about the nature of mental illness. Can people be regarded as psychotic merely because they hold eccentric beliefs about the universe and their own significance as prophets or teachers? What are the boundaries between sanity and madness? What does labelling someone psychotic really mean? Are our current psychiatric classifications adequate? These are not merely academic questions raised by a sceptical psychiatrist. I want to make a serious attempt to show that our dividing lines between sanity and mental illness have been drawn in the wrong place. The sane are madder than we think; the mad are saner.

Gurus are not the only type of human being to exemplify the need for revision of psychiatric categories. For example, consider the cases of two serial killers. Dennis Nilsen killed fifteen young men over a period of four years. He used to draw pictures of his victims after their deaths, and kept their remains under the floor boards or in his wardrobe. Jeffrey Dahmer killed seventeen people over a similar period. He dissected many of the corpses, boiled their heads, and ate parts of their bodies. The man in the street would deem both men insane on the grounds that men who commit serial murders on this scale and then behave as they did are so far removed from normal that they must be mad. I think the man in the street is right. But both murderers were deemed sane at their trials because they did not exhibit the signs and symptoms of schizophrenia or manic-depressive illness or suffer from any of the varieties of mental illness caused by drugs or physical disease. Multiple murderers constitute an extreme example of how grossly abnormal individuals can be considered sane by modern psychiatric taxonomy, and therefore responsible in law.

In addition, some confidence tricksters are misclassified as saner than they are. Confidence tricksters are often more abnormal mentally than those who prosecute or defend them realize. A successful confidence trickster requires a capacity to believe in his own phantasies which is beyond the reach of the ordinary person. If a man seems ebullient and charming, as many confidence tricksters do, the fact that such a person may also be grossly abnormal or chronically psychotic may escape notice. We tend to diagnose mental abnormality in the socially incompetent and overlook it or deny it both in the socially dominant and in the socially unobtrusive. Confidence tricksters who assume false identities for the purpose of extracting money from their victims sometimes become so obviously psychotic that they are transferred from prison to a psychiatric hospital. I well remember interviewing an elderly man in prison who had received many sentences for obtaining money on false pretences. He had never been regarded as suffering from mental illness; but, because I was interested in him, revealed a series of typical paranoid delusions in which he implicitly believed. He was perfectly well aware that he would be labelled psychotic and confined in a mental hospital if he told the prison doctors of his beliefs. Since he preferred a finite prison sentence to indefinite confinement in hospital, I had to promise to keep what he told me to myself. Perhaps this was yet another deception, but he gained nothing from it, so I am inclined to think that for once he was telling the truth. Some of the gurus whom we have considered hover on the brink between psychosis and confidence trickery. Jung used to say that there were many more schizophrenics in the community than is generally realized. 'These cases are partially camouflaged as obsessional neuroses, compulsions, phobias, and hysterias, and they are very careful never to go near an asylum.'[1] I think Jung was right.

Gurus usually go through a period of intense mental distress, sometimes amounting to mental illness, before they emerge with a revelation which both marks the end of their period of turmoil and also provides them with the new message which they preach or teach. In considering whether or not a guru is, or has been, mentally ill, we have to consider both the acute episode of distress through which he passes and also the settled convictions which succeed it. Unfortunately, detailed descriptions of the acute disturbance are often missing or incomplete, but there is no doubt that some gurus experience one or more periods of severe depression, sometimes alternating with elated episodes, whilst others pass through illnesses more closely akin to schizophrenia.

Some cases of mania or depression are so extreme that virtually all psychiatrists would agree about the diagnosis, and concur in believing that such people are mentally ill. So will the ordinary person. If someone who is generally equable becomes highly excited and irritable, talks incoherently, runs up large debts, engages in promiscuous sexual activity, and refuses to sleep, his friends will rightly consider him to be suffering from mental illness. A person who appears to be in the depths of gloom, who refuses to eat, who blames himself for trivialities, and who talks of suicide will, it is hoped, also be perceived as ill and in need of treatment. Ignatius's depression was originally precipitated by his injury, which had the effect of destroying his identity as a hidalgo. While at Manresa, he went through a period of depression of psychotic intensity, accompanied by suicidal thoughts. As I indicated earlier, the ecstatic 'consolations' which he described, together with his recurrent hallucinatory visions and voices, can be taken as manic or hypomanic phenomena, representing the opposite pole to depression.

Rajneesh's original period of illness, which occurred when he was adolescent, was probably a prolonged episode of depression which ended in a hypomanic state of ecstasy. He certainly suffered from at least two further periods of depression, one of which appears to have taken place before he began to deteriorate physically and mentally.

David Koresh also suffered from mood swings of pathological intensity in adolescence after being rejected by a girl whom he had made pregnant, sometimes believing himself to be especially evil, sometimes believing that he was uniquely favoured by God.

Jung's mental illness has been variously regarded, some believing it to be a prolonged period of depression, while others diagnose it as a schizophrenic episode. The same difficulty in diagnosis applies to Steiner's mid-life crisis.

Although many gurus go through a period of intense mental stress followed by recovery which may resemble manic-depressive illness, their behaviour after the crisis is over cannot easily be explained as characteristic of this type of mental disorder. One of the generally accepted features of manic-depressive illness is that it is intermittent. Between the episodes, most patients return to normality, unless the episodes recur so frequently that there is no time for complete recovery. But when gurus emerge from their acute illness they do not revert to what they were before. They become permanently changed people with a new set of beliefs and a new view of themselves and the world.

Can gurus be diagnosed as schizophrenic? Acute episodes of schizophrenia are distressing experiences which, more frequently than manic-depressive illness, leave behind permanent traces. Are the extraordinary views of themselves and the world which are propagated by gurus like Steiner and Gurdjieff the consequence of a schizophrenic illness?

Elizabeth L. Farr gives an unusually articulate account of her schizophrenic illness which demonstrates how bizarre experience prompts bizarre explanations. From the age of sixteen, she was ill for eight years, in and out of hospital, suffering from distorted perceptions, hallucinations, and delusions of a characteristic kind. She was diagnosed as suffering from catatonic schizophrenia. She heard voices speaking her thoughts and believed that her thoughts were audible to others because they were being broadcast. She also had visual hallucinations in which coloured designs which she called 'interference patterns' intruded themselves between her and whatever she was looking at. She began to think that she was a particularly sensitive person who perceived things which other people could not see. At times impersonal objects like lamps or chairs appeared to have personalities and to be trying to communicate with her. Her account of her high school search for an explanation demonstrates how urgent the need for the discovery of some sort of order becomes when the mind itself is chaotic.

In high school I became engrossed in religion, the occult, and the arts, as a possible way to help explain what was going on. The central driving force was to understand my experiences.

The delusions started insidiously. I do not know where religion, the occult, and the arts left off and where the crazy ideas started. All I know was that there had to be an explanation for my experiences and I had to be active in my pursuit of an Enlightenment to resolve the conflict between my reality and the reality that everybody else seemed to be experiencing. Everything had to be connected up somehow, I thought.[2]

In the context of a book about gurus, it is particularly interesting that she came to believe that she was approaching an 'enlightened state'. She believed that she would be required to leap from the seventh floor of a building and land on her head. She would then be put at a 'cosmic junction', at which her spirit would be taken from her body and transported to a parallel world in which she would receive the ultimate enlightenment. Ultimate enlightenment is exactly what many gurus claim to possess, and it is tempting to assume that such a claim is a consequence of an illness of schizophrenic type.

The illness from which Elizabeth Farr suffered required recurrent admission to hospital. From time to time it became obvious that she could not manage ordinary life in the community. It seems to me that, although no definite cerebral pathology has yet been established in schizophrenia, the perceptual distortions which Elizabeth Farr described were probably caused by some neurophysiological disturbance within the brain. Since her account closely corresponds with other accounts given by patients suffering from similar psychotic symptoms, it seems reasonable to conclude that this is a definable illness with a physical cause, even if we do not yet know what the cause may be. A recent review of the huge literature on brain research in schizophrenia concludes that 'schizophrenia may be characterised . . . by complex alterations in the normal reciprocal patterns of activation between anatomically related areas of the cerebral cortex.'[3] In other words, what is wrong is not a structural abnormality in one or other part of the brain, but a failure of co-ordinated communication between the different parts. For some years, research workers have been suggesting that schizophrenia may be related to poor or abnormal communication between the two hemispheres of the brain.

We all need to make sense out of our experience; but most of us have not been through the chaos of an acute schizophrenic breakdown, and have therefore not felt the need to find explanations of the world and our place in it which seem crazy to the ordinary person. Elizabeth Farr made a good recovery, and has been able to return to her career. It is interesting that she wrote of her schizophrenia:

> Although my illness was unpleasant, I cannot say that I completely regret that it happened. The psychosis was an experience in learning, problem-solving, and perceptual broadening that is an opportunity available to few.[4]

It is easy to appreciate that, if someone is suffering bizarre disorders of perception like those described by Elizabeth Farr, or like those described by Jung as occurring in his early childhood, the beliefs which appear to make sense of these disorders are likely to appear delusional to those who have not shared the same experience.

Jung's psychotic episode was also an experience in problem-solving. The distress through which he passed led to solutions which formed the foundation of his new psychological viewpoint, and which proved fruitful both for himself and for his many followers who embarked upon the same path of individuation. As we noted earlier, Jung was left with a number of beliefs which seem strange to those who do not believe in astrology, in synchronicity, or in paranormal psychological phenomena like clairvoyance. Such residual oddities are not uncommon after a period of psychotic illness, but do not detract from the value of Jung's discoveries. In his case, making sense out of his illness provided new, original insights which contributed both to the practice of psychotherapy and also to our understanding of human nature.

The kind of psychotic illness experienced by Elizabeth Farr and by Jung may last for some years, whether intermittently or not, but it is recognizably an illness to which the medical model can be applied. That is, it is something which afflicts a previously normal person from which they recover or nearly recover, comparable with developing and recovering from pulmonary tuberculosis, which may also leave some residual disability behind it. It is more difficult to view other forms of psychotic illness in the same light.

In the mental illness known as paranoid schizophrenia, perceptual distortions are less in evidence, although sufferers propound delusional systems which have much in common with each other. The patient usually believes that he is the subject of persecution, often by a specific group or organization like Freemasons, or Jews, or Roman Catholics, but sometimes by malign forces of evil which have no human form. These wicked people or devils torment the sufferer in various ways; sometimes using electrical machines to cause him to have bizarre physical sensations; sometimes inserting alien, obscene thoughts into his mind which could never have occurred to him naturally. They may have ways of broadcasting such thoughts so that other people have access to them. This is why people look askance at him in the street, perhaps muttering to each other that he looks peculiar. He has even heard voices accusing him of being sexually perverted. Given these circumstances, it is not surprising that he cannot get a job, that people do not recognize his special talents, and that he is rather isolated.

Because he is the subject of so much unwelcome attention, it follows that he must really be a person of consequence. Perhaps he is of royal descent, or a reincarnation of an Old Testament prophet. Prophets with a new message are usually rejected by the establishment – consider what happened to Jesus. He must certainly be someone very unusual indeed; is it even possible that he is the Messiah?

Grandiosity and isolation march hand-in-hand. Jung describes the case of a locksmith's apprentice who became mentally ill at the age of nineteen. He believed that he was in telephonic communication with the Mother of God and other important figures.

> He had never been blessed with intelligence, but he had, amongst other things, hit upon the magnificent idea that the world was his picture-book, the pages of which he could turn at will. The proof was quite simple: he had only to turn round, and there was a new page for him to see.
>
> This is Schopenhauer's 'world as will and idea' in unadorned, primitive concreteness of vision. A shattering idea indeed, born of extreme alienation and seclusion from the world, but so naïvely and simply expressed that at first one can only smile at the grotesqueness of it. And yet this primitive way of looking lies at the

very heart of Schopenhauer's brilliant vision of the world. Only a genius or a madman could so disentangle himself from the bonds of reality as to see the world as his picture-book.[5]

Paranoid schizophrenics generally see themselves as the centre of attention. The symbolist writer Anna Kavan describes this well.

Night had fallen, the lights glowed mistily through a thin haze. I looked at my watch and saw that the hour for the interview had almost arrived.

No sooner had I discovered this than a change seemed to come over everything. It was as though, in some mysterious way, I had become the central point around which the night scene revolved. People walking on the pavement looked at me as they passed; some with pity, some with detached interest, some with more morbid curiosity. Some appeared to make small, concealed signs, but whether these were intended for warning or encouragement I could not be sure. The windows, lighted or unlighted, were like eyes more or less piercing, but all focused on me. The houses, the traffic, everything in sight, seemed to be watching to see what I would do.[6]

This is self-absorption carried to extremes. The attention paid is usually hostile, but may also be benign. Some paranoid schizophrenics, for example, believe that the Royal Family is taking a special interest in them and sending them kindly messages. One of my patients, rightly perceiving that I was well-disposed toward him, was convinced that I was secretly conspiring with potential employers behind his back in order to find him a suitable job.

Paranoid delusions can also serve to explain the 'thought insertion' described by many patients. It may appear to such a patient that every time he speaks, the words which emerge are not those which he had intended. He may feel that if he is trying to think about a problem, his efforts are interrupted by unwanted thoughts which are irrelevant. Patients frequently complain of such disruption. They feel that they no longer have control over their thoughts or the words they speak. But where do these words and thoughts which seem so alien come from? Instead of supposing, as we do, that there is some malfunction of the speech centres of the brain, the patient expresses the delusion that some enemy has discovered ways of putting words into his mouth or thoughts into his head. This both explains his difficulties with speech and thought, and also, by blaming someone else, protects him from the realization that there is anything wrong with himself.

Thus, delusions are both explanatory and exculpatory. Many human beings are inclined to take personal credit for their successes, and to attribute their failures to bad luck, unfortunate circumstances, or malice. Students who do badly in examinations often attribute their failure to unfair examiners. When Gurdjieff had an automobile accident which nearly killed him, he did not admit that his own bad driving was to blame, but said that the accident was caused by a hostile power with which he could not contend. Delusions of persecution are an exaggerated expression of a tendency to blame others rather than the self which can be found in most people.

In trying to understand these mental phenomena, irrespective of their ultimate cause, it is helpful to assume that the emotional development of paranoid personalities has been halted at, or has regressed to, a very early stage resembling that of the infant who is both the centre of attention and also powerless; omnipotent and helpless at the same time. Psychoanalytic theorists describe this stage as one in which good and evil are sharply separated. The infant regards as wholly good those who fulfil his needs immediately, and as wholly bad those who do not respond instantly to his cries, or who fail to provide what he is yelling for. There is no room for compromise, or for the recognition that the same person can be good on one occasion and bad on another. Most of us grow out of this black and white view of other people and the world, but traces of it remain. When threatened by war, epidemics, earthquakes, famine and other disasters, many people regress to the so-called paranoid-schizoid stage of development, in which they will follow a guru-like leader whom they invest with magical powers for good, and at the same time find scapegoats whom they blame for the disaster and regard as wholly evil. Norman Cohn's classic book *The Pursuit of the Millennium* gives many examples of this reaction.[7] I described these phenomena in a chapter titled *The Ubiquity of Paranoia* in *Human Destructiveness*.[8]

The view that paranoid schizophrenia is a mental illness in which genetics, biochemical abnormalities, and possibly viral infection are all involved is in no way incompatible with the psychoanalytic view outlined above. Perhaps failure to mature beyond the paranoid-schizoid stage of development described by Melanie Klein, or regression to it, is actually caused by a virus, or by dietary deprivation in infancy. I want to emphasize that psychoanalytic descriptions of psychotic phenomena may be revealing and accurate, but do not necessarily involve accepting psychoanalytic theories of causation, which are often unconvincing. The important point is that paranoid delusions have a positive function. They make sense out of chaos within, and also preserve the subject's self-esteem. They are a creative solution to the subject's problems, albeit a creative solution which does not stand up to critical examination.

Henri Ellenberger introduced the term 'creative illness' to describe this phenomenon, and, in his book *The Discovery of the Unconscious*, applied the concept to Freud, to Jung, to Steiner, and to the physicist/philosopher Gustav Theodor Fechner. He described it as follows.

A creative illness succeeds a period of intense preoccupation with an idea and search for a certain truth. It is a polymorphous condition that can take the shape of depression, neurosis, psychosomatic ailments, or even psychosis. Whatever the symptoms, they are felt as painful, if not agonizing, by the subject, with alternating periods of alleviation and worsening. Throughout the illness the subject never loses the thread of his dominating preoccupation. It is often compatible with normal, professional activity and family life. But even if he keeps to his social activities, he is almost entirely absorbed with himself. He suffers from feelings of utter isolation, even when he has a mentor who guides him through the ordeal (like the shaman apprentice with his master). The subject emerges from his ordeal with a permanent transformation in his personality and the conviction that he has discovered a great truth or a new spiritual world.[9]

The creative illness experienced by Ignatius ended in precisely the way described by Ellenberger, with 'a permanent transformation in his personality and the conviction that he has discovered a great truth'; but, although the Inquisition expressed initial doubts, the truth which Ignatius discovered could be incorporated within the framework of the Christian religion. It is when a guru emerges from his creative illness with convictions which cannot be fitted into a generally accepted belief system that we tend to call his sanity into question, although a better test of whether or not he should be regarded as mentally ill is his social behaviour.

Paul Brunton is an example of a guru whose teaching was based upon a paranoid delusional system, but who maintained himself in the community rather than being committed to a mental hospital because his books won him followers who believed in him, and because he was a gentle character who posed no apparent threat to anyone else. Jeffrey Masson's book *My Father's Guru* is an invaluable picture of an extraordinary phenomenon.[10]

Paul Brunton was born on October 21, 1898, as Raphael Hurst. He was so ashamed of being half-Jewish that he had a cosmetic operation on his nose. He was also tiny, being only five foot high and alarmingly thin because of his frugal vegetarianism and insistence upon the importance of fasting. It is not surprising that such a person should entertain compensatory phantasies of being important. Every child has done so, although most grow out of the tendency. But Brunton discovered that he could write, just as Jim Jones and David Koresh discovered that they could harangue. Brunton's phantasies were reinforced and validated by the eager responses of his readers. He was a very successful writer. His first book, *A Search in Secret India*, recounted his travels in India in search of esoteric wisdom.[11] As we have seen, such travels are characteristic of potential gurus. A second book followed within a very short time. *The Secret Path* was first published in 1934, and by 1968 had reached its twenty-eighth impression.[12] Although careful scrutiny of his writings reveals them to be repetitive and based on wildly improbable premises, the writing itself is coherent. He published eleven books in all, the last being *The Spiritual Crisis of Man*,[13] which was published in 1952.

The general thrust of his prescription for attaining the higher wisdom is familiar. Modern man has lost touch with his inner self by being too preoccupied with material gain and the external world. Through meditation, asceticism, and the study of books like those written by Brunton, the dedicated disciple can attain a higher variety of consciousness akin to that described by the great Eastern sages of the past. Much of what Brunton has to say is quite sensible. I am sure that many people would benefit from the practice of meditation, even though they may not believe in the kind of enlightenment which Brunton said he had attained. Reincarnation is taken for granted in Brunton's writings; but belief in reincarnation is widespread throughout the world. Perhaps people hope that subsequent incarnations give them further chances to improve.

Brunton was evidently less guarded in speech than he was in his writings; for the beliefs which he propounded when living in the Masson household exhibit all the usual characteristics of a paranoid delusional system, and fulfilled the function of turning Raphael Hurst, an insignificant person with no special gifts, into Paul Brunton the teacher of esoteric wisdom whose doctrines are still promulgated by *The Paul Brunton Philosophical Foundation* in New York State.

Brunton exhibited many of the traits and forms of behaviour characteristic of gurus. He was secretive about his origins, and revealed nothing of his personal life in any of his books. If one claims, as he did, to have had many previous lives and to have come to earth from another planet, the less that is known about the actual circumstances of one's birth and childhood the better. Brunton's claim to wisdom largely rested upon memories derived from his previous incarnations and upon his assertion that higher beings residing in other parts of the universe had passed on their esoteric knowledge to him. He also said that he had been taught by a mysterious sage whom he met in Angkor, and that he had received a personal invitation to study in a 'Mongolian metaphysical school'. Near the beginning of *The Secret Path*, he wrote:

> I hoped to wander through the yellow deserts of Egypt and among the wisest sheikhs of Syria; to mingle with the vanishing fakirs of remote Iraq villages; to question the old Sufi mystics of Persia in mosques with graceful bulbous domes and tapering minarets; to witness the marvels performed by the Yogi magicians under the purple shadows of Indian temples; to confer with the wonder-working lamas of Nepal and the Tibetan border; to sit in the Buddhistic monasteries of Burma and Ceylon, and to engage in silent telepathic conversation with century-old yellow sages in the Chinese hinterland and the Gobi desert.[14]

This romantic nonsense might be more convincing if Brunton had been a linguist. He claimed to read Sanskrit, but actually knew only a few words. 'Silent telepathic conversation' was the only kind of conversation of which Brunton was capable with the sages he lists, since he could not speak their languages. Masson, who did actually study Sanskrit at Harvard because of Brunton's influence, wrote: 'He was just a hodgepodge of misread and misunderstood ideas from an ancient culture he did not know or understand.'[15]

Although Brunton was not a confidence trickster in the crude fashion of Jim Jones, he falsely claimed a Ph.D. from Roosevelt University in Chicago; an institution which disclaimed any knowledge of him. The title page of his book *The Wisdom of the Overself* describes the author as 'Paul Brunton Ph.D.' and the paperback edition of *The Secret Path* has 'Dr. Brunton' on the cover. There is no evidence that he had any higher education at all, although he claimed that he had studied philosophy at 'the Astral University' together with an American painter called Thurston whom he described as an 'advanced mystic' and 'a great occultist'.[16] In *The Wisdom of the Overself*, Brunton wrote: 'I went to great pains to explore the most recondite sources', but what these sources actually were is not revealed.[17]

Brunton had few possessions, and was not eager for wealth. He lived ascetically, drinking tea, but no coffee or alcohol, and abstaining entirely from meat. He always appeared frail and underweight. He taught that meditation could lead to higher wisdom and spiritual knowledge; but physical desires had to be mastered if the spirit was to flourish unimpeded. Brunton also taught that fasting and abstention from sex aided the disciple's path to enlightenment. However, like others who claim not to engage in sex, he never tired of talking about it, and had a fund of stories about how potential disciples had destroyed their chance of enlightenment by injudicious sexual indulgence. He himself was not notably chaste, since he married four times (twice to the same exceptionally beautiful woman) and fathered a son. He was also content to be supported financially and housed by his disciples. According to Masson, his father must have given Brunton around $100,000 over the years. Brunton never owned a home of his own.

His potential disciples were subjected to arbitrary tests, ostensibly as part of a process of selection. These tests consisted of carrying out tasks which might appear silly, but which had to be accepted willingly; an exhibition of power which we have already noted as characteristic of guru behaviour. Although Brunton was not cruel like Jones and Koresh, he exercised power over those who adhered to him by making them act as his servants. Like many gurus, he had disciples or students rather than friends. Masson's father, who for years was a completely subservient disciple, actually cooked meals and waited on Brunton, whilst at the same time paying the rent of the house in which Brunton was living. When Jeffrey Masson became Brunton's secretary, he had to minister to his obsessional frugality by cutting out any little bits of blank paper from letters he had received so that they could be used for writing notes. Brunton also had a compulsion to hoard string, and demanded that pieces which were too small to use again separately should be joined together.

Brunton convinced his followers that many previous lives had endowed him with special wisdom. He stated that both he and Jesus Christ had descended to earth from a realm inhabited by superior beings. He claimed that, at night, he could travel anywhere in his astral body. Like Jim Jones and David Koresh, Brunton thought that he was surrounded by enemies; but since these malignant forces who daily attacked him were mostly invisible, he did not resort to weapons. From time to time, these enemies were personified as Communists, who, he said, followed him from Tibet to California. However, the Communists were only one manifestation of much deeper evil forces who were trying to make him lose his mind. Although Brunton narcissistically claimed that he was particularly spiritually advanced, and that he possessed an aura of such strength that it protected him against evil assaults, he was also frightened of insanity. However, his paranoid delusions of persecution served to explain how it was that such a gifted and important person had not been even more successful, and thus preserved his self-esteem.

Some delusional systems are like fairy stories or science fiction. Although Jeffrey Masson eventually became disillusioned with Brunton, he was obviously very fond of him when he was a child, and thoroughly enjoyed the thrill of living in the same house as a man who had experienced many reincarnations and who had come to earth from Sirius. As Masson tells us, Paul Brunton gave the Masson family the impression that he was engaged in a spiritual campaign of which the details had to be kept secret. 'Enemies were lurking. The forces of evil were listening, waiting for their chance to infiltrate the headquarters of the forces of good . . . This was a universe as simply organized as a boy's adventure story.'[18]

Brunton's delusional system is a variation on the archetypal phantasy which we have already encountered in The Book of Revelation. It not only serves the function of elevating a nonentity to a position of great importance, but also, at least for its originator, is a way of making sense out of the chaos of a life which might otherwise appear senseless. Masson states that Brunton was not psychotic, because he knew what was real, but chose to ignore it in favour of the 'higher' reality to which he claimed access, but I do not think that Brunton could have been so convincing if he had not believed his phantasies to be true. We don't know if Brunton went through a period of doubt and distress from which he emerged with settled convictions; but, as in the case of Gurdjieff, his period of travel in India suggests that his search for esoteric wisdom was a search for a solution to his personal problems. His calm, untroubled certainty that he was a spiritually advanced person with miraculous powers cannot have been with him from childhood. People like Brunton make nonsense of conventional psychiatric diagnosis.

One of the major attractions of some of the faiths propounded by gurus is their simplicity. Many of us harbour a secret wish to be transported back to the world of the nursery, where black is black, and white is white; where the forces of good finally triumph over the forces of evil; where the righteous are taken up into heaven, whilst the wicked perish in the lake of fire. A good deal of the less sophisticated variety of fiction panders to our primitive taste for dividing the world into heroes and villains. Conan Doyle's invention of Sherlock Holmes and Professor Moriarty is an apt illustration. His protagonists are polar opposites; and Holmes's description of Moriarty fuels our paranoid phantasies.

He is the Napoleon of crime, Watson. He is the organizer of half that is evil and of nearly all that is undetected in this great city. He is a genius, a philosopher, and abstract thinker. He has a brain of the first order. He sits motionless, like a spider in the centre of its web, but that web has a thousand radiations, and he knows well every quiver of each of them. He does little himself. He only plans. But his agents are numerous and splendidly organized.[19]

Enjoyable as this is, we have to admit that its appeal is to an unregenerate child in ourselves who delights in such simplicities.

But the idea of a secret conspiracy aimed at undermining legitimate authority has such wide appeal that, when exploited by gurus and politicians, its effects may be disastrous. As Norman Cohn has argued, the great European witch-hunt, which began in the late sixteenth century and which lasted until around 1680, took place because witches came to be regarded as constituting a clandestine, heretical sect possessed of magical powers which was dedicated to the overthrow of Christianity and orthodox society.[20] Thousands of innocent women were accused, tortured, and burned because of widespread acceptance of a paranoid delusion.

One modern guru who, according to Michael Lind in the *New York Review of Books*, is trying to persuade his enormous audience that there is an international conspiracy, is the television evangelist, Pat Robertson. Robertson is a far-right Republican who ran for the Republican nomination in 1988. His Christian Coalition claims over a million members. Robertson postulates a satanic conspiracy which includes the Illuminati, a secret society which he says was launched in 1776 by a Bavarian professor named Adam Weishaupt. Robertson claims that the Illuminati took over the established 'Continental Order of Freemasons'. Financed by the Rothschilds, the society is alleged to have been responsible for the deaths of Louis XVI of France and Gustavus III of Sweden. Moses Hess, the German journalist who influenced both Marx and Engels, and who was one of the first proponents of Zionism, is said by Robertson to have been a member of the Illuminati, and to provide the connecting link between that sect and the beginning of world communism.

Norman Cohn, in another book, *Warrant for Genocide*, examines the myth of the Jewish world-conspiracy, and attributes its modern form to a French Jesuit, the Abbé Barruel. Barruel believed that the French Revolution was the culmination of the secret machinations of the medieval Order of Templars which had survived as a secret society pledged to abolish all monarchies, to overthrow the papacy, and to found a new world order which it would control. The heart of this conspiracy, its true leaders, were alleged by Barruel to be the Illuminati. However, as Cohn wrote: 'As for the obscure German group known as the Illuminati, they were not Freemasons at all but rivals of the Freemasons and had in any case been dissolved in 1786.'[21] Perhaps the Reverend Marion Gordon 'Pat' Robertson has been reading the wrong books. One possible source, according to Norman Cohn, is a book by a Scottish mathematician called John Robison entitled *Proofs of a Conspiracy against all the Religions and Governments of Europe, carried on in the secret meetings of Freemasons, Illuminati and Reading Societies.*

As we continue to examine Robertson's views recorded by Lind, we are soon launched into the mysterious realm of high finance, in which 'the money barons of Europe' profit by lending money to governments at compound interest so that those governments can build up armaments in order to be able to confront the Soviet threat with confidence. Robertson believes that these secret powers exaggerated Soviet strength in order that the United States should continue wasteful spending on armaments which required borrowing from international financiers. As Lind remarks: 'Robertson's elaborate conspiracy theories have little to do with ordinary evangelical Protestant theology. They are rooted, rather, in the underground literature of far-right populism that purports to interpret world history as dominated by Jews, Freemasons, and "international bankers." '[22] Although Robertson supports the State of Israel, Michael Lind is surely justified in saying that *The New World Order,* his best-selling book, 'purveys the Illuminati-Freemason-Communist-High Finance conspiracy theory of world history familiar from generations of anti-Semitic propaganda.'[23]

Belief in such conspiracy theories may have temporarily declined in Britain; but one only has to examine the thrillers of the 1920s and '30s to see how popular they once were. 'Sapper', Dornford Yates, and John Buchan are only three of the many writers who were overtly antisemitic. At the centre of the conspiracies which their heroes invariably foiled were Jewish bankers and armaments manufacturers intent on fomenting revolutions and causing wars in order to enrich themselves.

In 1920, both *The Times* and the *Spectator* published articles supporting the notion that there was a worldwide Jewish conspiracy
aimed at destroying Christianity and achieving world domination.[24]
As Lind's article demonstrates, such beliefs, barely concealed, are
still being propagated by an evangelist whose organization claims a
million members and whose votes the Republican Party cannot afford
to lose.

In the context of this book, paranoid people who find others to
share their delusions are of particular interest. I well remember a
man who used to stay up every night until after the programmes on
television had come to an end. He left his set switched on, and paid
close attention to the random flashes and points of light which
appeared on the darkened screen. He became convinced that inhabitants of another planet were trying to communicate with him. They
had important messages to deliver; messages which might save the
world from nuclear disaster. Many people with similar delusions
upset their relatives and friends and become so isolated that they end
up in a mental hospital. This man, however, joined an interplanetary
society where his delusions were taken quite seriously, and where
he was treated as a person of importance. Membership of the society
preserved him from breakdown. He was no threat to anyone, and
there was no reason to restrict his liberty. I cannot say what beliefs
the other members of the society held; but my patient was delighted
to find a group who did not consider him eccentric or insane.

Whilst writing this book I received a letter from someone
unknown to me who must remain anonymous. He kindly gave me
permission to quote the following paragraph.

Dear Sir,

   I have spent the last two years wrestling with my spirit and
overcoming all my weaknesses to become a perfect focus of
the Divine Principle. I believe a tradition exists in most religious
movements of people who master all their inner demons and
completely free themselves from sin to become completely
Instruments of God: Jesus Christ in the Christian tradition; the
prophet Muhammad in the Muslim tradition; the genuine Dalai
Lama in the Tibetan Buddhist tradition; and avatars of Vishnu/
Krishna in the Hindu tradition.

The writer goes on to tell me of self-inflicted damage to the fabric of his mind which needs to be corrected before he can be fully effective as a spiritual leader, and seeks my advice as to how he can get in contact with another Instrument of God who might be able to do this.[25] I am glad to say that, in his subsequent letter giving me permission to use this quotation, he reports that he has found what he was looking for and has been able to resolve his problems.

Gurus are not easily accommodated within our current psychiatric taxonomy. Neither their acute periods of mental distress nor the settled belief systems which follow can be dismissed as forms of insanity unless we are prepared to widen our concepts of insanity to a ridiculous extent. Gurdjieff and Steiner, though neither suffering from paranoid schizophrenia nor being psychotic in the sense of being socially disabled, share certain characteristics with patients whom psychiatrists would designate as paranoid. The condition described as *paranoia* is defined as 'A rare chronic psychosis in which logically constructed systematized delusions have developed gradually without concomitant hallucinations or the schizophrenic type of disordered thinking. The delusions are mostly of grandeur [the paranoiac prophet or inventor], persecution or somatic abnormality.'[26] In the most recent edition of the American Psychiatric Association's *Diagnostic and Statistical Manual of Mental Disorders* (DSM-IV), this diagnosis would now be *Delusional Disorder: Grandiose Type*. As I have indicated, it is indeed grandiose to create one's own cosmogony in total disregard of accepted scientific opinion. Both Steiner and Gurdjieff did this. As I recorded earlier, Gurdjieff stated that he had invented a special means for increasing the visibility of the planets and the sun and also for releasing energies that would influence the whole world situation. It is hard to imagine a more grandiose delusion. Steiner, in addition to inventing his own history of the universe, believed that he had special powers of observation which revealed the spiritual reality which lay behind material appearances. Brunton claimed that he was spiritually advanced because his many previous lives had endowed him with wisdom.

Such people cannot be deemed 'ill' in the sense in which Elizabeth Farr was ill, or even as ill as Koresh and Jones became toward the end of their respective missions. They are propounding belief systems which are wildly eccentric: they are narcissistic, isolated, and arrogant; but they do not suffer from perceptual distortions or thought disorder or any other symptoms which might lead one to suspect cerebral disease or malfunction. It is questionable whether people of this kind should be described under the heading of 'psychotic disorder', as they are at present.

The belief systems propounded by gurus like those of Steiner and Gurdjieff may be thought delusional, but so-called normal people also express eccentric ideas. For example, a substantial number of people believe that they have seen flying saucers, or that corn-circles are the work of aliens. But we do not judge such people to be psychotic unless there is other evidence of mental malfunction or social incompetence. For example, a professor of psychiatry at Harvard who had previously written an excellent biography of T. E. Lawrence suddenly shocked the psychiatric establishment by publishing a book called *Abductions* in which he revealed that he believed that a large number of his patients had been abducted by aliens who had removed them in space-ships and who often conducted rather nasty experiments on them, such as removing sperm from men and ova from women.[27] Dr. Mack's psychiatric colleagues will certainly consider him gullible to the point of absurdity, and will dismiss his beliefs about aliens as delusional. But, in the absence of other signs of mental illness, he cannot be deemed psychotic. The diagnosis of mental illness should not be made on the evidence of beliefs alone, however eccentric these may appear. I have tried to demonstrate that a new belief system, whether it is considered delusional or not, is an attempt at solving problems. Striving to make sense of strange mental experiences is only one example of the universal human desire to bring order out of chaos.

IX

CHAOS AND ORDER

THE SEQUENCE OF A PERIOD of distress followed by illumination is a characteristic human pattern which, while not necessarily amounting to illness, can be discerned in the process of creative discovery in the arts and the sciences, and also in religious conversion. It is striking that these different types of problem-solving cannot often be deliberately willed. Creative discovery, religious conversion, and the formation of delusional systems 'come to' people as a result of unconscious processes over which they have little voluntary control. The idea that a delusional system can be a solution to a problem was propounded in the last chapter, and may still be unfamiliar to some readers, although Freud indicated this in his paper on Schreber's paranoia as long ago as 1911.

> *The delusional formation, which we take to be the pathological product, is in reality an attempt at recovery, a process of reconstruction.*[1]

The experience of discord both in the external world and in the inner world of the psyche is characteristic of the human species, and so is the impulse to bring discord to an end by finding a new solution. Doubt and uncertainty are distressing conditions from which men and women passionately desire release. In his book *Cosmos, Chaos, and the World to Come*, the historian Norman Cohn demonstrates that the belief that the order of cosmos will triumph over the disorder of chaos is one of the fundamental beliefs of mankind.[2]

The eighteenth-century theologian and philosopher Johann Gottfried von Herder affirmed that the creation of integrated wholes, new unities, out of discrete data was the fundamental organizing activity of human nature. As a species, we are intolerant of chaos, and have a strong predilection for finding or inventing order. This is an inescapable part of our biological endowment. Konrad Lorenz described man as 'the specialist in non-specialization.' One might add that man's adaptation is by means of maladaptation, which is affirming the same peculiarity in different words. If we were perfectly adapted to the environment and the environment remained constant we might live in a state of blissful ignorance, unaware of any problems, but we should not be inventive because there would be no incentive to be so. As Rajneesh remarked: 'Man is the only unnatural animal – that's why religion is needed.'[3] Man, who is partially adapted to many different environments but fully adapted to none, is thereby pre-programmed always to search for something better, both materially and spiritually. This is why human achievements have been so remarkable. Man is a creative creature because he is spurred by doubt, by confusion, and by dissatisfaction with what is, both within and without. This compels him to use his imagination and to look for new ways of understanding himself and the world in which he lives. Since dissatisfaction is one spur to creativity, it is not surprising that some of the most highly creative human beings have been especially liable to intense mood swings or have manifested other signs of instability.

The distress of chaos followed by the relief of finding a new order is as typical of scientific and mathematical discovery as it is of the resolution of inner personal problems. Although scientists and mathematicians do not usually experience illness before reaching new insights, they often describe long periods of apparently fruitless pondering over a problem, only to find that the solution suddenly comes to them, perhaps when they are thinking about something else. The mathematician Carl Friedrich Gauss had been struggling unsuccessfully for two years to prove a mathematical theorem.

Finally, two days ago I succeeded, not on account of my painful efforts, but by the grace of God. Like a sudden flash of lightning, the riddle happened to be solved. I myself cannot say what was the conducting thread which connected what I previously knew with what made my success possible.[4]

Another mathematician, Henri Poincaré, describes the same phenomenon in relation to his work on Fuchsian functions. What these are will remain a mystery to non-mathematicians like myself, but Jacques Hadamard states that Poincaré's theory of Fuchsian groups and Fuchsian functions 'consecrated his glory'. After a period of vain endeavour and sleeplessness, he went on a geological excursion. It is characteristic of the creative process that putting the problem on one side and letting it simmer should bring the solution which conscious striving had failed to produce.

> The incidents of the travel made me forget my mathematical work. Having reached Coutances, we entered an omnibus to go some place or other. At the moment when I put my foot on the step, the idea came to me, without anything in my former thoughts having paved the way for it, that the transformations I had used to define the Fuchsian functions were identical with those of non-Euclidian geometry. I did not verify the idea; I should not have had time, as, upon taking my seat in the omnibus, I went on with a conversation already commenced, but I felt a perfect certainty. On my return to Caen, for conscience' sake, I verified the result at my leisure.[5]

A few days later, this insight was followed by another. After pondering some further mathematical problems, Poincaré was disgusted with his failure and went for a holiday to the seaside. A quite unexpected solution, 'with just the same characteristics of brevity, suddenness and immediate certainty' came to him when he was out walking.

Poincaré actually describes witnessing this usually unconscious process at work. One evening, having drunk black coffee, he said that ideas came to him in crowds. He then felt them collide until pairs of ideas interlocked and made a stable combination. This only happens after a great deal of preparatory work, so one must assume that the ideas are, as it were, held suspended in the mind, perhaps for very long periods. Poincaré imagines that the ideas from which the new solution will spring are

> something like the hooked atoms of Epicurus. During the complete repose of the mind, these atoms are motionless; they are so to speak, hooked to the wall; so this complete rest may be indefinitely prolonged without the atoms meeting and consequently without any combination between them.[6]

Then, when the mathematician starts to select and study those ideas from which the eventual solution will come, he shakes the atoms off the wall. They shoot about, and continue their spontaneous dance until new combinations are formed, and new patterns emerge. The mathematician has given the atoms their initial impetus, but the way in which they come together to form solutions takes place unconsciously.

Poincaré's account matches Graham Wallas's delineation of the stages of the creative process. Wallas's first stage is *Preparation*, in which the subject is consciously pondered and studied from every angle. The second stage is *Incubation*, in which conscious thought is abandoned, but during which some scanning and sorting process is going on unconsciously from which the new solution will emerge. The third stage is *Illumination*, in which the new solution appears. The fourth stage is *Verification*, in which the new solution is subjected to rigorous examination and, where possible, objective testing and replication by others.

Because *Incubation* and *Illumination* are not consciously controlled, the new solution 'comes to' the thinker, and it is not surprising that Gauss, quoted above, said that it was only by the grace of God that he finally succeeded in solving his problem. Whether or not religious language is used to describe the phenomenon of *Illumination* depends upon the thinker's prior convictions. A believer will thank God for providing him with a solution: an agnostic will marvel at the creative activity of the unconscious mind, which can scan, sort, and combine ideas in new ways. It is often difficult to persuade or cajole the unconscious into performing its task of finding solutions. As recorded above, problems may be incubating in the mind for years before illumination solves them. Artists and scientists have described a great many different procedures which they use to woo the unconscious, ranging from sleep to dealing a pack of cards or playing a Fauré duet.[7] Some of the procedures adopted can be regarded as forms of secular prayer.

Are inspirational solutions to scientific and mathematical problems ever wrong? Yes, certainly. Hadamard writes:

The feeling of absolute certitude which accompanies the inspiration generally corresponds to reality; but it may happen that it has deceived us. Whether such has been the case or not must be ascertained by our properly so-called reason, a task which belongs to our conscious self.[8]

Poincaré recorded that some of the ideas which came to him turned out to be erroneous. The mathematician and scientist must put his inspirations to the test; must verify the apparent solution or new idea, and of course he has the skill and training to do so. Such techniques of verification cannot be applied to works of art or to religious revelations, although I hope to show that both can be evaluated with the aid of reason.

The joy of solving a scientific problem can sometimes be accompanied by feelings akin to those experienced in religious revelation. C. P. Snow gives a vivid description of such an event in his early novel *The Search*. A young scientist has just received confirmation that his new discovery is correct. Science has already provided him with many rewarding moments, but this particular experience is different from any of them, different in kind, further from the self. Although Snow's account appears in a novel, we can be sure that his description is autobiographical.

> It was as though I had looked for a truth outside myself, and finding it had become for a moment part of the truth I sought; as though all the world, the atoms and the stars, were wonderfully clear and close to me, and I to them, so that we were part of a lucidity more tremendous than any mystery.[9]

Snow's young scientist records that, before he experienced this 'tranquil ecstasy', he had sneered at the mystics who described being at one with God or part of the unity of things. After that afternoon, although he would have interpreted the experience differently, he thought he knew what they meant. I do not suppose that this often happens to scientists or mathematicians engaged in research. Because their field of study is external and impersonal, there is no obvious connection between their work and their interior life. However, I believe that finding an answer to a mathematical or scientific problem also has its internal repercussions within the psyche. There is a mysterious level of mental activity at which solving a problem in the external world resonates within the mind itself and perhaps relieves internal tensions. Kant perceived that our picture of reality must always be incomplete, and perhaps distorted, because we can never transcend the limitations imposed by our concepts of space, time and causality. As human beings, our perception is inevitably restrained, and to an unknown extent invalidated, by these subjective categories. We can perhaps go further, and declare that, however objective a scientist may try to be, his picture of the universe is bound to be conditioned to some extent, not only by the fact of being human in the Kantian sense, but also because his established beliefs form part of the structure of his own psyche.

For example, Newton found great difficulty in explaining how gravity operated, because it involved bodies acting upon one another at great distances without mutual contact or the mediation of anything resembling the hypothetical interstellar ether in which he no longer believed. Some authorities consider that Newton resolved this problem by attributing gravitational phenomena to the direct intervention of God. If he had not believed in God, he would have had to reach different conclusions about gravity. Although Newton's religious beliefs were unorthodox, his conviction that God could and would directly intervene in the running of the universe prevented him from considering other possibilities and thus brought his enquiries to a halt.

New discoveries in science and mathematics often consist of a synthesis between theories or concepts which have hitherto been regarded as unconnected. Newton's discovery of universal gravitation depended upon linking the laws of motion of the planets with the laws of motion of objects upon earth. Poincaré's discovery depended upon his recognizing that two supposedly different mathematical entities were identical. But both Newton's and Poincaré's imaginative leaps required mathematical verification which only conscious persistence and skill could provide. Physicists are still searching for a field theory which will unify all the forces of nature because they imagine that such a unity must exist, even if they cannot yet express it theoretically and mathematically. The problem nagged Einstein for forty years, and he died without finding a solution.

Both Einstein and Newton exhibited many oddities of personality. Einstein was an isolated child who remained detached and somewhat solitary throughout his life. At the age of sixteen, he exhibited sufficient evidence of stress and depression to obtain a doctor's certificate stating that his mental state required that he leave school in Munich and join his parents in Italy; but he never had a psychotic breakdown. Newton experienced a psychotic episode in 1693, when he was just over fifty, following a period of insomnia and loss of appetite.[10] He believed that his friends were plotting against him and broke off his relationship with Pepys. A letter to the philosopher Locke reveals that, during his illness, he believed that Locke had been attempting to 'embroil him with women'. Newton made a good recovery after a few months, which makes it likely that his illness was primarily an episode of depression, with paranoid ideas as a secondary feature.

Both Newton and Einstein were able to abandon current paradigms and create new models of the universe. This depended upon their making unconventional links between concepts which might have been dismissed as crazy if they had been unable to prove them mathematically. In both cases, the intense drive to make sense out of the universe may have been related to an incipient feeling of chaos within. As we noted when discussing Jung's breakdown, confusion between the internal world of the subject and the external world may prompt a quest for the discovery of a new order.

These examples demonstrate that personal factors cannot be entirely excluded from science; and I do not think it absurd to claim that, when a scientist makes a discovery and cries 'Eureka', he is celebrating the birth of a new order within his own mind as well as an addition to cosmic order. It is difficult to avoid falling in love with one's own new ideas. As Thomas S. Kuhn has shown in *The Structure of Scientific Revolutions*, the paradigms of science become so entrenched within the mind that they are sometimes almost as difficult to argue with or supersede as are the delusions of the insane or the faith of the religious believer.[11] This observation in no way disparages the methods of science; the need for objectivity, for verification, and, where possible, for prediction. Subjective factors creep in to scientific discovery and achievement, however rigorously the scientist attempts to exclude them; but, because he is a member of the scientific community, with a shared set of values and the knowledge that any new solution to a problem is going to be subjected to rigorous scrutiny by his peers, he cannot claim the infallibility with which a religious convert or a guru proclaims his own new insight.

For example, the scientists in the United States who thought that they had discovered a new way of producing endless amounts of energy from 'cold fusion' had to climb down because no one could replicate their results. It seems likely that they believed that they had really made an important discovery, and that they must have been triumphant for a while. They finally had to admit that they had been mistaken; but who is to say 'No' to the new discoveries of a guru?

We have to remember that many scientific theories of the past which seemed to have explanatory validity at the time have turned out to be false, and could sometimes be called delusional. One example is the so-called interstellar 'ether' which was supposed to permeate space and provide a medium through which gravitational and other forces could be transmitted, but which, as we saw above, was rejected by Newton. Another is the eighteenth-century belief that a substance called 'phlogiston' was lost during burning from everything combustible. Neither the ether nor phlogiston actually exist; but their imagined existence served as an explanation for some physical phenomena until better theories came along to replace them. Those of us who do not understand modern physics may be forgiven for smiling at a world which supposedly consists of particles so small that their existence has to be deduced rather than observed, and which last only for minute fractions of a second that can hardly be measured. If a modern physicist were to be transported back to the seventeenth century, he might find it hard to persuade his scientific colleagues that his vision of the universe was not delusional. But today we take it for granted that something like the apparently crazy world of sub-atomic particles actually exists, because we are convinced that most physicists are both honest and sane, and because they set up experiments which can be repeated and verified. However much physicists may disagree with each other, there is a consensus about the nature of the world and about scientific method, and a constant interchange of ideas and information. Revolutionary theories of the universe may at first appear as crazy as the delusions of the insane, but, if they stand up to scientific scrutiny, will finally be incorporated into the scientific edifice. No physicist expects that whatever he says will be accepted without question.

The works of artists, musicians, and writers are more obviously and immediately concerned with their subjective emotions, but the recurrent pattern of the creative quest in both science and the arts is the same, and those who are impelled to follow this path are motivated by similar forces. Writers, particularly poets, are commonly afflicted by severe, recurrent depression, and their work can often be partially interpreted as a way of relieving their distress, a search for tranquillity. In both *The Dynamics of Creation* and *Solitude*, I have described how the creative imagination can exercise a healing function. 'By creating a new unity in a poem or other work of art, the artist is attempting to restore a lost unity, or to find a new unity, within the inner world of the psyche, as well as producing work which has a real existence in the external world.'[12] If we accept the idea that being less than perfectly adapted to the external world is part of man's biological endowment which stimulates his imagination, it is not surprising that so many of the people who develop the most fertile imaginations are driven by inner tensions. As Graham Greene affirmed, and many other writers have echoed, 'Writing is a form of therapy.'[13]

The solutions which writers and other artists find to both aesthetic and personal problems may not, at first sight, resemble the solutions arrived at by mathematicians and scientists, but both groups describe the creative process in similar terms. A period of intense concentration, of studying all the various aspects, is followed by a fallow period in which the problem or the new idea is put on one side, and allowed to simmer without conscious interference. In the case of writers, this fallow period is often one of quite severe depression, in which the writer feels bereft, exhausted, inept, and hopeless. This period is analogous to the period of mental distress or physical illness which, in the case of gurus, precedes revelation. In the case of writers and musicians, the fallow period is generally succeeded by the birth of a new idea; an aesthetic solution which is incorporated in a work of art, which is then published or otherwise displayed. The artist himself is, for the moment, usually convinced of the rightness of his solution. This never lasts, for a new problem always presents itself. In both science and the arts, the work is never done. No active scientist or artist ever rests upon his laurels for long. There is always another scientific problem to be solved, another novel to be written, another string quartet to be completed.

Of course, works of art cannot be proved to be erroneous or correct, like scientific hypotheses, but if they are well-constructed and touch a common chord within our shared humanity, they are appreciated and welcomed, and recognized as valuable. Most artists are content with this, and do not insist that their admirers confine their appreciation to their own works without extending it to other artists working in the same field. Today, an exaggerated emphasis upon the romantic insistence on individual fulfilment has led to many musical compositions, sculptures, and paintings being so sub-jective and so removed from the mainstream of art that they are only appreciated by a minority. In music, we have witnessed the decline of rigorously composed serial music because it touches the hearts of so few, and because it is so difficult to remember. In the visual arts, doubt has been thrown on the worth of many objects, or piles of objects, claiming to be called sculpture. Any creative production must be appreciated by a few people other than the artist himself if it is to be recognized as a work of art. Otherwise, the artist risks the accusation of madness or of totally failing to communicate, which comes to the same thing. If they want their work to be appreciated in their lifetimes, both artists and scientists must remain 'part of the main'.

The answers which gurus provide are, for the most part, all-embracing. That is, gurus are not like artists or scientists in working away at successive problems, each requiring a new solution. Their answers are holistic, embracing the human condition and life itself. Such answers are often no more than generalizations from their own subjective experience. As we have seen, some of these revelations appear to be so eccentric, so out of touch with accepted opinion about the world, that we regard them as evidence of mental illness. But normal people also have deeply irrational holistic experiences in which the distress of inner conflict and the sense of being improperly adjusted to the world temporarily disappear. As I suggested earlier, the sane are madder than we realize.

The mystical 'consolations' described by Ignatius are of particular interest in this context. It will be recalled that on one occasion he saw 'the plan of divine wisdom in the creation of the world'. These consolations are an example of an irrational spiritual experience, usually felt and remembered as deeply impressive. Neither psychotic delusions nor religious faith nor being in love can be shaken by argument. Nor can spiritual experience. A person has either had such an experience or he has not. Mystical states may be short-lived, but they leave an indelible imprint. Even when dissociated from any religious faith, they are remembered and treasured, and their return is longed for. Sometimes they occur in the course of meditation. In spite of becoming completely disillusioned with Rajneesh as a guru, Hugh Milne, his former bodyguard, was able to write:

> On several occasions I reached that true bliss and abundant joy which comes from a deep meditative state. This meditative space was incomparably beautiful and worth anything to experience. Those who dismiss 'evil cults' have no idea at all how rapturous this state can be, and how no other pleasure can compare with it. Most people who have spent any time in a religious cult will have tasted this bliss, and it is what keeps them coming back for more.[14]

In another book, I discussed the mystical experiences which many people have experienced when alone: 'Intimations of Immortality', as Wordsworth called them.[15] These moments of perfect harmony, in which the self and the world seem at one, are precious recollections which imprint themselves on the memory.

Ecstatic experiences are described by a variety of writers, including Walt Whitman, Edmund Gosse, Arthur Koestler, A. L. Rowse, Bernard Berenson and C. S. Lewis. This list demonstrates that the experience in question is as likely to happen to unbelievers as to the religious. Bernard Berenson, as one might predict, records his experience in relation to the visual.

> For years I had been inquiring, excavating, dredging my inner self, and searching in my conscious experience for a satisfying test. I needed a test to apply to the artifacts that I thought I admired but could not hypnotize or habituate myself to enjoy with complete abandon, while the worm of doubt kept gnawing at the felicity of the ideal paradise. Then one morning as I was gazing at the

leafy scrolls carved on the door jambs of S. Pietro outside Spoleto, suddenly stem, tendril and foliage became alive and, in becoming alive, made me feel as if I had emerged into the light after long groping in the darkness of an initiation. I felt as one illumined, and beheld a world where every outline, every edge, and every surface was in a living relation to me and not, as hitherto, in a merely cognitive one. Since that morning, nothing visible has been indifferent or even dull. Everywhere I feel the ideated pulsation of vitality, I mean energy and radiance, as if it all served to enhance my own functioning.[16]

In his partly autobiographical poem 'Childe Harold's Pilgrimage', Byron records feelings of unity with nature.

Are not the mountains, waves, and skies, a part
Of me and of my soul, as I of them?
Is not the love of these deep in my heart
With a pure passion? should I not contemn
All objects, if compared with these? and stem
A tide of suffering, rather than forego
Such feelings for the hard and worldly phlegm
Of those whose eyes are only turn'd below,
Gazing upon the ground, with thoughts which dare not glow?[17]

When Admiral Byrd spent the winter of 1934 alone at an advanced weather base in the Antarctic, he had a mystical experience during one of his daily walks and described it in terms of music.

Harmony, that was it! That was what came out of the silence – a gentle rhythm, the strain of a perfect chord, the music of the spheres, perhaps.
   It was enough to catch that rhythm, momentarily to be myself a part of it. In that instant I could feel no doubt of man's oneness with the universe . . . The universe was a cosmos, not a chaos; man was as rightfully a part of that cosmos as were the day and night.[18]

Here is an example taken with permission from a response to a research enquiry.

My first ecstatic experience occurred when I was about eight or nine years old, and I still remember it vividly. It followed an intense childish disappointment at not being allowed to accompany my father and sister on a walk which was considered too long for me – we were on holiday in the country at the time. I shed tears, lay on my bed in misery, and then may have fallen asleep. When I got up, I suddenly experienced a complete change of mood in which all feelings of disappointment suddenly vanished, to be replaced by peace, serenity, and a kind of inner happiness which is almost indescribable. I joined my mother in the garden, perfectly content to be alone with her, and feeling that she must have had such experiences herself; that I did not need to explain anything. She would certainly have explained it in religious terms, and I think I probably would have done so at that age; perhaps believing that God had reached down to remove my pain. As I write this, the experience is still so vivid that tears (of relief and happiness) come into my eyes!

Since then, I have had several more such experiences. Some have been connected with music. One occurred when the duet from Don Giovanni 'Là ci darem la mano' was running in my head. For a whole morning – much longer than my other spiritual experiences – this music transformed my feelings about the world and myself so that I perceived the world as beautiful whilst feeling an inner calm and serenity. I can begin to recapture the feelings by recalling the music; but they are no more than a pale shadow of the experience itself.

I count them as the most valuable experiences of my life. At one with oneself, mankind, and the universe; 'Surprised by Joy'; the most wonderful, beautiful experiences one can imagine.[19]

Another example recorded by William James comes from the memoirs of Baroness Malwida von Meysenbug (1816–1903). She was an early campaigner for the rights of women, a socialist, and a friend of Wagner. She was also hostess to Nietzsche and Paul Rée in the winter of 1876 in Sorrento, when Nietzsche had his last encounters with Wagner.

I was alone upon the seashore as all these thoughts flowed over me, liberating and reconciling; and now again, as once before in distant days in the Alps of Dauphiné, I was impelled to kneel down, this time before the illimitable ocean, symbol of the Infinite. I felt that I prayed as I had never prayed before, and knew now what prayer really is: to return from the solitude of individuation into the consciousness of union with all that is, to kneel down as one that passes away, and to rise up as one imperishable. Earth, heaven, and sea resounded as in one vast world-encircling harmony. It was as if the chorus of all the great who had ever lived were about me. I felt myself one with them, and it appeared as if I heard their greeting: 'Thou too belongest to the company of those who overcome.'[20]

The state of being in love often includes the sense of complete unity with another person, if not necessarily with the universe. It is also a totally irrational experience. Indeed, Freud referred to the state of being in love as a kind of madness, as 'the normal prototype of the psychoses,'[21] and lovers used to be referred to as 'moonstruck' in reference to the ancient belief that Luna, the moon, caused lunacy. We tend to treat infatuated lovers with the same tact that we extend to believers whose faith we do not share, and to madmen whose delusions we perceive as absurd. We know that there is no point in arguing with someone who is in love. We may think the object of infatuation to be totally unworthy of such devotion, but it is quite useless to say so. The most reasonable and equable people are not immune to love's charms and delusions. Although disappointed love can be excruciating, never to have been in love is to have missed a vital experience. The historian Edward Gibbon, whose autobiography and style of writing reveal him to have been the epitome of eighteenth-century urbanity, describes his early love for Suzanne Curchod as something to be proud of.

I understand by this passion the union of desire, friendship and tenderness, which is inflamed by a single female, which prefers her to the rest of her sex, and which seeks her possession as the supreme or the sole happiness of our being. I need not blush at recollecting the object of my choice; and though my love was disappointed of success, I am rather proud that I was once capable of feeling such a pure and exalted sentiment.[22]

Gibbon, while recognizing that sexual desire is an essential ingredient of the state of being in love, does not make the mistake of reducing the condition to nothing but sexual infatuation. To be in love is 'a pure and exalted sentiment' because it is as much concerned with the search for unity as it is with sex. Those who have experienced the sense of unity with the universe and have also felt the sense of unity with a beloved person know that these experiences are the same. This description comes from a private letter, again reproduced with the author's permission.

> When I was first in love with H—. I had the experience of being entirely at one with her. There was no anxiety to impress or compete; just a deep joy at loving and being loved; a tranquil ecstasy. I was so certain of our complete mutual understanding that, when we went to church together, I found myself flooded with tears – whether of relief or joy, I cannot tell. Such ecstasies do not last for very long; but the memory of that serene certainty is still precious and continues to colour our subsequent friendship.[23]

Although being in love may last for a considerable period of time, it does not usually persist with its initial intensity. Like other irrational experiences, or periods of mental illness, it may open doors of perception which otherwise might have remained closed. As in the instance just quoted, it may pave the way toward a new and valuable intimacy with another person.

Those who have had ecstatic experiences of the kind described have no doubt of their significance. Ecstasies cannot be quantified or replicated (although a few people claim to be able to summon them at will). For some, ecstasies may create a foundation for religious belief. Romain Rolland, writing to Freud complaining of Freud's dismissal of religion as illusion, suggested that what he described as the 'oceanic' feeling of being at one with the external world was the origin of religious sentiments. In reply, Freud, who had never experienced such a feeling himself, interpreted it as an extreme regression to a very early state; that of the infant at the breast before he has learned to distinguish himself from either his mother or the external world. The two views are not incompatible.

For agnostics, these transient perceptions of a wonderful unity reveal something about the creative search for answers and solutions which is so characteristic a feature of the human condition. The transience of ecstatic experiences of unity should be welcomed, not deplored. It is better to travel hopefully than to arrive. One of the disadvantages which religious revelations and delusional systems have in common is their rigidity and their permanence. The believer invests so much in his belief system that he can neither modify it nor subject it to rational argument. The sceptic who continues to search, but who only intermittently finds, is less hampered. If, during his quest, he is granted a glimpse of that perfection of wholeness for which he is seeking, he should count himself extremely fortunate.

I suggested earlier that Ignatius's ecstatic consolations could be regarded as manic or hypomanic phenomena; the counterpart to his periods of depression. But although some manic-depressives undoubtedly have mystical experiences, I doubt whether all such experiences can be classified as hypomanic. Manic-depressive illness in its severest manifestations is a definable mental disorder which is strongly genetically determined, but we have to remember that there are less severe mood disorders which ultimately shade off into normality. Those who exhibit mood swings of more than usual intensity, but who cannot be deemed psychotic at any point in the cycle are said to be suffering from cyclothymic disorder. It is easy to recognize that there is a continuum between manic-depressive illness and normality, for we all go through periods of depression and periods of elation of varying intensity.

It is not so generally recognized that many apparently normal people have experienced symptoms which are considered characteristic of schizophrenia, or at least closely allied with whatever 'schizophrenia' may be. There is a continuum between normal and schizophrenic, just as there is between normal and manic-depressive. We know that proneness to schizophrenia is strongly determined by heredity, as is manic-depressive illness. The lifetime expectation for schizophrenia in the general population is about one per cent, but the risk of schizophrenia in the immediate relatives of schizophrenics – parents and siblings – is about ten times as high. When both parents are schizophrenic, the risk of any child they have becoming so is about forty per cent. If one of a pair of identical twins becomes schizophrenic, the risk of the other becoming so is about fifty per cent; a finding which supports the idea of a hereditary component but also demonstrates that heredity is not the only factor involved. If schizophrenia was entirely genetic in origin, identical twins would show a hundred per cent rather than fifty per cent concordance.

Not everyone is equally liable to develop psychotic disorders of schizophrenic type; but if the idea of a continuum between psychotic and normal is accepted, one might expect to find that there were normal people who exhibited traits of personality predisposing or akin to schizophrenia, and one would expect that such people would be particularly likely to be found amongst the relatives of schizophrenics. This is in fact the case. Research has demonstrated that many normal people will admit to having experienced mild symptoms resembling schizophrenic experience; feelings of unreality, 'telepathic' thoughts; auditory or visual hallucinations; distorted, paranoid thinking. There is an awkwardly named dimension of personality recognized by psychologists as *schizotypy* which is taken as indicating the possession of traits similar to those found in schizophrenics, and which might indicate the possibility of schizophrenic illness in the face of stress. Some of these traits have a positive aspect.

Both schizophrenics and schizotypical personalities often report a feeling of being overloaded by incoming stimuli. They may be oversensitive to light and noise, and feel distressed if, for example, they are in a crowded room where many conversations are going on at once. Such people may also be plagued by a feeling that too many different thoughts are crowding the mind at the same time. I believe that this may be one motive force impelling creativity. Muddle is so unpleasant that it demands sorting out. The creative act of bringing order out of chaos provides relief.

Thought disorder, defined as a disturbance in the organization, control, and processing of thoughts, is one of the most striking clinical features of schizophrenia. Signs of thought disorder include irrelevant responses, disconnected ideas, vagueness, and the use of peculiar words, a phenomenon already referred to in the chapter on Gurdjieff. Conceptual boundaries are blurred, and the associations between one idea and another are so subjective and tangential that the observer cannot follow the schizophrenic's train of thought. Yet unexpected associations, the discovery of connections between concepts or phenomena hitherto unperceived, are essential elements of creative thinking in science, and literature has been enriched by the eccentric use of language. The language employed by James Joyce in *Ulysses* and *Finnegans Wake* is sometimes reminiscent of schizophrenic discourse, and it is appropriate to recall that Joyce's daughter Lucia was schizophrenic. A number of studies have demonstrated that the relatives of schizophrenics (who share a high proportion of the same genes) are more likely to engage in creative pursuits than the relatives of normal people. No one suggests that full-blown schizophrenia is anything but destructive; but a latent disposition to schizophrenia may be related to originality and prompt creative discovery.

It is also the case that those who rate high in measures of schizotypy are those most liable to have spiritual experiences. M. C. Jackson, who has demonstrated this in *A study of the relationship between psychotic and spiritual experience*,[24] lists the major features of such experience. There is considerable overlap with William James's definition of the states of mind which he calls mystical; but Jackson adds some characteristics, taken from his reading of over five thousand modern accounts of spiritual experience. William James defines mystical states of mind in terms of four characteristics. These are:

Ineffability; meaning the difficulty of expressing the experience in words.

Noetic quality. The experience is also a state of knowledge; an insight into what is felt as new depths of truth.

Transiency. Most mystical states cannot be sustained beyond an hour or two.

Passivity. The person feels that his own will is in abeyance, and sometimes feels guided or controlled by some power external to himself.

Jackson adds peacefulness, the sense of tranquillity to which I have already referred. He also refers to changed sense of time or space, anomalous perceptions, an awareness of an altered state of consciousness, and a sense of having achieved a new perspective on life and its problems. Unity with nature or with the universe as a whole is a common accompaniment.

A brief recapitulation of some of the ideas so far advanced may be helpful at this point. Gurus go through a period of stress, sometimes amounting to a psychotic illness, which is brought to an end by the revelation of a new truth which dispels confusion, brings order, and provides relief. This sequence of events is comparable with the creative process in mathematics and science, which also begins with the nagging discomfort of perceiving problems and difficulties, but which is ended by the construction of new hypotheses which bring together facts or theories which have hitherto seemed incompatible.

The same process takes place in the creation of works of art, which often involves a period of depression or other stress before the artist feels that he can order his material in a way which makes him feel that he has finally 'got it right.' I quoted Herder's proposal that the creation of new unities, integrated wholes out of discrete data, was the fundamental organizing activity of human nature; and I suggested that human beings were motivated to create such wholes because their lack of exact adaptation to any one environment left them dissatisfied and always in search of a perfection which they could never reach.

In the chapter entitled *The Divided Self* in *The Varieties of Religious Experience*, William James discusses the ways in which mental discordance can become converted into inner unity and peace.

> But to find religion is only one out of many ways of reaching unity; and the process of remedying inner incompleteness and reducing inner discord is a general psychological process, which may take place with any sort of mental material, and need not necessarily assume the religious form . . . For example, the new birth may be away from religion into incredulity; or it may be from moral scrupulosity into freedom and licence; or it may be produced by the irruption into the individual's life of some new stimulus or passion, such as love, ambition, cupidity, revenge, or patriotic devotion. In all these instances we have precisely the same psychological form of event, – a firmness, stability, and equilibrium succeeding a period of storm and stress and inconsistency.[25]

The new truths proclaimed by gurus are holistic solutions which are sometimes so eccentric that they cannot be accommodated within a generally accepted belief system and are therefore labelled delusions. But before dismissing gurus as madmen, it is salutary to recall that so-called normal people also have holistic experiences in which conflict and distress temporarily disappear. Ecstasies are one variety of such experience; being in love is another. Both resemble delusions in that they are not susceptible to rational argument or criticism. Some of the most deeply felt, important human experiences are entirely irrational.

X

DELUSION AND FAITH

ANOTHER DEEPLY FELT, important human experience which is also irrational is the phenomenon of conversion. We have already encountered this in the case of Ignatius, although he would probably have acknowledged a nominal Christianity before his illness turned him into a passionate believer. Conversion to a religious faith brings with it a huge sense of relief. It may appear as if a burden had been laid down, and as if a higher power had taken over the direction of the subject's life. William James wrote of conversion:

> But since, in any terms, the crisis described is the throwing of our conscious selves upon the mercy of powers which, whatever they may be, are more ideal than we are actually, and make for our redemption, you see why self-surrender has been and always must be regarded as the vital turning-point of the religious life, so far as the religious life is spiritual and no affair of outer works and ritual and sacraments.[1]

William James gives a number of examples illustrating self-surrender. Two taken from Edwin D. Starbuck's *Psychology of Religion* run as follows. "I simply said: 'Lord I have done all I can; I leave the whole matter with Thee;' and immediately there came to me a great peace. – Another: 'All at once it occurred to me that I might be saved, too, if I would stop trying to do it all myself, and follow Jesus: somehow I lost my load.'"[2]

More subtle, and therefore more compelling, is the conversion to Roman Catholicism of John Henry Newman. *Apologia pro Vita Sua* is his own account of his spiritual progress which, because it is a prose masterpiece, has become a classic. Here is what he wrote about the relief which followed his joining the Church of Rome.

From the time that I became a Catholic of course I have no further history of my religious opinions to narrate. In saying this, I do not mean to say that my mind has been idle, or that I have given up thinking on theological subjects; but that I have had no variations to record, and have had no anxiety of heart whatever. I have been in perfect peace and contentment; I never have had one doubt. I was not conscious to myself, on my conversion, of any change, intellectual or moral, wrought in my mind. I was not conscious of former faith in the fundamental truths of Revelation, or of more self-command; I had not more fervour; but it was like coming into port after a rough sea; and my happiness on that score remains to this day without interruption.[3]

In the last chapter, I suggested that the sceptic, who may have intermittent glimpses of unity, but who does not embrace a holistic solution to life's problems, is following the course set by both artists and scientists, whose searches go on throughout their lives, and who never reach a final conclusion. But what religions provide and what gurus proffer are holistic solutions. Religious faith is an answer to the problem of life, not to a series of intellectual puzzles or artistic dilemmas; and, even when Jung, Freud and Steiner claimed to be applying the methods of science, it is clear that they were actually promoting belief systems which are much more akin to religious faiths than they were inclined to acknowledge. Sceptics appear to be in a minority. The majority of mankind want or need some all-embracing belief system which purports to provide an answer to life's mysteries, and are not necessarily dismayed by the discovery that their belief system, which they proclaim as 'the truth', is incompatible with the beliefs of other people. One man's faith is another man's delusion.

I have attempted to show that there is a continuity between psychotic experience and normal behaviour. Manic-depression, clear-cut in its extreme form as a definable recurrent illness, shades off into the less severe 'cyclothymic disorder', and can be seen to be related to the periods of minor depression and elation which are part of the experience of the average, normal person. There is also a continuity between manifest schizophrenic illness like that of Elizabeth Farr, or that of Jung's locksmith apprentice, and the 'delusional disorder' of Steiner and Gurdjieff, with Brunton's paranoid state hovering uneasily somewhere between the two; and many normal people admit to intermittent symptoms resembling those described by schizophrenics. I have also underlined the idea that delusions are attempts at solving problems. Delusions are both exculpatory and explanatory: they preserve self-esteem by blaming others; interpret anomalies of perceptual experience in ways which diminish the threat of mental chaos; and, when grandiose, give a much-needed injection of self-confidence to a person who might otherwise feel isolated and insignificant. Religious faiths serve similar functions in the economy of the psyche.

Delusions have been defined as

abnormal beliefs held with absolute conviction; experienced as self-evident truths usually of great personal significance; not amenable to reason or modification by experience; whose content is often fantastic or at best inherently unlikely; and which are not shared by those of a common social and cultural background.[4]

If we accept this definition, it follows that whether a belief is considered to be a delusion or not depends partly upon the intensity with which it is defended, and partly upon the numbers of people subscribing to it.

As Bhagwan Shree Rajneesh was reported as saying:

There are fictions when the society supports you, there are fictions when nobody supports you. That is the difference between a sane and an insane person; a sane person is one whose fiction is supported by the society. He has manipulated the society to support his fiction. An insane man is one whose fiction is supported by nobody; he is alone so you have to put him in the madhouse.[5]

Religious faiths conform to the definition of delusions given above in every respect except one: they cannot be defined as abnormal because world faiths are shared by large numbers of people, whether or not they come from similar social and cultural backgrounds. This underlines my contention that we should not diagnose anyone as psychotic because they express eccentric or delusional beliefs, unless they are also exhibiting other signs of mental disorder or social incompetence.

If we return to the definition of delusions we see that religious faiths are also 'beliefs held with absolute conviction', or else they are not faiths at all. Of course believers intermittently have doubts; but the fact that they regard doubts as enemies with which to contend rather than rationally justified queries attests the basic strength of their convictions. Faith is experienced as being of such great personal significance that, for the believer, it constitutes the hub around which everything in life revolves. Faiths are no more amenable to reason than are delusions, although it is arguable that, unlike delusions, they can be modified by experience to some extent. Faith may alter over the years. It may grow, deepen, change; but unless altogether abandoned, it remains a belief system which affects the whole of the way life is lived. In the same way, delusional systems usually affect the whole of an individual's behaviour and perception of himself.

It is because of this holistic, all-embracing characteristic that it is just as difficult to argue with religious faith as it is to argue with paranoid delusions.

Both sets of beliefs are connected to some extent with the preservation of self-esteem, with the conviction of being 'special'. The self-esteem of the ordinary person is closely bound up with personal relationships. We value ourselves because our spouses, children, and friends appear to be fond of us, enjoy our company, or profess love for us. The person who becomes a Christian has, in addition, the belief that God loves and values him. This is both a bonus and an insurance. The believer is, to some extent, protected from the tragedies of personal existence. The impact of bereavement and failure, however poignant, is modified by the conviction that God's love will continue, however dire the circumstances. Faith really can protect people against horrors. For example, those who held rigid, simple religious beliefs were better able to resist Communist attempts at indoctrination than doubting intellectuals.[6]

But faith is even more important to those in whose lives, for whatever reason, affectionate relationships play little part. Gurus have often been isolated as children, and tend to be introverted, narcissistic, and more interested in what goes on in their own minds than in relationships with others. These traits of personality encourage the development of phantasies. Imagination flourishes best in solitude. The cosmogonies elaborated by Gurdjieff and Steiner can be attributed to a highly developed talent for phantasy made possible by isolation. If their ideas had been discussed with others and critically examined at an early stage, they could not have been sustained. As it was, their ideas became grandiose delusions which could be described as private faiths. It is not surprising that such faiths are not open to argument. If self-esteem entirely depends upon a private faith or upon a delusional system, that faith or system is so precious that it must not be shaken. No one can afford a total loss of self-esteem, and those who come close to doing so when in the throes of severe depression often commit suicide.

Returning to the definition of delusions, we can say that the content of religious faith is often 'fantastic or at best inherently unlikely.' In Christianity, for example, we can point to the Virgin Birth and the Resurrection as being fantastic because they are so contrary to biological principles. Many Eastern religions teach the reincarnation of the soul, which seems inherently unlikely. There is no objective evidence for either religious faith or delusions. No one can demonstrate the existence of God. Faiths cannot be tested by experiment, proved or disproved. We have seen that delusional systems support self-esteem; so do religious faiths. For example, it is hard for us to accept that most human beings are functionally replaceable. Each one of us is unique; but only a few men and women of genius are irreplaceable. Most human beings will be forgotten a few years after their death. Nature is prodigal. There are far too many human beings in the world; and the majority are totally unmemorable. If we are lucky, our friends and relatives will miss us for a while, but very few of us achieve any permanent memorial. This is difficult to tolerate. The dying Keats, in despair at the lack of recognition accorded him by his countrymen, desired that his name should be left off his tombstone and only these words engraved upon it: 'Here lies one whose name was writ in water.' If so wonderfully gifted a poet as Keats could thus express his disillusion, what is it possible for the ordinary person to say about himself? 'I lived, I died, I know not why. I shall not be remembered.'

But the case is different if, for example, one can adopt the Christian faith. For Christianity asserts that every human being, however humble, is precious in the eyes of God. A man may have been abandoned by family and friends; he may be a failure, a down-and-out alcoholic, a misfit, a sinner whom the world will not forgive. But if he has faith that God loves him, and that, if he repents, God will forgive him, he is protected against despair, and the horror of nonentity. Many of the early converts to Christianity must have embraced this faith because it affirmed that quite ordinary people, of no particular gifts or consequence in society, were yet of value in the eyes of God. Nietzsche repudiated Christianity on a number of different grounds, including its insistence on the superiority of soul over body and its tendency to label sexuality as evil. Another reason for his rejection was the idea that the humble and meek should be exalted; the very opposite of Nietzsche's belief that the strong deserved to flourish.

> Jesus (or Paul), for example, found how small people lived in the Roman province – a modest, virtuous, pinched life. He offered an exegesis, he read the highest meaning and value into it and with this also the courage to despise every other way of life.[7]

T. S. Eliot wrote: 'Human kind cannot bear very much reality.' The inability to bear the reality of one's own transience and unimportance constitutes one powerful motive for adopting a religious faith; for the Christian God is alleged to value each person as an unique individual, and the doctrine of the immortality of the soul is confirmation that this uniqueness will not disappear. In some other faiths, continuity of the individual is assured by reincarnation until the point is reached at which the preservation of individuality is no longer seen as of any importance. It is not surprising that people cling so tightly to belief systems which reassure and support them so effectively. When discussing the inevitability of death with John Freeman at the end of his 'Face to Face' interview in 1959, Jung said that the unconscious, threatened with a complete end, disregarded it. 'You know, when I think of my patients, they all seek their own existence and to assure their existence against that complete atomisation into nothingness, or into meaninglessness. Man cannot stand a meaningless life.'[8] But some of us cannot adopt a faith just because it may be psychologically desirable for us to believe: we need some evidence that it is true. Life is not meaningless to those who live it to the full, even if they do not believe in the immortality of the soul.

Many people have been brought up to believe that a religious faith is desirable. If we cannot bring ourselves to believe, or have abandoned a former religious allegiance, believers, who are today more tolerant than they used to be, extend their sympathy. Faith, we are told, moves mountains. Faith will see one through all the tribulations of life. It will comfort one in affliction, give meaning to existence, provide hope for the future, and promise salvation and eternal life in heaven. But Nietzsche regarded faith as a kind of weakness.

> Faith is always coveted most and needed most urgently where will is lacking; for will, as the affect of command, is the decisive sign of sovereignty and strength. In other words, the less one knows how to command, the more urgently one covets someone who commands, who commands severely – a god, prince, class, physician, father confessor, dogma, or party conscience.[9]

If the title guru had been in common use in Nietzsche's day, he would surely have added it to his list of those who command.

Idiosyncratic belief systems which are shared by only a few adherents are likely to be regarded as delusional. Belief systems which may be just as irrational but which are shared by millions are called world religions. When comparing the beliefs held by psychotics with the religious beliefs held by normal people, it is impossible to say that one set of beliefs is delusional while the other is sane. If we reconsider the beliefs about the universe put forward by Gurdjieff and Steiner, we can say with confidence that their beliefs are so bizarre, so out of touch with the consensus of informed, educated opinion, that the ordinary person will conclude that such men must be mad and that their beliefs are delusions. These are the beliefs of people who inhabit desert islands of the mind; so remote from the thoughts and opinions of others that they are unaffected by them. In spite of this, neither man was a psychiatric case, nor likely to become one. Both Gurdjieff and Steiner attracted followers who no doubt believed, or still believe, in their extraordinary histories of the universe; but the numbers are so small that it is reasonable to regard these disciples as harmless eccentrics and to designate both cosmogonies as delusional.

However, there are estimated to be more than a thousand million Christians in the world. It would be insufferably arrogant and absurd to say that all these people are deluded or misguided. Yet the Virgin Birth, the Resurrection, the immortality of the soul and the resurrection of the body are doctrines which, though integral parts of the Christian faith, are as incredible to the biologically minded sceptic as Gurdjieff's beliefs about the moon, or Steiner's cosmic beings. If there were only a hundred believing Christians in the world, we should think them quite as eccentric as those who are convinced that everything which Gurdjieff or Steiner affirmed was literal truth. When members of the Church of England attend Morning Prayer, they are required to repeat the Apostles' Creed or some modern version of it listing the same beliefs. This Creed may be unfamiliar to some readers and I will therefore quote it in full.

I believe in God the Father Almighty, Maker of Heaven and Earth: And in Jesus Christ his only Son our Lord; Who was conceived by the Holy Ghost, Born of the Virgin Mary, suffered under Pontius Pilate, Was crucified, dead, and buried; He descended into hell; The third day he rose again from the dead; He ascended into Heaven, And sitteth on the right hand of God the Father Almighty; From thence he shall come to judge the quick and the dead.

I believe in the Holy Ghost; the holy Catholick Church; The Communion of Saints; The Forgiveness of Sins; The resurrection of the Body, And the Life everlasting. Amen.

How many of those calling themselves Christians believe the literal truth of these propositions? Modern Christians, including bishops and other members of the Anglican Church, try to justify their repetition of the Creed by affirming that its propositions are to be taken metaphorically. The Holy Ghost, for example, can be taken as indicating that the spirit of Jesus lives on, just as we might say that the spirit of Plato's philosophy still influences us. The story of the Resurrection can be perceived in the same way: the man who died is resurrected in the hearts of those who love him. The Virgin Birth is an archetypal myth which is not confined to Christianity. Early Christian missionaries, when they discovered that the people whom they had come to convert had their own versions of the Incarnation, thought that the devil must have been perverting their teaching.[10] Many contemporary Christians would surely agree that the Virgin Birth is the way that we tend to think about the origin of heroes, rather than a literal account of what happened. A former Bishop of Birmingham, interviewed in 1993, freely admitted that he did not believe in the Virgin Birth, although, surprisingly, he did believe in the literal truth of the Resurrection.[11] It is easy for an agnostic to accept the validity of much of the teaching of Jesus, but it must be hard for some Christians to repeat a creed which includes belief in the resurrection of the body and eternal life after death. Those of us who were brought up as Christians are so accustomed to hearing and repeating the Creed that we tend to disregard its actual content.

Some scientists and philosophers who are religious believers can separate their professional thinking from their faith so that the two, as it were, occupy separate compartments within the mind. They bring to mind Tertullian's famous statement: 'And the Son of God died, which is immediately credible because it is absurd. And buried he rose again, which is certain because it is impossible.'[12] Agnostic colleagues find it difficult to empathize with the deliberate espousal of irrationality by someone who is usually rational in professional and academic life; but they generally, though not invariably, avoid entering into arguments which they recognize as futile, and treat the person concerned with exactly the same degree of tolerance which any decent person extends to the delusions of the psychotic or the moonstruck idealisations of the lover.

Scientists demand experimental evidence, replication, and proof before they will accept a new hypothesis. Science could not progress unless every advance is questioned. But, as Thomas S. Kuhn has shown in *The Structure of Scientific Revolutions*, it is often difficult for scientists to abandon established and familiar concepts because they have become articles of faith rather than remaining as provisional hypotheses. Even the most sceptical scientist must 'believe in' whatever paradigm underpins his research. Problems cannot be investigated or even perceived without some conceptual framework, but all such frameworks must be able to be overturned. There should be no articles of faith in science, unless it be the faith that no discovery, no law, is so absolute that it cannot be superseded.

In practice scientists do not usually exhibit such total scepticism. For example, some scientists are such passionate advocates of evolution by natural selection that their writings display the fervour of a missionary preaching a gospel. Darwin's hypothesis has such explanatory power, makes sense of so much that was previously obscure, that it easily becomes elevated into a principle which *must* be right. Even the most rational human beings show a strong propensity toward adopting a faith which a critically based philosophical training cannot wholly expunge. A very large number of people profess beliefs which cannot be proved, which lack any objective support, and which, to those who do not share them, appear crazy. I am inclined to think that we all have such notions. Even the most rational agnostic secretly harbours beliefs which are deeply irrational, especially in areas concerned with self-esteem and love. We like to think that we are irreplaceable, and so we believe it, even though we rationally appreciate that we shall soon be forgotten. Many of us harbour transient grandiose delusions that we are more important than we actually are.

Towards the end of his great book, William James tries to define 'under all the discrepancies of the creeds, a common nucleus to which they bear their testimony unanimously'. He concludes that

> there is a certain uniform deliverance in which religions all appear to meet. It consists of two parts: –
>
> 1. An uneasiness; and
>
> 2. Its solution.
>
> 1. The uneasiness, reduced to its simplest terms, is a sense that there is *something wrong about us* as we stand.
>
> 2. The solution is a sense that *we are saved from the wrongness* by making proper connection with the higher powers.[13]

But 'the higher powers' need not be perceived as deities. As I indicated in the last chapter, those who are gifted enough to be creative artists or research scientists or mathematicians know that they are indeed dependent upon powers which are not of their own making.

The examples already given demonstrate that solutions to aesthetic and scientific problems are often the product of mental processes which are beyond conscious control. I believe that sorting, scanning, and trying to make sense out of experience is going on in our minds all the time. We get glimpses of such a process when we remember our dreams, or when we enter a state of reverie in which we no longer exercise control over our thoughts. In this sense we are all dependent upon higher powers. Anyone engaged in creative work must acknowledge such dependence unless he is so conceited that he lacks any insight into how his mind functions. To believe that one's own ego is capable of anything and everything is to be ridiculously inflated. Nietzsche, who lost the Christian faith in which he had been raised, and who announced the death of God, nevertheless retained a need to acknowledge a superior power. In *Beyond Good and Evil*, he refers to the artist's need for spiritual discipline, for

> protracted *obedience* in *one* direction: from out of that there always emerges and has always emerged in the long run something for the sake of which it is worthwhile to live on earth, for example, virtue, art, music, dance, reason, spirituality – something trans-figuring, refined, mad and divine.[14]

But Nietzsche's obedience is to ideas and ideals, not to a human being. It is one thing to acknowledge an allegiance to an ideal or to trust the higher powers within the mind itself: it is quite another to submit to a guru who is *Human, All too Human*, – as Nietzsche named one of his books. Some gurus like Steiner and Ignatius remain honest, sincere, and apparently little affected by the adoration of disciples. Others, like Rajneesh, become corrupt. But the person who becomes a disciple 'falls for' a particular guru without being able to distinguish between dross and gold. The process is equivalent to falling in love, or to the occurrence of 'transference' in psycho-therapy. None of us is immune to such phenomena. It would be quite wrong to dismiss all disciples of gurus as immature or neurotic. I happen to think that elevating a human being into a 'higher power' who possesses spiritual insight not given to ordinary mortals is dangerous and misguided; but I can envisage circumstances in which I might succumb. In the East, gurus or Masters are much more acceptable than they are to western Protestants or agnostics. It is taken for granted that the aspirant to enlightenment needs a superior figure; a Master who will direct and guide him. Perhaps Buddhist and Hindu cultures are better at selecting gurus than we are, because gurus are more embedded in the culture, and their existence more taken for granted.

A naïve American couple who had read some of my writings once called on me. The interview ended with the man saying: 'Dr. Storr, I guess you are our idea of a wonderful person.' I should have said 'I'm not *my* idea of a wonderful person,' but I was so embarrassed that all I did was to mutter some disclaimer. It seems to me that many gurus are only too willing to be regarded as wonderful persons. I doubt if they are much troubled by embarrassment at the adulation they receive, although they may be corrupted by it. Gurus, as I hope I have shown in this book, differ widely from each other; but they share the apparent conviction that they *know*, and that their personal revelation applies to everyone. Emerson, in his essay on *Self-Reliance*, thought this characteristic of genius.

> To believe your own thought, to believe that what is true for you in your private heart is true for all men, – that is genius.[15]

My own view is that this is not genius but narcissism; self-absorption hovering on the brink of madness. In the case of gurus, it seems to be the consequence of isolation. Gurus go through a period of intense stress or mental illness, and come out on the other side with what generally amounts to a delusional system which, because of their lack of friends with whom ideas could be discussed on equal terms, is elaborated in solitude. The ideas they have, unlike those of scientists or mathematicians, are not exposed to critical scrutiny, or subjected to the authority of an established church. They then seek disciples. Acquiring disciples who wholeheartedly embrace the guru's system of ideas is the final proof of his superiority; the confirmation of his phantasies about himself. Confidence tricksters are convincing because they have come to believe in their own fictions. Gurus are convincing because they appear sure that they are right. They have to believe in their own revelation or else their whole world collapses. The certainty shown by gurus should, paradoxically, be the aspect of their behaviour which most arouses suspicion. There is reason to think that all gurus harbour secret doubts as well as convictions, and that this is why they are driven to seek disciples. Richard Webster writes:

> Classically, however, the Messiah's quest for some external confirmation of his secret identity has also manifested itself in a more common form – in the desire to attract followers, and having done so, to make huge demands of loyalty, as if to test the obedience of his disciples, and to prove his own supernatural ascendancy by the quality and completeness of the submission he can command.[16]

This is certainly true of some of the gurus discussed in this book. Unless, like Ignatius, gurus persuade their followers to join an established church, they offer faiths which are entirely dependent on belief in the guru himself. Self-surrender to something or someone who appears more powerful than the individual's weak ego or will is an essential feature of conversion. People who give up their independence to a guru's direction feel a similar sense of relief, but put themselves at greater risk.

Agnostic intellectuals usually value independence of thought and freedom of expression very highly. One of the things which they find shocking about those who join new religious movements is the abrogation of personal responsibility and the subjection of independent judgement to that of the guru. John Carswell thought it appalling that Orage, the leading English editor of his day, should 'owe obedience to an Armenian magus', namely Gurdjieff. When people discover that those who join the Unification Church have their marriage partners chosen for them by Sun Myung Moon, and are forbidden to have sexual relationships before marriage or for some time afterwards, they recoil at this abandonment of personal freedom. Many who are not Roman Catholics shudder when they see the words *Nihil Obstat* on the flyleaf of a book by a Catholic writer. Cannot anyone write what he pleases under the law, without having to submit his writings to a censor who may, for all he knows, be bigoted or insensitive? But Catholics, especially those who follow the teachings of Ignatius, believe that obedience to authority is virtuous self-abnegation; and it is clear that it is with great relief that many people surrender their own judgement to a figure deemed to be superior. Rajneesh was described as a man to whom one only had to say 'I leave everything to you,' and everything would be taken care of.

Gurus are isolated people, dependent upon their disciples, with no possibility of being disciplined by a Church or criticized by contemporaries. They are above the law. The guru usurps the place of God. Whether gurus have suffered from manic-depressive illness, schizophrenia, or any other form of recognized, diagnosable mental illness is interesting but ultimately unimportant. What distinguishes gurus from more orthodox teachers is not their manic-depressive mood swings, not their thought disorders, not their delusional beliefs, not their hallucinatory visions, not their mystical states of ecstasy: it is their narcissism.

The reader will have understood that I am not a Freudian disciple, but this does not prevent me from appreciating many of the ideas which Freud had to offer. His paper *On Narcissism: An Introduction* is considered by his editors to be among the most important of his writings. Freud begins his discussion of narcissism with a discussion of paranoid schizophrenia (he actually uses the term 'paraphrenia', but this is no longer current usage).

Such patients, Freud claims, 'display two fundamental character-istics: megalomania and diversion of their interest from the external world – from people and things.'[17] He goes on to say that this interest, or libido, which has been withdrawn from the external world is directed toward the subject's own ego. It is this which warrants the use of the term 'narcissism'. Freud proposes that the narcissism of paranoid schizophrenics is a secondary phenomenon; an exagger-ation of the self-absorption found in normal children which he names primary narcissism. 'The charm of a child lies to a great extent in his narcissism, his self-contentment and inaccessibility, just as does the charm of certain animals which seem not to concern themselves about us, such as cats and the large beasts of prey.'[18] We expect small children to be self-absorbed and demanding. A baby has to be the centre of attention if its needs are to be met, and we do not assume that small children will be in any way concerned about how the adults who look after them are feeling or what their needs may be. All babies are megalomaniacs. Small children require a great deal of love without being able to reciprocate. A small child loves its mother so long as she provides what the child needs; but we do not expect the child to show the kind of concern for its mother's feelings which we do expect an adult lover to show toward the object of his love. At this narcissistic stage in emotional development the aim is to be loved rather than to love anyone else.

Those who remain narcissistic in adult life retain this need to be loved and to be the centre of attention together with the grandiosity which accompanies it. This is characteristic of gurus. Even ostensibly humble gurus like Rudolf Steiner retain grandiose beliefs in their own powers of perception and their own cosmogonies. The need to recruit disciples is an expression of the guru's need to be loved and his need to have his beliefs validated; but, although he may seduce his followers, he remains an isolated figure who does not usually have any close friends who might criticize him on equal terms. His status as a guru demands that all his relationships are *de haut en bas*, and this is why gurus have feet of clay.

XI

TO WHOM SHALL
WE TURN?

MOTHER MEERA

EURIPIDES PUTS INTO the mouth of Orestes the precept which constitutes the epigraph to this book. 'The wisest men follow their own direction and listen to no prophet guiding them.' But this is a counsel of perfection, more honoured in the breach than in the observance. The fact is that many, if not most, human beings sometimes feel the need for someone to whom they can turn when perplexed. Of course we all need experts to guide us through the mazes of civilized living; accountants, solicitors, electricians, plumbers. But the perplexities which concern us here are to do with the meaning of life. Why is it that human beings, even when fully adult, look to others for guidance rather than making up their own minds about problems to which there are no unequivocal answers?

Perhaps it is inappropriate to call any human being 'fully adult.' The term *neoteny* refers to the evolutionary process by which human beings have retained certain characteristics into adult life which, in other primates, belong to an early stage of development. Thus, mature human beings have the facial appearance and relatively large brains which are found in the foetuses of subhuman primates. Neoteny is sometimes called *foetalization*. It preserves the flexibility which tends to disappear with full maturity. We remain malleable because we retain some of our childhood characteristics in adult life. This ensures that old humans are better at learning new tricks than old dogs.

One of the defining characteristics of human beings is that their adaptation to the world depends principally upon learning rather than upon those built-in behaviour patterns which govern the lives of creatures lower down the evolutionary scale. The development of speech has made possible the transmission of culture. Man's infancy and childhood, relative to his total life-span, has been prolonged by evolution, with the consequence that there is additional time for learning to take place. Learning does not cease with the end of childhood. Many of us continue to learn all our lives, and enjoy doing so. Now that so many people are surviving into old age, a modern western society cannot be considered advanced unless it provides adequate facilities for adult education.

Our predisposition to go on learning is adaptive, but remaining teachable into adult life demands the retention of some characteristics of childhood, amongst which is a tendency to overestimate the teacher. Children learn best from teachers they respect and look up to. Although adults can make use of teachers merely as technical experts, they probably learn faster if they like their instructor and are impressed with his or her knowledge and expertise. If a pupil is learning carpentry or the use of computers, the personal qualities and sensibilities of the teacher may be relatively unimportant. This is not so when the pupil studies subjects more closely connected with human emotions. Although musicologists may be able to teach their subject as an intellectual exercise, the appreciation and performance of music itself cannot be effectively taught except by someone to whom music is emotionally meaningful. Musical executants who may long have outstripped their teachers technically often look back on those teachers with deep admiration and affection. Musical insight is akin to 'spiritual' insight: the teacher who has it is revered or even idolized. This is even more clearly the case with gurus who profess insight into life itself and teach how it should be lived. Disciples often attribute almost magical powers to their gurus. It is a form of idealization which is even more dangerous than falling in love.

Psychotherapists are familiar with the occurrence of transference, a phenomenon first described by Freud as the process by which a patient attributes to his analyst attitudes and ideas that derive from previous authority figures in his life, especially from his parents. Later, the term became extended to include the patient's total emotional attitude toward the analyst. Freud at first regarded transference with distaste. He wanted psychoanalysis to be an impersonal quest for truth in which the relationship between patient and analyst was entirely professional and objective rather than personal. The role he wanted to assume was that of a mountain guide. Instead, he found that his patients made him into an idealized lover, a father figure, or a saviour.

The phenomenon of transference is not confined to the relation-ship between a psychotherapist and a patient. We are all liable to project subjective feelings of love and hate upon authority figures, whether these be gurus, political leaders, or teachers. I think that this is an inevitable though undesirable consequence of retaining the ability to learn into adult life. It is one striking aspect of our 'immaturity'. Madame Cornuel wrote 'No man is a hero to his valet'; but leaders are inevitably regarded as heroes or villains by those who do not know them intimately. In the United States, President Kennedy was absurdly overestimated both during his life-time and posthumously. It is only quite recently that his character and achievements have been called into question and accorded objective scrutiny by historians. In Great Britain, although their numbers are shrinking, there are still people who idealize the Queen and other members of the royal family. The tendency to overestimate promi-nent persons is not confined to the disciples of gurus; it is a human failing shared by us all.

Certainty is hugely seductive, and certainty is offered by all suc-cessful leaders: it is an important part of their charisma. This is a book about spiritual rather than political leaders, but successful politicians share some of the characteristics of gurus, even if they preach no gospel. As every politician realizes, the image is more compelling than the reality. Charles de Gaulle was a charismatic politician who believed in himself as a personification of France. Winston Churchill was, as he said himself, the roar of the lion, the voice of England. Both de Gaulle and Churchill were superb orators, but it was their inner conviction, comparable with that of gurus, which made them charismatic. When Churchill finally became Prime Minister in 1940 at the age of sixty-five, he said to his doctor: 'This cannot be accident, it must be design. I was kept for this job.'[1] Like religious gurus, political leaders sometimes believe that they are chosen by God. If they had been total failures, we might well dismiss both de Gaulle's and Churchill's beliefs about themselves as grandiose delusions.

In Britain during the Second World War, Winston Churchill was idolized as the saviour of the country. When Britain faced Nazi Germany alone in 1940 and the threat of imminent invasion hung over us all, Churchill's dogged courage, resilience, defiance, and gift for rhetoric braced and invigorated a people who might rationally have concluded that they were bound to be defeated. 'Churchill's well-nigh miraculous achievement during the dire summer months of 1940 was to convert the nation to a mystical faith in its own providential destiny.'[2] The study of Churchill throws light on that mysterious quality of charisma which is so characteristic of gurus, and also shows that idealization may, under certain circumstances, have positive uses. Churchill, like some of the gurus we have been looking at, found reality in what his doctor called his 'inner world of make-believe'.[3] Because this inner world was clearly one in which he had a heroic mission to fulfil, he was able to impose it upon almost the whole British population at a time when a hero was desperately needed. Churchill was intensely narcissistic. Although many of those who worked with him and for him adored him, he showed an extraordinary obtuseness about the feelings of other people. As I wrote in my essay on Churchill:

> In 1940, Churchill became the hero that he had always dreamed of being. It was his finest hour. In that dark time, what England needed was not a shrewd, equable, balanced leader. She needed a prophet, a heroic visionary, a man who could dream dreams of victory when all seemed lost. Winston Churchill was such a man; and his inspirational quality owed its dynamic force to the romantic world of fantasy in which he had his true being.[4]

At the end of the war, Churchill was rejected by the electorate in favour of a Labour administration which, it was widely felt, would better tackle the task of reconstruction. Churchill felt this rejection as base ingratitude, but I think that the electorate were percipient in realizing that Britain no longer needed a prophet or a saviour.

I recall meeting Sir Oswald Mosley. His political stance and particularly his antisemitism were anathema to me; but, at a dinner party, the first impression he made was of a courteous, old-fashioned aristocrat with beautiful manners. Mosley had immense charm. The conversation turned from family matters to Northern Ireland. I forget what Mosley said, but he instantly propounded a series of measures which he insisted that the British government ought at once to adopt if they were ever to solve this long-running, apparently insoluble problem. That evening, I saw charisma in action. Although Mosley had long been discredited, I began to understand why, in his early days, he had been hailed as a future Prime Minister. He was so convincing that one began to feel that he might be right. After all, no politician had any idea how to deal with the I.R.A. or what should be done about Ulster. Perhaps, I felt, we should follow Mosley's lead in dealing with this particularly intractable problem, even though we might recoil in distaste from his Fascist past; perhaps Mosley really *knew*. Against my own better judgement, I became fleetingly impressed by a man whose former policies I hated, simply because he appeared so sure that he was right.

I have not listed Hitler as a guru because he does not qualify as a spiritual teacher, but he manifested many of the characteristics of the worst gurus, including the use of apocalyptic language and a paranoid insistence on the Jews as the evil enemy, the Anti-Christ striving to destroy the noble Aryan Redeemer. As J. P. Stern points out, Hitler's speeches used 'a solemn declamatory style superimposed upon the intimately personal language of Luther's New Testament'.[5] His rhetoric persuaded his audience to connive at his self-dramatization as a messianic figure: his portrayal of the Jew as the source of all evil provided them with a scapegoat who could be blamed for the problems and failures of society. Given the state of Germany during the 1920s and early '30s, it is not surprising that Hitler attracted an enthusiastic following.

Creative artists who found new movements may also exhibit some of the characteristics of the guru, although their message is aesthetic rather than religious. The composer Richard Wagner displayed many of the characteristics of the disreputable type of guru. He was unscrupulous financially, insisting on luxury even when he had no money to pay for it. He was also unscrupulous sexually, although, like Rajneesh, he was probably no great performer. He craved adulation and demanded that his adherents should afford him devotion and complete fidelity. Even as a boy of seventeen, he was looking for a companion 'to whom I could pour out my inmost being to my heart's content, without my caring what the effect might be on him'.[6] Wagner had to dominate and was incapable of a relationship on equal terms. He had only disciples, no true friend. After he had parted from his first wife, there was no one who could criticize him or contradict him without being deemed a traitor.

Characteristically, he exploited his disciples. When Nietzsche was temporarily bewitched by him, Wagner used him to run errands, buy Christmas presents, and undertake other menial chores. As soon as he had completed the poem of the *Ring*, he insisted on reading all four sections over two days to patient followers, and repeated these readings over and over again to any who would listen. This was Wagner's form of the interminable haranguing to which some gurus submit their disciples. Wagner was widely cultured, hugely well-read, marvellously gifted as a composer, and extraordinarily imaginative. He was one of the most charismatic human beings who have ever lived. Even those, like Nietzsche, who rebelled or became disillusioned with him, acknowledged that they could never forget the magic of his personality or the enchantment of his music. Wagner was also narcissism personified. He had to be right: he *knew*.

These four examples of charismatic people who were not gurus in the sense of preaching a religious message, underline the disagreeable fact that many of those who are most obviously charismatic are, from the human point of view, deeply flawed characters who should be regarded with extreme caution. Their persuasive, impressive power is a product of their grandiose conviction of their own importance. They need to dominate in order to confirm their own status. David Aberbach has suggested that, in many cases, charisma is related to bereavement or other personal traumata within the family. The new identity which emerges from the personal crisis through which charismatic gurus pass may be of someone who belongs to the whole world rather than to a secure family; someone who belongs to everyone, and therefore to no one. This certainly explains the charismatic person's lack of close personal relationships in some instances.[7] But the millions who flocked to support Hitler from 1933 onwards would not have been deterred by the suggestion that they were being misled by the charisma of a paranoiac. Social disruption and misery invariably throw up leaders of this type, as Norman Cohn has demonstrated.[8] Both Churchill and Hitler, in their entirely different ways, demonstrate the accuracy of Norman Cohn's observation. If a society is sufficiently disrupted, or seriously threatened, politicians who promise to restore order or save the society from its enemies become transformed from men of affairs into magical, guru-like saviours.

In psychoanalytic terms, the desire to submit to a guru's guidance or to acquire a religious faith is conventionally explained as the persistence of a childhood need for a father. In *Civilization and Its Discontents*, Freud wrote:

> The derivation of religious needs from the infant's helplessness and the longing for the father aroused by it seems to me incontrovertible, especially since the feeling is not simply prolonged from childhood days, but is permanently sustained by fear of the superior power of Fate. I cannot think of any need in childhood as strong as the need for a father's protection.[9]

We expect that a child who is inexperienced in the ways of the world to turn to a parent for guidance. The very young perceive that their parents know more about life's problems than they do, and it may take years for a child to realize that his parents are not omniscient but fallible. A lingering hope that somewhere there is someone who *knows* persists in the recesses of the minds of most of us, which manifests itself more obviously when people are distressed or ill. As I wrote earlier, the compelling need to attract disciples demonstrates that the certainty exhibited by gurus is more apparent than real, but it is difficult for someone who is seeking spiritual guidance to appreciate this. Is it possible to distinguish the kind of guru who should be regarded with suspicion from someone to whom it is reasonable to turn as a genuine guide? It is easier to point to those who should be avoided than to recommend reliable mentors.

The gurus who should be regarded as potentially dangerous are those who are authoritarian and those who are paranoid. These two characteristics march hand in hand. I would like to add another; the capacity for oratory; perhaps the most dangerous weapon in a guru's armoury. Gurus like Koresh and Jones harangued their disciples into submission, submerging them in a flood of words. Since many gurus are concerned far more with their own dominance than with anything else, it is not surprising that many become corrupt, both sexually and financially. As I have indicated, surrender to God or to some abstract guiding principle is not only seductive but understandable and, in some instances, valuable. Surrender to a human guru is fraught with risk. Rajneesh required complete surrender of all that had previously been held dear, even a follower's former identity, which is why his disciples were given new names. Even Ignatius demanded unquestioning obedience to religious superiors.

Eileen Barker, who has done so much to dispel the mystery surrounding new religious movements, and who draws attention to their virtues as well as to their dangers, agrees that gurus who make important decisions about converts' lives should be regarded with caution. Gurus who exercise personal control over their disciples' money, dress, personal possessions and sexual partners are particularly to be avoided. The same is true of leaders who claim divine authority, and leaders or movements who pursue a single goal in a single-minded manner. We should be alert to situations in which converts are dependent on the movement for definitions and the testing of reality. A movement which cuts itself off, either geographically or socially, from the rest of society is suspect. So is a 'movement drawing sharp, unnegotiable boundaries between "them" and "us", "godly" and "satanic", "good" and "bad" – and so on.'[10] These boundaries are characteristic of the paranoid picture of the world which I outlined earlier. The movements led by Jim Jones and David Koresh provide obvious examples.

Some gurus become more and more inaccessible, even to their disciples, because they are primarily self-absorbed and not really concerned with friendship or the problems of their followers. Rajneesh is a striking example. Gurdjieff's intense concentration on Fritz Peters when the latter was severely depressed is one example of a guru manifesting personal concern. But this encounter was a matter of forceful persuasion rather than exploration and personal understanding. Gurus who are never personally available should be avoided. Rudolf Steiner continued to be able to devote himself to others even when he had achieved a large following, and so did Ignatius and Jesus. But both Freud and Jung became more concerned with theory and less interested in therapy as they got older.

Self-surrender to a guru who will relieve one from the burdens of personal responsibility and provide a new belief system is not the only attraction of joining a new religious movement. It is heartening for many people to belong to a group professing the same allegiance.

The survivors of Jonestown did not regret their stay in that disastrous settlement, and some recalled it as a paradise. Many of the young followers of Rajneesh enjoyed the companionship, as well as the sexual freedom, which they experienced at the ranch in Oregon. The mostly young, mostly middle-class English disciples of the Unification Church of the Reverend Sun Myung Moon welcomed the feeling of belonging to a movement which aimed at spiritual ideals not envisaged by ordinary Western society. They seem to have been initially attracted by the happy atmosphere, smiling faces, and apparently loving community. The Moonies share the belief that Moon is a messiah who can lead the way to establishing the Kingdom of Heaven upon earth.

In any society, there will always be people who are disillusioned with what the orthodox churches have to offer. Many who join new religious movements are young idealists who rightly feel that modern western society is so materialistic and competitive that spiritual values have been shelved in favour of the pursuit of wealth. It is surely significant that the phrase 'standard of living' is always taken to indicate a material standard, more champagne and smoked salmon; not a spiritual standard, which would include better education and greater cultural opportunities.

There is no doubt that joining a group of like-minded contemporaries working toward a common end is life-enhancing. As we have seen, it is possible to become completely disillusioned with a particular guru and yet look back with nostalgia on the exhilaration which accompanies comradeship and being welcomed into a community. As Eileen Barker wrote in her book *New Religious Movements* (NRMs),

> Perhaps those who are willing to learn from the NRMs could become more aware of the desire of many young people to *give*. In a world of specialisation, bureaucracy and social welfare, it is not always easy for young people with idealism to know how to expend their undirected energy for the good of others. Some churches, some schools and some community centres do tap this energy. So do some NRMs.[11]

But such movements are bound to have leaders, and as my accounts of some of these leaders have demonstrated, they vary in quality and in integrity to an astonishing extent.

There is another aspect of group membership which is sometimes deplorable. Disciples who are certain that their particular guru has revealed 'the truth' are apt to become arrogant, insensitive, and dismissive of those who do not share their beliefs. The *sannyasins* of Rajneesh behaved badly both in India and Oregon, thinking themselves superior to the local residents.

Edmund Gosse's description of being brought up by parents who were ardent Plymouth Brethren is an unsurpassed account of a childhood overshadowed by bigotry. An early interest in literature prompted Gosse to buy a book containing the poetry of Ben Jonson and Christopher Marlowe. The latter poet entranced him, but his father denounced the book as abominable. The Plymouth Brethren seriously believed that only members of their tiny sect were sure of salvation and eternal life, and that all Catholics, for example, were doomed to perpetual torment after death.[12] One might assume that modern esoteric groups were more tolerant, until one recalls the teaching of David Koresh, who persuaded his followers that a Second Coming was imminent in which he himself would become king of Israel, while God and his army of immortals slaughtered all the wicked of the earth, beginning with the Christian church.

However, one can say something about the qualities of teachers and spiritual guides who can be relied on. The best teachers of adults are non-authoritarian. They may inform, suggest, advise; but they realize that every individual is different and that, in the end, men and women have to discover their own paths and form their own opinions. The word *education* is related to the Latin verb *educere,* which means 'bring out, develop from a latent condition'.[13] The teaching enterprise is exactly that; and the good teacher is delighted when a former pupil goes beyond what has been taught to make some original contribution which may be more important than anything the teacher has achieved. This desirable outcome requires a certain modesty on the part of the teacher, combined with a capacity to relate to the pupil as an individual. The same considerations apply, or should be applied, to analytical psychotherapy. Jung's description of how an analyst should behave to his patient is as far removed from the didactic stance of authoritarian gurus as it is possible to be. The following quotation is from a lecture given in 1932, while he was still very interested in psychotherapy.

> If the doctor wants to guide another, or even accompany him a step of the way, he must *feel* with that person's psyche. He never feels it when he passes judgment. Whether he puts his judgments into words, or keeps them to himself, makes not the slightest difference. To take the opposite position, and to agree with the patient offhand, is also of no use, but estranges him as much as condemnation. Feeling comes only through unprejudiced objectivity. This sounds almost like a scientific precept, and it could be confused with a purely abstract attitude of mind. But what I mean is something quite different. It is a human quality – a kind of deep respect for the facts, for the man who suffers from them, and for the riddle of such a man's life. The truly religious person has this attitude.[14]

The good teacher retains integrity because he is more interested in his subject and in his pupil than in himself. If a scholar is dedicated to the study of history, or mathematics, or philosophy, his enthusiasm will communicate itself to the pupil, and both will be embarked together on a search for the truth which transcends personal considerations. The same applies, with even more cogency, to a religious or spiritual quest. This obedience to 'something transfiguring, refined, mad and divine', as Nietzsche put it,[15] tends to protect the teacher-pupil relationship, although transgressions sometimes occur. Mutual concern with something greater than the individual tends to prevent too much concentration on the interpersonal relationship and exploitation of the weaker by the stronger.

It might be assumed that good teachers or spiritual guides lack charisma because of their modesty; but this is not always the case. My friend, the composer Alan Ridout, wrote to me while I was engaged on this book:

> I think it highly necessary to draw a distinction between human beings such as you are describing – ones riddled with narcissism – and the genuinely holy ones who also have 'charisma'.

He describes attending a service in Canterbury Cathedral when the Pope visited England. He was duly impressed with the Pope,

> But the figure who really shook me I was not expecting at all. I hadn't even thought about him. It was Cardinal Hume. He was neither looking about him nor behaving in any abnormal, or even special, way. Yet as he passed I felt an aura of extraordinary 'holiness' about him. Something marked him as quite, quite special – to me anyway. And thinking about it, as I have often done in the year since, it was that he *lacked* any kind of self-consciousness – such as most people *would* feel if having to process before a huge crowd with every 'big name' in the land. In fact his manner was characterised by a genuine humility which, in the context, was sufficiently different from the others to be tremendously striking.[16]

I am inclined to agree with this assessment of Cardinal Hume, who is said to have been reluctant to assume high office when first appointed Cardinal. What is particularly interesting is that so apparently selfless a person is perceived as charismatic. In the introduction I said that genuine virtue is usually unobtrusive, and that morally superior individuals influence others by their private behaviour rather than by haranguing crowds or acquiring disciples. This example shows that there is a charisma of goodness, as well as a charisma of power.

Sometimes what the potential disciple is seeking from a guru is maternal love, especially if death or separation has deprived a young child of the mother's presence. In his book *Hidden Journey*, Andrew Harvey gives an extraordinarily interesting and moving account of a series of ecstatic experiences which were induced by his meetings with a seventeen-year-old girl called Meera. Since she remained silent during their first meetings, she was far from behaving like a conventional guru, but his experience with her throws light upon devotion to gurus in general. Sceptics might allege that she was no more than a beautiful living image upon which devotees could project their needs and wishes; and it is the case that Andrew Harvey has since repudiated her on the grounds that she does not accept his homosexuality as a valid way of life. But there is no doubt that, at the time, Andrew Harvey found something for which he had been looking since childhood; something which, as he freely admits, was akin to the peace and security which he had felt in the presence of his mother when he was a small child in Delhi, but which had been taken from him when, at the age of six-and-a-half, she left him at boarding school a thousand miles away.

> India gave me a mother, then took her away. Years later, I found in India another Mother in another dimension, and the love I had believed lost returned. Without that first wound I would not have needed love so much or been prepared to risk everything in its search. Without the memory of a human tenderness I might never have accepted the passion that awoke in my being when I met the woman who has transformed me. From the deepest wound of my life grew its miraculous possibility.[17]

At the age of nine, Harvey left India for fifteen years to be educated in England. Since he was highly intelligent, he won a scholarship to Oxford, gained a first-class degree, and was elected a Fellow of All Souls; perhaps the highest academic accolade which is ever granted to a young person in England. But the wound remained, and neither the poetry he wrote, the alcohol he drank, nor the sexual relationships upon which he embarked, did anything to heal it. Recurrent thoughts of suicide drove him, when he was twenty-five, to return to India. He was not seeking salvation, but simply hoping to recapture some of the happiness he remembered from childhood, which had never returned. Psychiatrists are familiar with the plight of English children who have been prematurely removed from home in order that they may be sent to a boarding school. The misery is often prolonged; the damage done is sometimes irreparable.

A chance meeting with Jean-Marc Frechette, a French Canadian who was visiting an ashram in Pondicherry ripened into friendship. Following his example, Harvey began regular meditation, and was at last rewarded with a 'consolation', as Ignatius would have called it; a kind of joy which he had never before experienced. He began to hear strange sounds, to see visions, and to realize that he was embarked upon a journey of discovery for which the sophisticated rationalism of intellectual life in Oxford had been no preparation.

Harvey began to read the works of Aurobindo, the deceased guru to whose ashram his friend Jean-Marc was attached. Sri Aurobindo, born in 1872, had been educated in Cambridge, where he obtained a senior scholarship in classics, and won many prizes. He later became professor of English literature in Baroda College. After involvement in India's struggle for independence, during which he was arrested, he abandoned politics and spent the rest of his life in the pursuit of enlightenment and in writing books on his religious quest. To Harvey's surprise and delight, one of Aurobindo's books was *The Mother*, 'a vision of the Divine Mother, of God as the mother, so radical, so potent, so all-embracing that it overturned and transformed completely everything I had hitherto understood of God'.[18] Jean-Marc told him:

> This is the time of the return of the Mother. Goethe foresaw it at the end of *Faust* when Faust was redeemed by the Mothers. Ramakrishna knew it. Even the Catholics seem to know it in the increasing sacred importance they are giving to Mary. She is returning to save a tormented creation.[19]

Had he known it, Jean-Marc Frechette could have added Jung to his list. Jung thought that the proclamation by Pope Pius XII in 1950 of the dogma of the bodily Assumption of the Virgin into heaven was the most important religious event since the Reformation.

> The logical consistency of the papal declaration cannot be surpassed, and it leaves Protestantism with the odium of being nothing but a *man's religion* which allows no metaphysical representation of woman . . . Protestantism has obviously not given sufficient attention to the signs of the times which point to the equality of women.[20]

Jung, who died in 1961, might have been pleased to see that English Protestantism took a step toward recognizing the equality of women by allowing their ordination as priests in 1994.

Jean-Marc believed that the return of the Divine Mother would be manifested by her actual embodiment in a human being. When he suggested this, Andrew Harvey responded by saying that he did not believe in reincarnation. Harvey returned to academic life, but, in November 1978, received a letter from Jean-Marc summoning him back to India in order to meet a young woman whom he described as a Master. On Christmas Day 1978, Jean-Marc took Harvey to the house in Pondicherry in which Meera was living. Eight or nine others awaited her appearance. When she came, she sat on a chair, saying nothing.

> One by one, in silence, the people in the room went up to kneel to her and let her take their heads between her hands and then look into her eyes. The silence she brought with her into the room was unlike any I had ever experienced – deeper, full of uncanny, wounding joy.[21]

Andrew Harvey knelt in his turn, and had a vision of Velásquez's painting *Mary as Queen of Heaven*, but with Meera taking the place of the Spanish woman in the original. The eyes which stared into his were calm and compassionate. Later, he had a vision of Aurobindo's face in golden light. Each evening he returned for the same ritual. As a poet, a novelist, and an intellectual, nearly everything he had learned had come to him through words.

> But in Meera's silence I returned to a deeper learning, the one I experienced in music when my whole being was addressed, the one I had known as a child, sitting reading by my mother as she slept, or playing canasta with her on the beach, watching the sea.
> Fears struck at me, and doubts, but always every evening Meera would remove them, simply by being herself, seated in her chair with such simple love. I had no idea who or what she was; I knew only that she was something I had never seen before, and that I was more at home with her than with anyone else.[22]

Harvey was far too intelligent not to know how his repeated mystical experience would appear to others.

> I had lost a mother as a child, and now, with suspicious completeness, found another one who would never abandon me and on whom I could project any magical fantasy I wished because she was remote and silent and herself engaged in a fantasy that matched mine. That this interpretation was absurd didn't stop it from being powerful; its cold voice tormented me.[23]

Harvey presumably rejects this interpretation as absurd because he believes that accepting it would invalidate his experience as 'magical fantasy'. But others who have had closely similar experiences know that they can occur with other people who are not perceived as reincarnations of the Divine Mother but simply as loving and beloved human beings.

When Harvey asked Meera's guardian what her teaching actually was, since she did not speak, Mr. Reddy replied: 'Union in silence with all Being and action flowing from that Silence in enlightened joy . . . What the soul wants is ecstasy and knowledge; the Mother gives both'.[24] Harvey repeatedly refers his experiences with Meera back to his childhood experiences with his mother, and then seems to reject the idea that they can be interpreted in this way. But many children who are lucky enough to have mothers to whom they are very close, and who seem to understand them completely, are likely to feel a sense of unity with the mother and the same sense of unity with a world in which they are cared for and free from anxiety about the future. This is surely the reason that Jesus said:

> Let the little ones come to me; do not try to stop them; for the kingdom of God belongs to such as these. I tell you that who-ever does not accept the kingdom of God like a child will never enter it.[25]

As we saw in Chapter 9, Freud considered ecstatic experiences of unity to be an extreme regression to an early infantile state; that of the infant at the breast who has not yet learned to distinguish between himself, the mother, and the external world; a state already described by Tennyson.

> The baby new to earth and sky,
> What time his tender palm is prest
> Against the circle of the breast,
> Has never thought that 'this is I:'
> But as he grows he gathers much
> And learns the use of 'I' and 'me',
> And finds 'I am not what I see,
> And other than the things I touch.'[26]

It does not seem to me that Harvey's mystical experiences are invalidated if some of them can be interpreted as recapturing a state of bliss experienced in early childhood. What would be interesting is to know what effect Meera might have upon a person who had never experienced the security of maternal love and understanding. Do such states inevitably depend upon recall, or can they be induced *de novo*?

Meera's silence is the most riveting thing about her. All the other gurus whom we have considered, with the possible exception of Ignatius, were fluent speakers who were able to preach, harangue, or talk without notes, sometimes for hours at a time. But Meera said nothing, thus opening the path to self-discovery rather than proclaiming a doctrine. It may sound ridiculous to suggest that, if someone must seek a guru it is best to choose one who does not speak, but I mean it at least half seriously. I am reminded of a patient whom I was treating who once lay on the couch for fifty minutes without saying anything at all. Partly out of curiosity, partly out of a sense that something important was taking place, I also said nothing. The atmosphere was peaceful and happy. At the end of the session, she said that this had been the best of all our meetings so far.

I am inclined to think that when psychotherapy heals, as it sometimes does, it may be because the psychotherapist has provided a secure haven, a maternal enclave, in which the patient is for a time removed from the troubles of the world, and, like a happy child, can feel totally accepted, confident, and free to grow. It seems to me that psychotherapists, of whichever sex, are often cast in the role of the perfect mother – the Divine Mother or archetypal mother, if you prefer to call her so – and that this may be a necessary part of the healing process. I don't think that this way of looking at the process of healing diminishes its importance; nor do I think that such an interpretation diminishes Meera. The fact that so young a girl can play such a role at all argues that she must be a remarkable person with an intuitive understanding of others and a wonderful serenity. Those who believe her to be a reincarnation of the Divine Mother will no doubt dismiss what I have written as crassly imperceptive; but I am not in any way questioning the validity of that which Meera made possible for Harvey, only its interpretation.

We live at a time when, in England, belief in orthodox Christian doctrine is in decline. Less than 2.5 per cent of the population regularly attend church on Sunday. As the Bishop of Oxford said in an interview: 'We in Western Europe are now in a post-Christian society.'[27] It might be assumed that, as a consequence, more people are susceptible to the allure of new religious movements and the teachings of gurus. I am not convinced that this is the case. In the United States, where it is said that a far higher proportion of the population go to church than do so in this country, new religious movements flourish with more vigour than they do in England. So do television evangelists, from whose dubious ministrations we in England have so far been spared. Most of the new religious movements which have emerged since the 1950s originated in North America or India. Moreover, history reveals that the guru with a new revelation is a perennially recurring figure. Some have been even more bizarre than David Koresh. Aldous Huxley records the case of the Swiss Anabaptist Thomas Schucker, who claimed that he was divinely guided to cut off his brother's head, and did so in the sight of a large audience which included his father and mother. Those who are tempted to follow a guru often seem to try one after another, for ever looking for a new revelation or a new path to salvation which they never quite reach. Gurus will continue to flourish as long as they can gain disciples; but those disciples are, in my view, looking for what they want in the wrong place.

If there is one lesson I have learned from writing this book, it is that one should never judge a person to be insane or even unreliable only because he holds bizarre beliefs. Most people in the world subscribe to belief systems for which there is no evidence and which do not stand up to critical evaluation. The diagnosis of insanity must include an assessment of the individual's social behaviour and relationships with other human beings.

If there is one message I want to convey, it is to distrust characters who are both deeply self-absorbed and also authoritarian. No one *knows* in the sense that Gurdjieff or Rajneesh or Jung believed that they *knew* and were supposed to *know* by their disciples. All authorities, whether political or spiritual, should be distrusted, and extremely authoritarian characters who divide the world into 'us' and 'them', who preach that there is only one way forward, or who believe that they are surrounded by enemies, are particularly to be avoided. It is not necessary to be dogmatic to be effective. The charisma of certainty is a snare which entraps the child who is latent in us all.

If anyone is in urgent need of help or guidance, let him find someone who will listen rather than preach; someone who will encourage him to look inward and find out what he as a unique individual thinks and believes, rather than accepting some guru's dogma. If anyone is looking for the joy of working with others toward a common goal, let him join one of the many organizations devoted to helping refugees, the poor, the sick, and the unfortunate. Such organizations need no guru, and those who join them need have no religious affiliation. The wish to help one's fellow men is not confined to believers.

It is over a hundred years since Nietzsche first published *Die Fröhliche Wissenschaft* (The Gay Science), but what he wrote is an appropriate note on which to end this book.

> *The meaning of our cheerfulness.*- The greatest recent event — that "God is dead," that the belief in the Christian god has become unbelievable — is already beginning to cast its first shadows over Europe . . . Why is it that even we look forward to the approaching gloom without any real sense of involvement and above all without any worry and fear for *ourselves*? Are we perhaps still too much under the impression of the *initial consequences* of this event — and these initial consequences, the consequences for *ourselves*, are quite the opposite of what one might perhaps expect. They are not at all sad and gloomy but rather like a new and scarcely describable light, happiness, relief, exhilaration, encouragement, dawn.
>
> Indeed, we philosophers and "free spirits" feel, when we hear the news that "the old god is dead," as if a new dawn shone on us; our heart overflows with gratitude, amazement, premonitions, expectation. At long last the horizon appears free to us again, even if it should not be bright; at long last our ship may venture out again, venture out to face any danger; all the daring of the lover of knowledge is permitted again; the sea, *our* sea, lies open again; perhaps there has never been such an "open sea". – [28]

References

INTRODUCTION

1. Sigmund Freud, *Civilization and its Discontents*, translated by James Strachey in collaboration with Anna Freud, assisted by Alix Strachey and Alan Tyson, Standard Edition, Volume XXI (London: Hogarth Press and Institute of Psycho-Analysis, 1961) pp. 83-4.
2. Anthony Storr, *Solitude* (London: HarperCollins, 1989).
3. Eileen Barker, *New Religious Movements* (London: HMSO, 1992), p. 13.

CHAPTER I

1. Tim Reiterman & John Jacobs, *Raven* (New York: Dutton, 1982), p. 45.
2. Ibid., p. 147.
3. Eileen Barker, *New Religious Movements* (London: HMSO, 1992), pp. 14-15.
4. Shiva Naipaul, *Journey to Nowhere* (Harmondsworth: Penguin, 1982), pp. 144-7.
5. Tim Reiterman & John Jacobs, op. cit., p. 177.
6. David Leppard, *Fire and Blood* (London: Fourth Estate, 1993), p. 12.
7. Ibid., p. 140.
8. Martin King & Marc Breault, *Preacher of Death* (London: Penguin Group, Signet, 1993), p. 309.
9. William Shaw, *Spying in Guru Land* (London: Fourth Estate, 1994), p. 207.
10. William Shaw, op. cit., p. 201.
11. Martin King & Marc Breault, op. cit., p. 78.
12. Martin King & Marc Breault, op. cit., p. 308.

CHAPTER II

1. James Moore, *Gurdjieff: The Anatomy of a Myth* (Shaftesbury: Element Books, 1991).
2. P. D. Ouspensky, *In Search of the Miraculous* (New York: Harcourt Brace, 1949), p. 36.
3. P. D. Ouspensky, op. cit., p. 66.
4. G. I. Gurdjieff, *Views from the Real World* (London: Routledge & Kegan Paul, Arkana, 1984), p. 69.
5. Fritz Peters, *Gurdjieff* (London: Wildwood House, 1976), pp. 292-3.
6. J. G. Bennett, *Gurdjieff: Making a New World* (London: Turnstone Books, 1973), p. 79.
7. James Moore, 'Gurdjieffian Groups in Britain', *Religion Today*, Volume Three/Number Two, May-September 1986.
8. Thomas and Olga de Hartmann, *Our Life with Mr. Gurdjieff* (London: Penguin, Arkana, 1992), p. 26.
9. Alan W. Watts, *The Way of Zen* (London: Thames and Hudson, 1957), p. 199.

10. Eugen Bleuler, translated by Joseph Zinkin, *Dementia Praecox or The Group of Schizophrenias* (New York: International Universities Press, 1950), p. 156.
11. Ibid. p. 157.
12. James Moore, *Gurdjieff: The Anatomy of a Myth* (Shaftesbury: Element Books, 1991), p. 42.
13. Ibid., pp. 42-3.
14. J. G. Bennett, op. cit., p. 275.
15. G. I. Gurdjieff, *All and Everything* (London: Routledge & Kegan Paul, 1950), p. 82.
16. P. D. Ouspensky op. cit., p. 85.
17. Ibid., p. 85.
18. J. G. Bennett, op. cit., p. 250.
19. P. D. Ouspensky, op. cit., p. 57.
20. J. G. Bennett, op. cit., p. 251.
21. Ibid., p. 82.
22. James Moore, op. cit., p. 41.
23. G. I. Gurdjieff, *Meetings with Remarkable Men*, translated by A. R. Orage (London: Routledge & Kegan Paul, 1963), p. 87.
24. J. G. Bennett, op. cit., p. 121.
25. Fritz Peters, op. cit., pp. 81-2.
26. Fritz Peters, op. cit., pp. 270-4.
27. Ibid., p. 259.
28. J. G. Bennett, op. cit., p. 148.
29. Fritz Peters, op. cit., p. 30.
30. James Moore, op. cit., p. 261.
31. René Zuber, *Who Are You Monsieur Gurdjieff?*, translated by Jenny Koralek (London: Routledge & Kegan Paul, 1980), p. 3.
32. Fritz Peters, op. cit., p. 27.
33. J. G. Bennett, op. cit., p. 154.
34. J. G. Bennett, op. cit., p. 163.
35. Meryle Secrest, *Frank Lloyd Wright* (New York: Knopf, 1992), p. 61.
36. Ibid., p. 431.
37. James Moore, op. cit., p. 365.
38. Meryle Secrest, op. cit., p. 510-511.
39. Joseph Rykwert, 'Towards a well-distributed world', *Times Literary Supplement*, May 6, 1994, p. 16.
40. James Moore, op. cit., p. 205.
41. John Carswell, *Lives and Letters* (London: Faber & Faber, 1978), p. 213.
42. Fritz Peters, op. cit., p. 242.
43. J. G. Bennett, op. cit., p. 165.
44. C. S. Nott, *Teachings of Gurdjieff*, (London: Routledge & Kegan Paul, 1961), p. 56.
45. Claire Tomalin, *Katherine Mansfield* (London: Penguin, 1988), pp. 232-3.

CHAPTER III

1. Eileen Barker, *New Religious Movements* (London: HMSO, 1992), p. 203.
2. Ralph Rowbottom, *Independent on Sunday*, 7th August, 1994, p. 16.
3. Hugh Milne, edited by Liz Hodgkinson, *Bhagwan: The God that Failed* (London: Sphere Books, 1987), p. 13.
4. Bhagwan Shree Rajneesh, *The Supreme Understanding: Reflections on Tantra*. edited by Ma Yoga Anurag, compiled by Swami Amrit Pathik (London: Sheldon Press, 1978), p. x.
5. James S. Gordon, *The Golden Guru* (Massachusetts: The Stephen Greene Press, 1988), p. 52.
6. Bernard Levin, *The Times*, 8 April 1980, p. 12.
7. Bhagwan Shree Rajneesh, *The Mustard Seed: Reflections on the Sayings of Jesus*, edited by Swami Satya Deva, compiled by Swami Amrit Pathik (London: Sheldon Press, 1978), p. 488.
8. Ibid., p. 157.
9. Bhagwan Shree Rajneesh, *The Supreme Understanding*, p. 112.
10. Ibid., p. 193.

11. Bhagwan Shree Rajneesh, *Meditation: The Art of Ecstasy*, edited by Ma Satya Bharti (London: Sheldon Press, 1978), p. 147.

12. Bhagwan Shree Rajneesh, *The Supreme Understanding*, op. cit., p. 10.

13. Ibid., p. 64.

14. Ibid., p. 96.

15. Ibid., p. 213.

16. Bhagwan Shree Rajneesh, *Meditation*, op. cit., p. 233.

17. Frances Fitzgerald, *Cities on a Hill* (London: Picador, 1987), p. 297.

18. Bernard Levin, *The Times*, 9 April 1980, p. 14.

19. Bhagwan Shree Rajneesh, *Meditation*, op. cit., p. 136.

20. Bhagwan Shree Rajneesh, *The Mustard Seed: Reflections on the Sayings of Jesus*, edited by Swami Satya Deva, compiled by Swami Amrit Pathik (London: Sheldon Press, 1978), pp 4, 8.

21. Frances Fitzgerald, op. cit., p. 275.

22. James S. Gordon, op. cit., p. 182.

23. Hugh Milne, op. cit. p. 274.

24. Bernard Levin, *The Times*, 10 April, 1980.

CHAPTER IV

1. Henri F. Ellenberger, *The Discovery of the Unconscious*, (New York: Basic Books, 1970), p. 685.

2. Rudi Lissau, *Rudolf Steiner* (Stroud: Hawthorn Press, 1987), p. 33.

3. A. P. Shepherd, *A Scientist of the Invisible* (Edinburgh: Floris Books, 1983), p. 66.

4. Ibid., p. 3.

5. Antonina Vallentin, *Einstein*, translated by Moura Budberg (London: Weidenfeld & Nicolson, 1954), p. 11.

6. Johannes Hemleben, *Rudolf Steiner: A Documentary Biography*, translated by Leo Twyman (East Grinstead: Goulden, 1975), p. 16.

7. Quoted in Jeremy Bernstein, *Einstein* (New York: Viking Press, 1973), pp. 172-3.

8. Rudolf Steiner, *The Philosophy of Freedom*, translated by Michael Watson (London: Rudolf Steiner Press, 1964), p. 89.

9. Ibid., p. 14.

10. Ibid., p. 70.

11. Ibid., p. 90.

12. Ibid., p. 119.

13. Henri Ellenberger, *The Discovery of the Unconscious* (New York: Basic Books, 1970), p. 685.

14. Rudolf Steiner, *Knowledge of the Higher Worlds. How Is It Achieved?* translated by D. S. Osmond and C. Davy (London: Rudolf Steiner Press, 1969), p. 65.

15. Ibid., p. 42.

16. Ibid., pp. 35-6.

17. Johannes Hemleben, op. cit., p. 88.

18. A. P. Shepherd, op. cit., p. 152.

19. Rudolf Steiner, *Occult Science - An Outline*, translated by George and Mary Adams (London: Rudolf Steiner Press, 1969), p. 11.

20. Ibid., p. 65.

21. Ibid., p. 108.

22. Rudolf Steiner, *Reading the Pictures of the Apocalypse*, translated by James H. Hindes (New York: Anthroposophic Press, 1993), p. 100.

23. Ibid., p. 40.

24. Ibid., p. 82.

CHAPTER V

1. C. G. Jung, *Letters*, Volume 1, 1906-1950, translated by R. F. C. Hull, selected and edited by Gerhard Adler in collaboration with Aniela Jaffé (London:

Routledge & Kegan Paul, 1973), p. 203.

2. C. G. Jung, *The Zofingia Lectures*, translated by Jan van Heurck, introduced by Marie-Louise von Franz, Collected Works, Supplementary Volume A, (London: Routledge & Kegan Paul, 1983), pp. 3-19.

3. Anthony Storr, 'Why Psychoanalysis is not a Science,' in *Churchill's Black Dog and Other Phenomena of the Human Mind* (London: Collins, 1989), pp. 207-227.

4. Gerhard Wehr, *Jung: A Biography*, translated by David M. Weeks (Boston: Shambhala, 1987), p. 29.

5. C. G. Jung, *Memories, Dreams, Reflections*, edited by Aniela Jaffé, translated by Richard and Clara Winston (London: Collins and Routledge & Kegan Paul, 1963), p. 327.

6. Ibid., pp. 31-2.

7. Ming T. Tsuang, *Schizophrenia: The Facts* (Oxford: Oxford University Press, 1982), p. 98.

8. Ibid., p. 4.

9. Vincent Brome, *Jung: Man and Myth* (London: Macmillan, 1978), p. 301.

10. C. G. Jung, M. D. R., p. 169.

11. Eugen Bleuler, *Dementia Praecox or The Group of Schizophrenias*, translated by Joseph Zinkin (New York: International Universities Press, 1950), p. 255.

12. C. G. Jung, M. D. R., p. 181.

13. Ibid., p. 184.

14. John Kerr, *A Most Dangerous Method* (New York: Knopf, 1993), p. 503.

15. C. G. Jung, M. D. R., p. 191.

16. John Kerr, 'Madnesses,' *London Review of Books*, 23 March, 1995, pp. 3-6.

17. C. G. Jung, *The Zofingia Lectures*, translated by Jan van Heurck, edited by William McGuire, The Collected Works, Supplementary Volume A (London: Routledge & Kegan Paul, 1983), p. 88.

18. Friedrich Nietzsche, *Thus Spoke Zarathustra*, translated by R. J. Hollingdale, *Zarathustra's Prologue*, 5 (Harmondsworth: Penguin, 1969), p. 46.

19. Anthony Storr, *Jung* (New York: Routledge, 1991), p. 83.

20. C. G. Jung, *The Freud/Jung Letters*, edited by William McGuire, translated by Ralph Manheim and R.F.C. Hull (London: Hogarth Press and Routledge & Kegan Paul, 1974), Letter 178J, p. 294.

21. Quoted in John Kerr, op. cit., p. 172.

22. C. G. Jung, 'Psychotherapists or the Clergy', in *Psychology and Religion: West and East*, translated by R. F. C. Hull, Collected Works, Vol. 11 (Routledge & Kegan Paul, 1958), p. 331.

23. Ibid., p. 334.

24. Richard Noll, *The Jung Cult* (Princeton: Princeton University Press, 1994), p. 291.

25. C. G. Jung, *Psychotherapists or the Clergy*, op. cit., p. 347.

26. C. G. Jung, *The Archetypes and the Collective Unconscious*, translated by R. F. C. Hull, Collected Works, Volume IX, Part 1 (London: Routledge & Kegan Paul, 1968), p. 79.

27. David Peat, *Synchronicity* (New York: Bantam Books, 1987), p. 94.

28. C. G. Jung, *The Zofingia Lectures*, translated by Jan van Heurck, edited by William McGuire, The Collected Works, Supplementary Volume A (London: Routledge & Kegan Paul, 1984), p. 41.

29. Ibid.
30. David Peat, op. cit.
31. C. G. Jung, *The Freud/Jung Letters*, op. cit., Letter 259J, p. 427.
32. Edgar Wind, Letter to Professor Jack Good, 12 January 1970. By kind permission of Mrs. Margaret Wind, who retains the copyright.
33. C. G. Jung, *Flying Saucers: A Modern Myth*, translated by R. F. C. Hull, in *Civilization in Transition* (London: Routledge & Kegan Paul, 1964), Collected Works, Vol. 10, p. 311.
34. C. G. Jung, *Memories, Dreams, Reflections*, op. cit., p. 328.
35. Anthony Storr, *Music and the Mind* (London: HarperCollins, 1992).
36. Roger Scruton, 'Modern Philosophy and the Neglect of Aesthetics,' in Peter Abbs, editor, *The Symbolic Order* (London: The Falmer Press, 1989), p. 27.

CHAPTER VI

1. Ernest Gellner, *The Psychoanalytic Movement* (London: Paladin, 1985), p. 5.
2. Ibid.
3. Henri F. Ellenberger, *The Discovery of the Unconscious* (New York: Basic Books, 1970), p. 444.
4. Peter Gay, *Freud: A Life for Our Time* (London: Dent, 1988), p. 104.
5. Sigmund Freud, *The Complete Letters of Sigmund Freud to Wilhelm Fliess*, translated and edited by Jeffrey Moussaieff Masson (Cambridge, Mass. Harvard University Press, 1985), p. 417.
6. Ibid., p. 272.
7. Quoted in Frank J. Sulloway, *Freud, Biologist of the Mind* (New York: Basic Books, 1979), p. 85.
8. Sigmund Freud, *The Aetiology of Hysteria*, translated by James Strachey in collaboration with Anna Freud, assisted by Alix Strachey and Alan Tyson, Standard Edition, Volume III (London: The Hogarth Press and The Institute of Psycho-Analysis, 1962), p. 199.
9. Ibid., p. 203.
10. Sigmund Freud, *The Future of an Illusion*, Standard Edition, Volume XXI, 1961, p. 56.
11. Quoted in Ernest Jones, *Sigmund Freud: Life and Work*. Volume Two (London: The Hogarth Press, 1955), p. 168.
12. Phyllis Grosskurth, *The Secret Ring* (New York: Addison-Wesley, 1991), p. 25.
13. Richard Webster, *Why Freud Was Wrong* (London: HarperCollins, 1995), p. 365.
14. Peter Gay, *Freud: A Life for Our Time* (London: J. M. Dent, 1988), p. 369.
15. Frederick Crews, 'The Unknown Freud', *The New York Review of Books*, Vol XI, No. 19, November 18, 1993 pp. 55–66.
16. Jeffrey Moussaieff Masson, op. cit., pp. 456–7.
17. Janet Malcolm, *The Impossible Profession* (New York: Knopf, 1981), p. 83.
18. Anthony Storr, *Freud* (Oxford: Oxford University Press, 1989), p. 104.
19. Sigmund Freud, *The Question of a Weltanschauung*, Standard Edition Volume XXII, 1964, p. 159.
20. Ibid., p. 180.

CHAPTER VII

1. Margaret Hebblethwaite, *Finding God in All Things*, (London: Fount, 1987), p. 11.

2. Philip Caraman, S. J. *Ignatius Loyola* (London: Fount, 1994) p. 27.
3. William James, *The Varieties of Religious Experience* (London: Longmans, Green, 1903), p. 410.
4. C. G. Jung, *The Structure and Dynamics of the Psyche*, translated by R. F. C. Hull, Collected Works, Volume 8 (London: Routledge & Kegan Paul, 1969), pp. 196-198.
5. Philip Caraman, op. cit., p. 40.
6. Ronald A. Knox, *Enthusiasm* (Oxford: Clarendon Press, 1950), p. 245.
7. W. W. Meissner, *Ignatius of Loyola* (New Haven: Yale University Press, 1992), p. 91.
8. W. W. Meissner, op. cit., p. 210.
9. Stanley Milgram, *Obedience to Authority* (New York: Harper & Row, 1974).
10. Anthony Storr, *Human Destructiveness*, Second Edition (London: Routledge, 1991), pp. 107-9.
11. William James, op. cit., p. 312.
12. W. W. Meissner, op. cit., p. 280.
13. Ibid., p. 285.
14. William James, op cit., p. 410.
15. Norman Cohn, *Cosmos, Chaos, and the World to Come* (New Haven and London: Yale University Press, 1993).
16. Ibid., p. 78.
17. *The New English Bible*, Matthew 4, 17 (Oxford University Press, Cambridge University Press, 1970), The New Testament, p. 6.
18. E. P. Sanders, *The Historical Figure of Jesus* (London: Allen Lane The Penguin Press, 1993), p. 183.
19. Op. cit., *The New English Bible*, Matthew 24, 29-31, pp. 34-5.
20. E. P. Sanders, op. cit., p. 60.
21. Op. cit., *The New English Bible*, Mark 8, 28-29, p. 54.
22. Ibid., pp. 64-5.
23. Humphrey Carpenter, *Jesus* (Oxford: Oxford University Press, Past Masters, 1980).
24. Op. cit., *The New English Bible*, Mark 3, 33-35.
25. Geza Vermes, *The Religion of Jesus the Jew* (London: SCM Press, 1993), p. 192.
26. Op. cit., *The New English Bible*, Luke 18, 10-14.
27. Ibid., Matthew 6, 6, p. 9.
28. Norman Cohn, op. cit., p. 201.
29. Op. cit., *The New English Bible*, Matthew 7, 28-9, p. 11.
30. Ibid., Mark 15, 39, p. 66.
31. Geza Vermes, op. cit., p. 168.
32. Op. cit., *The New English Bible*, Mark 15, 34-5, p. 66.
33. Salomon Reinach, *Orpheus: A History of Religions*, translated by Florence Simmonds (London: Routledge, Revised Edition, 1931), pp. 252-3.

CHAPTER VIII

1. C. G. Jung, 'On the Psychogenesis of Schizophrenia', in *The Collected Works of C. G. Jung*, Volume 3, translated by R. F. C. Hull, edited by Herbert Read, Michael Fordham, & Gerhard Adler (London: Routledge & Kegan Paul, 1960), p. 247.
2. Elizabeth L. Farr, 'Introduction: A personal account of schizophrenia', in Ming T. Tsuang, *Schizophrenia: The Facts* (Oxford: Oxford University Press, 1982), pp. 1-2.
3. S. E. Chua and P. J. McKenna, *Schizophrenia - a Brain Disease?* British Journal of Psychiatry (1995), **166**, 563-582.
4. Elizabeth L. Farr, op. cit., p. 9.
5. C. G. Jung, *Two Essays on Analytical Psychology*, translated by

R. F. C. Hull, Collected Works, Volume 7 (London: Routledge & Kegan Paul, 1953), p. 141.

6. Anna Kavan, edited by Brian W. Aldiss, *My Madness* (London: Picador Classics, 1990), p. 15.

7. Norman Cohn, *The Pursuit of the Millennium* (London: Secker & Warburg, 1957).

8. Anthony Storr, *Human Destructiveness*, Second Edition (London: Routledge, 1991).

9. Henri Ellenberger, *The Discovery of the Unconscious* (New York: Basic Books, 1970), pp. 215-6.

10. Jeffrey Moussaieff Masson, *My Father's Guru* (Reading, Massachusetts, Addison-Wesley Publishing, 1993).

11. Paul Brunton, *A Search in Secret India* (London: Rider, 1983).

12. Paul Brunton (Dr. Brunton), *The Secret Path* (London: Rider, 1969).

13. Paul Brunton, *The Spiritual Crisis of Man* (London: Rider, 1952).

14. Paul Brunton, *The Secret Path* (London: Rider, 1969), p. 14.

15. Jeffrey Moussaieff Masson, op. cit., p. 160.

16. Jeffrey Moussaieff Masson, op. cit., p. 85.

17. Paul Brunton, *The Wisdom of the Overself* (London: Rider, 1943), p. 8.

18. Jeffrey Moussaieff Masson, op. cit., p. xiv.

19. Sir Arthur Conan Doyle, *Sherlock Holmes: The Complete Short Stories* (London: John Murray, 1928), p. 540.

20. Norman Cohn, *Europe's Inner Demons* (New York: Basic Books), 1975.

21. Norman Cohn, *Warrant for Genocide* (London: Eyre & Spottiswoode, 1967), p. 26.

22. Michael Lind, 'Rev. Robertson's Grand International Conspiracy Theory', *New York Review of Books*, Volume XLII, no. 2, 21-5, February 2, 1995.

23. Ibid., p. 25.

24. Anthony Storr, *Human Destructiveness*, Second Edition (London: Routledge, 1991), pp. 132-3.

25. Private communication.

26. World Health Organization: *Mental Disorders: Glossary and guide to their classification in accordance with the Ninth Revision of the International Classification of Diseases.* (WHO: Geneva, 1978), p. 31.

27. John E. Mack, *Abductions: Human Encounters with Aliens* (New York: Simon & Schuster, 1994).

CHAPTER IX

1. Sigmund Freud, *Notes on a Case of Paranoia*, translated by James Strachey in collaboration with Anna Freud, assisted by Alix Strachey and Alan Tyson, Standard Edition, Volume XII (London: The Hogarth Press and The Institute of Psycho-Analysis, 1958), p. 71.

2. Norman Cohn, *Cosmos, Chaos, and the World to Come* (London: Yale University Press, 1993).

3. Bhagwan Shree Rajneesh, *The Supreme Understanding: Reflections on Tantra*, edited by Ma Yoga Anurag, compiled by Swami Amrit Pathik (London: Sheldon Press, 1978), p. 213.

4. Jacques Hadamard, *The Psychology of Invention in the Mathematical Field* (New Jersey: Princeton University Press, 1945), p. 15.

5. Ibid., p. 13.

6. Ibid., p. 47.

7. Rosamond E. M. Harding, *An*

Anatomy of Inspiration (Cambridge: Heffer, 1940), p. 30.

8. Jacques Hadamard, op. cit., p. 56.

9. C. P. Snow, *The Search* (London: Gollancz, 1934), p. 127.

10. Anthony Storr, *Isaac Newton*, in *Churchill's Black Dog and other phenomena of the human mind* (London: HarperCollins, 1989), pp. 93-96.

11. Thomas S. Kuhn, *The Structure of Scientific Revolutions* (Chicago: Chicago University Press, 1962).

12. Anthony Storr, *Solitude* (London: HarperCollins Flamingo, 1989), p. 123.

13. Graham Greene, *Ways of Escape* (Harmondsworth: Penguin Books, 1981), p. 211.

14. Hugh Milne, *Bhagwan: The God that Failed*, edited by Liz Hodgkinson (London: Sphere Books, 1987), p. 128.

15. Anthony Storr, *Solitude* (London: HarperCollins,1989).

16. Bernard Berenson, *Aesthetics and History* (London: 1950), pp. 68-70.

17. Lord Byron, 'Childe Harold's Pilgrimage', Canto the Third, LXXV (London: John Murray, 1816), p. 42.

18. Richard E. Byrd, *Alone* (London: Ace Books, 1958), pp. 62-3.

19. Private communication.

20. Quoted in William James, *The Varieties of Religious Experience* (London: Longmans, Green, 1903), p. 305.

21. Sigmund Freud, *Totem and Taboo*, translated by James Strachey in collaboration with Anna Freud, assisted by Alix Strachey and Alan Tyson, Standard Edition Volume XIII (London: The Hogarth Press and The Institute of Psycho-Analysis), p. 89.

22. Edward Gibbon, edited by G.

Birkbeck Hill, *Memoirs of My Life and Writings* (London: Methuen, 1900), p. 105.

23. Private communication.

24. M. C. Jackson, *A study of the relationship between psychotic and spiritual experience*, Thesis for D. Phil., Oxford University, 1991.

25. William James, *The Varieties of Religious Experience* (London: Longmans, Green, 1903), pp. 175-6.

CHAPTER X

1. William James, *The Varieties of Religious Experience* (London: Longmans, Green, 1903), p. 210.

2. Ibid., p. 208.

3. John Henry Newman, edited by Maisie Ward, *Apologia pro Vita Sua* (London: Sheed and Ward, 1976), p. 160.

4. P. Mullen, *The phenomenology of disordered mental function*, in *Essentials of Postgraduate Psychiatry* (London: Academic Press, 1979).

5. Hugh Milne, *Bhagwan: The God that Failed*, edited by Liz Hodgkinson (London: Sphere Books, 1987), p. 128.

6. Joost A. M. Meerloo, *Mental Seduction and Menticide* (London: Cape, 1957), p. 50-1.

7. Friedrich Nietzsche, *The Gay Science*, translated by Walter Kaufmann (New York: Vintage Books, 1974), **353**, p. 296.

8. C. G. Jung, *Face to Face*, interview with John Freeman, October 1959, B.B.C. Script.

9. Friedrich Nietzsche, op. cit., **347**, p. 289.

10. Joseph Campbell, *The Hero with a Thousand Faces* (New York: Pantheon, Bollingen Foundation, 1949), p. 309.

11. Mary Loudon, *Revelations* (London: Hamish Hamilton, 1994), pp. 155-6.
12. C. G. Jung, *Psychological Types*, translated by R. F. C. Hull and H. G. Baynes, in *The Collected Works*, Volume Six (London: Routledge & Kegan Paul, 1971), pp. 12-13.
13. William James, op. cit., p. 508.
14. Friedrich Nietzsche, *Beyond Good and Evil*, translated by R. J. Hollingdale (Harmondsworth: Penguin, 1973), **188**, p. 93.
15. Ralph Waldo Emerson, *Self-Reliance*, in *Ralph Waldo Emerson*, edited by Richard Poirier (Oxford: Oxford University Press, 1990), p. 131.
16. Richard Webster, *Why Freud was Wrong* (London: HarperCollins, 1995), p. 301.
17. Sigmund Freud, *On Narcissism*, translated by James Strachey, in collaboration with Anna Freud, assisted by Alix Strachey and Alan Tyson, Standard Edition, Vol. XIV (London: Hogarth Press and the Institute of Psychoanalysis, 1957), p. 74.
18. Ibid., p. 89.

CHAPTER XI

1. Lord Moran, *Churchill: The Struggle for Survival 1940-1965* (London: Constable, 1966), p. 776.
2. Piers Brendon, *Winston Churchill* (London: Secker & Warburg, 1984), p. 142.
3. Lord Moran, op. cit., p. 778.
4. Anthony Storr, *Churchill's Black Dog and Other Phenomena of the Human Mind* (London: Collins, 1989), p. 49-50.
5. J. P. Stern, *Hitler: The Führer and the People* (London: Fontana, 1975), p. 89.
6. Quoted in Ernest Newman, *Wagner as Man and Artist* (London: Gollancz, 1963), p. 38, n. 2.
7. David Aberbach, *Surviving Trauma* (London: Yale University Press, 1989), pp. 124-141.
8. Norman Cohn, *The Pursuit of the Millennium* (London: Secker & Warburg, 1957).
9. Sigmund Freud, *Civilization and Its Discontents*, translated and edited by James Strachey, in collaboration with Anna Freud, assisted by Alix Strachey and Alan Tyson (London: The Hogarth Press and The Institute of Psycho-Analysis, 1961), Standard Edition, Volume XXI, p. 72.
10. Eileen Barker, *New Religious Movements* (London: HMSO, 1992), p. 137.
11. Eileen Barker, op. cit., p. 136.
12. Edmund Gosse, *Father and Son* (London: The Folio Society, 1972), p. 204.
13. T. F. Hoad (editor), *The Concise Oxford Dictionary of Etymology* (Oxford: Oxford University Press, 1986), p. 142.
14. C. G. Jung, *Psychotherapists or the Clergy*, in Volume 11, The Collected Works, *Psychology and Religion: West and East*, translated by R. F. C. Hull (London: Routledge & Kegan Paul, 1958), **519**, pp. 338-9.
15. Friedrich Nietzsche, *Beyond Good and Evil*, translated by R. J. Hollingdale (Harmondsworth: Penguin, 1973), **188**, p. 93.
16. Alan Ridout, personal communication.
17. Andrew Harvey, *Hidden Journey* (London: Rider, 1991), p. 10.
18. Ibid., p. 25.

19. Ibid., p. 26.
20. C. G. Jung, *Answer to Job*, in *Psychology and Religion: West and East*, translated by R. F. C. Hull, Collected Works, Vol. 11 (London: Routledge & Kegan Paul, 1958), **753**, p. 465.
21. Andrew Harvey, *Hidden Journey*, op. cit., p. 33.
22. Ibid., p. 35.
23. Ibid., p. 49.
24. Ibid., p. 53.
25. *The New English Bible*, St. Luke, 15-17 (Oxford and Cambridge University Presses, 1970), p. 99.
26. Alfred Tennyson, *In Memoriam A.H.H. XLV*, *The Poems of Tennyson*, edited by Christopher Ricks (London: Longman, 1969), p. 902.
27. Mary Loudon, *Revelations* (London: Hamish Hamilton, 1994), p. 373.
28. Friedrich Nietzsche, *The Gay Science*, translated by Walter Kaufmann (New York: Vintage Books, 1974), pp. 279-280.

Bibliography

Aberbach, David, *Surviving Trauma*, London: Yale University Press, 1989.

Bancroft, Anne, *Modern Mystics and Sages*, London: Paladin, 1978.

Barker, Eileen, *The Making of a Moonie*, Oxford: Blackwell, 1984.

Barker, Eileen, *New Religious Movements*, London: HMSO, 1993.

Beckford, James A., *Cult Controversies: The Societal Response to the New Religious Movements*, London: Tavistock Publications, 1985.

Bennett, John G., *Gurdjieff*, London: Turnstone Books, 1973.

Bennett, John G., *Gurdjieff: A Very Great Enigma*, Three Lectures, New York: Samuel Weiser, 1973.

Boyle, Nicholas, *Goethe*, Volume I, Oxford: Oxford University Press, 1992.

Caraman, Philip, *Ignatius Loyola*, London: HarperCollins, 1990.

Carpenter, Humphrey, *Jesus*, Oxford: Oxford University Press, 1980.

Carswell, John, *Lives and Letters*, London: Faber & Faber, 1978.

Chadwick, Peter, *Borderline*, London: Routledge, 1992.

Claridge, Gordon, *Origins of Mental Illness*, Oxford: Blackwell, 1985.

Copley, Samuel, *Portrait of a Vertical Man*, London: Swayne Publications, 1989.

Costello, Charles G., (Editor), *Symptoms of Schizophrenia*, New York: John Wiley, 1993.

Cotton, Ian, *The Hallelujah Revolution*, London: Little, Brown, 1995.

Davy, John, *Hope, Evolution and Change*, Stroud: Hawthorn Press, 1985.

De Hartmann, Thomas and Olga, edited by T.C. Daly and T.A.G. Daly, *Our Life with Mr Gurdjieff*, London: Penguin, Arkana, 1992.

Eagle, Morris N., *Recent Developments in Psychoanalysis*, New York: McGraw-Hill, 1984.

Ellenberger, Henri F., *The Discovery of the Unconscious*, New York: Basic Books, 1970.

Evans, Christopher, *Cults of Unreason*, London: Harrap, 1973.

Fitzgerald, Frances, *Cities on a Hill*, London: Picador, 1987, New York: Simon & Schuster, 1986.

Goodwin, Frederick K. and Jamison, Kay Redfield, *Manic-Depressive Illness*, New York: Oxford University Press, 1990.

Gordon, James S., *The Golden Guru*, Lexington, Mass: Stephen Greene Press, 1988.

Grosskurth, Phyllis, *The Secret Ring*, New York: Addison-Wesley, 1991.

Gurdjieff, G., *All and Everything*, London: Routledge & Kegan Paul, 1950.

Gurdjieff, G., *Meetings with Remarkable Men*, London: Routledge & Kegan Paul, 1963.

Gurdjieff, G., *Views from the Real World*, London: Routledge & Kegan Paul, Arkana, 1984.

Harvey, Andrew, *Hidden Journey*, London: Rider, 1991.

Harvey, Andrew, *A Journey in Ladakh*, London: Picador, 1993.

Hay, David, *Religious Experience Today*, London: Mowbray, 1990.

Hebblethwaite, Margaret, *Finding God in All Things: The Way of Saint Ignatius*, London: HarperCollins, 1987.

Hemleben, Johannes, translated by Leo Twyman, *Rudolf Steiner*, East Grinstead: Henry Goulden, 1975.

Huxley, Aldous, *Ends and Means*, London: Chatto & Windus, 1938.

Isherwood, Christopher, *My Guru and His Disciple*, Harmondsworth: Penguin, 1981.

Jackson, M.C., *A Study of the Relationship between Psychotic and Spiritual Experience*, D.Phil. Thesis, 1991, University of Oxford.

James, William, *The Varieties of Religious Experience*. London: Longmans, Green, 1903.

Johnson, Paul E. & Wilenz, Sean, *The Kingdom of Matthias*, New York: Oxford University Press, 1994.

King, Martin and Breault, Marc, *Preacher of Death*, London: Signet Books, 1993.

Knox, Ronald A., *Enthusiasm*, Oxford: Clarendon Press, 1950.

Kramer, Joel & Alstad, Diana, *The Guru Papers*, Berkeley: North Atlantic Books/Frog, 1993.

Laski, Marghanita, *Ecstasy*, London: Cresset Press, 1961.

Lean, Garth, *Frank Buchman*, London: Constable, 1985.

Leppard, David, *Fire and Blood*, London: Fourth Estate, 1993.

Lissau, Rudi, *Rudolf Steiner*, Stroud: Hawthorn Press, 1987.

Loudon, Mary, *Revelations*, London: Hamish Hamilton, 1994.

Masson, Jeffrey Moussaieff, *My Father's Guru*, Reading, Mass: Addison-Wesley, 1993.

McCreery, Charles, *Schizotypy and Out-of-the-Body Experiences*, D.Phil. Thesis, 1993. University of Oxford.

Meissner, William W., *Ignatius of Loyola*, New Haven: Yale University Press, 1992.

Milne, Hugh, *Bhagwan: The God That Failed*, London: Sphere Books, 1983.

Moore, James, *Gurdjieff*, Shaftesbury, Dorset: Element Books, 1991.

Mullan, Bob, *Life as Laughter*, London: Routledge & Kegan Paul, 1983.

Naipaul, Shiva, *Journey to Nowhere*, Harmondsworth: Penguin, 1982.

Newman, John, Henry, *Apologia pro Vita Sua*, edited by Maisie Ward. London: Sheed and Ward, 1976.

Nott, C.S., *Teachings of Gurdjieff: The Journal of a Pupil*, London: Routledge & Kegan Paul, 1961.

Ouspensky, P.D., *In Search of the Miraculous*, New York: Harcourt, Brace & World, 1949.

Paffard, Michael, *Inglorious Wordsworths*, London: Hodder & Stoughton, 1973.

Rajneesh, Bhagwan Shree, edited by Ma Satya Bharti, *Meditation: The Art of Ecstasy*, London: Sheldon Press, 1980.

Rajneesh, Bhagwan Shree, edited by Ma Yoga Anurag, compiled by Swami Amrit Pathik, *The Supreme Understanding: Reflections on Tantra*, London: Sheldon Press, 1978.

Rajneesh, Bhagwan Shree, edited by Swami Satya Deva, compiled by Swami Amrit Pathik, *The Mustard Seed: Reflections on the Sayings of Jesus*, London: Sheldon Press, 1978.

Reavis, Dick J., *The Ashes of Waco*, New York: Simon & Schuster, 1995.

Reed, T.J., *Goethe*, Volume I, Oxford: Oxford University Press, 1985.

Ruthven, Malise, *The Divine Supermarket*, London: Vintage Books, 1991.

Sanders, E.P., *The Historical Figure of Jesus*, London: Allen Lane, The Penguin Press, 1993.

Secrest, Meryle, *Frank Lloyd Wright*, New York: Knopf, 1992.

Shaw, William, *Spying in Guru Land*, London: Fourth Estate, 1994.

Steiner, Rudolf, translated and introduced by Michael Wilson, *The Philosophy of Freedom, The Basis for a Modern World Conception*, London: Rudolf Steiner Press, 1964.

Steiner, Rudolf, translated by D.S. Osmond and C. Davy, *Knowledge of the Higher Worlds – How Is It Achieved?* London: Rudolf Steiner Press, 1969.

Steiner, Rudolf, translated by George and Mary Adams, *Occult Science – An Outline*, London: Rudolf Steiner Press, 1989.

Tomalin, Claire, *Katherine Mansfield: A Secret Life*, London: Penguin, 1988.

Underhill, Evelyn, *Mysticism*, London: Methuen, 1911.

Vermes, Geza, *The Religion of Jesus the Jew*, London: SCM Press, 1993.

Walker, Kenneth, *A Study of Gurdjieff's Teaching*, London: Cape, 1957.

Washington, Peter, *Madame Blavatsky's Baboon*, New York: Schocken, 1995.

Webster, Richard, *A Brief History of Blasphemy*, Southwold: Orwell Press, 1990.

Webster, Richard, *Why Freud Was Wrong: Sin, Science and Psychoanalysis*, London: HarperCollins, 1995.

Welch, William J., *What Happened In Between*, New York: George Braziller, 1972.

Wilson, Andrew N. *Jesus*, London: HarperCollins, 1993.

Wilson, Colin, *Rudolf Steiner*, Wellingborough: Aquarian Press, 1985.

Young, Julian, *Nietzsche's Philosophy of Art*, Cambridge: Cambridge University Press, 1992.

Young-Bruehl, Elisabeth, *Creative Characters*, New York: Routledge, 1991.

Zuber, René, translated by Jenny Koralek, *Who Are You Monsieur Gurdjieff?* London: Routledge & Kegan Paul, 1980.

Index

Aberbach, David, 220
Abraham, Karl, 118
Adler, Alfred, 117
Ahura Mazda (deity), 140–1
American Psychiatric Association: *Diagnostic and Statistical Manual of Mental Disorders*, 170
Anderson, Margaret, 23, 36
Angra Mainyu (or Ahriman; deity), 140
Antelope, Oregon, 60
Anthroposophical Society, 67
Anthroposophy, 67, 73
Anurag, Ma Yoga, 47
archetypes, 98–9, 103
artists: and creative process, 183–4, 193
astral body, 78
astrology, 102–3, 157
Aurobindo (Ghose), Sri, 227–8
authority figures (leaders), 217–21, 224, 232

Barker, Eileen: on charismatic leaders, xvii, 222; on People's Temple, 8; on Rajneesh, 47; *New Religious Movements*, 223
Barruel, Abbé, 167–8
Bartoli, Michel, 139
Bennett, John Godolphin, 23, 26–7, 31–2, 34, 36, 38, 41; *Gurdjieff: Making a New World*, 26
Berenson, Bernard, 185
Bharti, Ma Satya, 57
Blake, William, 73
Blakey, Deborah, 8
Blavatsky, Helena Petrovna, 76–7
Bleuler, Eugen, 29, 90
Bohm, David, 100
Bollingen series (books), 97
Borsh, Father Dean, 24
Branch Dravidian Seventh Day Adventists, 13; *see also* Koresh, David

Breault, Marc, 13, 15–17
Breuer, Josef, 111–13
Breuil, Abbé Henri-Edouard-Prosper, 36
Brill, A. A., 94
British Psycho-Analytical Society, 121
Brücke, Ernst, 109
Brunton, Paul (*born* Raphael Hurst), 162–6, 198; *A Search in Secret India*, 162; *The Secret Path*, 162–4; *The Spiritual Crisis of Man*, 162; *The Wisdom of the Overself*, 164
Buchan, John, 168
Buddha: as guru, xiii–xiv; Rajneesh on, 52–3
Byron, George Gordon, 6th Baron: 'Childe Harold's Pilgrimage', 186

C. G. Jung Institute, Zurich, 85
Caiaphas (high priest), 143
Camphill homes for the handicapped, 81
Carpenter, Humphrey: *Jesus*, 139, 143, 146
Carswell, John, 40, 209
Carter, Rosalynn, 6
Catholicism: and obedience, 209
causality, 99–100
Ceauşescu, Nicolae, 3
Chaikin, Eugene, 7
Chanon, Jean, 132
charisma, xvi–xvii, 217–20, 225–6, 233
children: self-absorption, 210–11; and need for father, 221
Christianity: and faith, 201–1; beliefs, 204–5; world appeal, 204; *see also* Catholicism
Churchill, Sir Winston S., 217–18, 220
Cohn, Norman: on witches, 167; on leaders, 220; *Cosmos, Chaos, and the World to Come*, 139, 141, 145, 175; *The Pursuit of the Millenium*, 159; *Warrant for Genocide*, 167–8
collective unconscious, 98
combat myths, 140–1

249

confidence tricksters, xiv, 11, 33, 35–6, 153;
  see also Gurdjieff
conspiracy theories, 167–9
conversion, 197
creative illness, xix, 161; see also individual
  sufferers
creativity (human), 175–8, 183–4, 190–3
Crews, Frederick, 119
Cuéllar, Velásquez de, 129–30
Curchod, Suzanne, 188
cyclothymic disorder, 198
Cyriax, James, 57

Dahmer, Jeffrey, 152
Darwin, Charles, 206
Davis, Angela, 6
delusion, 198–200, 206
Devaraj (Rajneesh's doctor), 61
dictators, 3
Dominic, St, 131
Dornach, Switzerland: Goetheanum, 80
Doyle, Sir Arthur Conan, 166
dreams, 111–12
Dynamic Meditation, 54

ecstasy see mystical/ecstatic experience
Eder, David, 23
Edison, Thomas, 76
education, 224–5; see also learning
Ego: Steiner's view of, 78
Einstein, Albert, 69–72, 180–1
Eitingon, Max, 118
Eliot, T. S., 23, 202
Elizabeth II, Queen, 217
Ellenberger, Henri, xix, 73, 111, 161; The
  Discovery of the Unconscious, 161
Ellsberg, Daniel, 6
Emerson, Ralph Waldo: Self-Reliance, 208
'ether' (medium), 182
Etheric body, 78
Euripides, 215

faith, 200–6
Farr, Elizabeth L., 89, 155–7, 170, 198
Fechner, Gustav Theodor, 161
Ferdinand II (of Castile), King of Spain, 130
Ferenczi, Sandor, 115, 117–18
Ferstel, Baroness Marie von, 119–20
Fitzgerald, Frances, 55, 58
Fliess, Wilhelm, 110–12, 116
foetalization, 215

folie à deux, 18
Fonda, Jane, 6
Forel, Auguste, 112
Francis I, King of France, 130
Francis of Assisi, St, 131
Franz, Marie-Louise von, 96
Frechette, Jean-Marc, 227–9
Freeman, John, 97, 202
Freemasons, 167–8
Freud, Sigmund: on narcissism, xv; on
  mental divisions, 78; and Jung, 85–6, 90,
  93–4; personal secrecy, 88; and
  psychoanalytic theory, 109–11,
  114–17, 120, 123; scientific claims,
  109–10, 118; career, 111, 118–20;
  'creative illness', 111–12, 161; theories of
  sexuality, 112–14; and transference, 114,
  216; rejects religion, 115; personal
  relations, 116–17; certainties, 117–19;
  persuasiveness, 118–19; influence, 120,
  122–5; on patients, 122; cases, 123–4; on
  delusion, 175; on love as madness, 188;
  rejects ecstatic experience, 189, 230;
  theorising, 222; The Aetiology of Hysteria,
  113; An Autobiographical Study, 117;
  Civilization and Its Discontents, 221; The
  Future of an Illusion, 115; The Interpretation
  of Dreams, 111–12, 115; Introductory
  Lectures, 118; New Introductory Lectures,
  124; On Narcissism, 210; 'The Question
  of a Weltanschauung', 124
Fuchsian functions, 176–7

Gandhi, Mohandas Karamchand
  (Mahatma), 50
Garnett, David, 23
Gaulle, Charles de, 217
Gauss, Carl Friedrich, 176, 178
Gay, Peter, 111, 118
Gellner, Ernest: The Psychoanalytic
  Movement, 109
Gibbon, Edward, 188–9
Goethe, J. W. von, 72–5
Gomperz, Elise, 119
good and evil, conflict of, 141
Gordon, Dr James S., 10, 48, 54
Gosse, Sir Edmund, 185, 224
Greene, Graham, 183
Gurdjieff, Georgei Ivanovitch: as
  confidence trickster, 11, 33–6, 43; life
  and travels, 23–5, 27–8, 166; ideas,
  beliefs and teachings, 25–6, 28–9, 31,
  35–8, 42–3, 52, 171, 204, 232; invented

language and cosmogony, 29–33, 36, 41, 43, 79, 101, 170, 191, 200, 204–5; attention to others, 36–7, 123, 222; personal habits and behaviour, 37–8, 160; treatment of followers, 38–41, 209; influence on Rajneesh, 47, 51, 53, 58; delusions, 160, 170, 198; *All and Everything*, 33, 35, 41–2; *Meetings with Remarkable Men*, 23–4
gurus: defined, xiii–xix; exploitation of followers, xviii; mental states, 151–5, 162, 170, 193–4; apparent certainties, 208–9, 221, 232; followers' submission to, 209–10, 216, 221–2; qualities, 210–11, 218, 221; isolation, 222
Gustavus III, King of Sweden, 167
Guyana *see* Jonestown

Hadamard, Jacques, 177–8
Harries, Richard Douglas, Bishop of Oxford, 232
Hartmann, Olga de, 27, 35, 38
Hartmann, Thomas de, 27, 38
Harvey, Andrew, 226–31
Heap, Jane, 23, 36
Heisenberg, Werner, 99–100
Herder, Johann Gottfried von, 175, 193
Hess, Moses, 167
Hitler, Adolf, 219–20
homosexuality: Rajneesh condemns, 52; Andrew Harvey's, 226
Honofrio, St, 131–2
Hume, Cardinal Basil, Archbishop of Westminster, 226
Huxley, Aldous, 232
hysteria: Freud on, 112–14

Ignatius, St *see* Loyola, St Ignatius of
Illuminati, 167–8
'implicate order', 100
'Inner Circle of Humanity', 26
Inquisition, Holy, 135, 137
Institute for the Harmonious Development of Man *see* Prieuré, Château du
International Fraternity for Ethics and Culture, 93
'Invisible Hierarchy', 27
Isabella I (of Castile), Queen of Spain, 129

Jackson, M. C., 192
James, William, 187, 192, 197; *Varieties of*

Religious Experience, 136, 138, 193, 206
Jesuits (Society of Jesus), 129, 135–7
Jesus: as guru, xiii–xiv; in Book of Revelation, 14; Rajneesh on, 52–3; Steiner on, 73, 77; and good-evil conflict, 141–2; teachings, 141–7, 158; in gospels, 142, 144, 147–8; devotion to others, 222; on children, 230
Jews: and world conspiracy, 167–9; Hitler's portrayal of, 219
John the Baptist, 141, 143
Jones, Ernest, 118
Jones, Jim: heads People's Temple, 4–12, 18–19, 50, 162, 222; paranoia, 4, 11, 151, 165, 170; oratory and preaching, 5–6, 10, 221; as confidence trickster, 11, 164; and Koresh, 15–16
Jones, Jimmy (JJ's adopted son), 11
Jones, Marceline (JJ's wife), 6, 12
Jones, Stephan (JJ's son), 9, 12
Jonestown, Guyana, 4, 7–8, 10–12, 18, 223
Joyce, James, 192
Jung, Carl Gustav: attitude to religion, 51, 54, 85, 87–8, 93–6, 103–4, 198; and personal growth, 67; on spiritual world (*pleroma*), 77, 99; break with Freud, 85, 90, 94–5, 117–18; 'creative illness', 85, 88–92, 161; ideas and teachings, 85–6, 93–105; life, 87–9; self-absorption, 87, 104; mental state and hallucinations, 88–92, 154, 157, 181; psychological aims, 88; mistresses, 91, 97; on magic and occult, 101–3, 157; lectures on Loyola's *Spiritual Exercises*, 134; on schizophrenics, 153, 158; on inevitability of death, 202; theorising, 222; on behaviour towards patients, 224–5; on importance of women, 228; certainties, 232; *Answer to Job*, 96; *On the Psychology and Pathology of So-called Occult Phenomena*, 101; *Septem Sermones ad Mortuos*, 2, 99
Jung, Revd Paul Achilles, 88

Kant, Immanuel, 72, 98, 180
Kavan, Anna, 159
Keats, John, 201
Kekulé, Friedrich August von, 71
Kennedy, John F., 217
Kerensky, Alexander, 27
Kerr, John, 92
Kingdom of God (or Heaven), 141–2, 144
Klein, Melanie, 121, 161
Knapp, Alfred, 93

Knox, Ronald, 134
Koestler, Arthur, 185
Koguzki, Felix, 69
Koresh, Cyrus (DK's son), 16
Koresh, David: life and beliefs, 4, 12–19, 60, 162, 222, 224; mental state, 12–13, 17, 139, 154, 165, 170; oratory, 14, 221
Koresh, Rachel (DK's wife), 16
Krafft-Ebing, Richard von: Textbook of Psychiatry, 86
Krishnamurti, Jiddu, 59
Kuhn, Thomas S: The Structure of Scientific Revolutions, 181, 205

Labbu (Sumerian sea dragon), 140
Laing, R. D., xviii, 49, 91
L'Amour, Louis, 58
Lascaux, France, 36
Laxmi, Ma Yoga (Rajneesh's disciple), 54
Lazovich, Olgivanna Ivanovna see Wright, O. I.
learning (human), 215–16
Leppard, David: Fire and Blood, 13–14
Levin, Bernard, 51, 54–5, 62
Lewis, C. S., 185
Lind, Michael, 167–9
Locke, John, 181
Lopez, Vincent, 9, 11
Lorenz, Konrad, 175
Louis XVI, King of France, 167
love, 188–90, 194
Lovelock, Derek, 16
Loyola, St Ignatius of: background and career, 129–31, 135; leg injury, 130–1; conversion to religious life, 131–3, 162, 197; 'creative illness', 131, 161–2; visions and ecstatic 'consolations', 131–5, 137–8, 184, 190, 227; health and mental state, 132–3, 137, 139, 151, 154; contemplation, 134; teachings and faith, 135–9; integrity, 207; and established church, 209; devotion to others, 222; Spiritual Exercises, 134–5, 137
Ludolph of Saxony: Life of Christ, 131
Lueger, Karl, 119
Luther, Martin, 133, 138

McCormick, Fowler, 97
Mack, John E: Abductions, 171
madness, 152–4; see also paranoid schizophrenia; schizophrenia
Mahesh Yoga, Maharishi, 27

Mairet, Philip, 33
Malcolm, Janet, 121
manic-depression, 190, 198
Mansfield, Katherine, 23, 42
Mao Tse-tung, 3, 105
Marxism, 124
Mary, Virgin, 228
Masson, Jeffrey: My Father's Guru, 162–6
'Masters of Wisdom', 26
mathematics: discovery in, 176–81, 193, 206
Meera, Mother, 226, 229–31
Meissner, William W., 135
Mellon, Paul, 97
Meysenbug, Baroness Malwida von, 187
Milgram, Stanley: Obedience to Authority, 136
Milne, Hugh, 47, 55, 57, 59–60, 185; Bhagwan, 60
Moon, Sun Myung, 209, 223
Moore, James, 26–7, 30
Mosley, Sir Oswald, 218–19
Muhammad the Prophet, xiii
mystical/ecstatic experience, 185–90, 192, 194, 230–1
myth: Jung on, 98

Naipaul, Shiva, 8, 10
Nájera, Duke of, 130
narcissism, xv, 208, 210–11, 220
Naturphilosophie, 73–5
neoteny, 215
Newman, Cardinal John Henry: Apologia pro Vita Sua, 197–8
Newton, Sir Isaac, 73, 180–2
Nicoll, Maurice, 23
Nietzsche, Friedrich: influence on Jung, 88; loss of faith, 103–4, 202–3, 207; and Baroness von Meysenbug, 187; and Wagner, 220; on religion, 225; Beyond Good and Evil, 207; Die Fröhliche Wissenschaft, 233; Human, All too Human, 207; Thus Spake Zarathustra, 92
Nilsen, Dennis, 152
Noll, Richard: The Jung Cult, 95–6

obedience, 136–7
Oedipus complex, 111–12
Oeri, Albert, 87
Orage, A. R., 23, 39–41, 209
Orage, Jessie (née Dwight), 41
Oregon state: Rajneeshpuram (commune), 57–61

Ouspensky, Peter Damien, 23–4, 32, 40, 101; *In Search of the Miraculous*, 31, 33

paranoid schizophrenia, 157–61, 170, 210
Paul Brunton Philosophical Foundation, New York State, 163
Pauli, Wolfgang, 100
Peat, David: *Synchronicity: The Bridge Between Matter and Mind*, 101
People's Temple, 4, 6–8, 10
Pepys, Samuel, 181
Peters, Fritz, 34–8, 222
'phlogiston', 182
Pius XII, Pope, 228
Plato, 77, 99–100
pleroma, 77, 99
Plymouth Brethren, 224
Poincaré, Henri, 71, 176–80
Prieuré, Château du: Institute for the Harmonious Development of Man, 28, 35–6, 38–41
problem solving, 176–82, 207
psychoanalysis, 109–11, 115–17, 120–5
Psychological Club, Zurich, 95
psychotherapy, 122–3

Rajneesh, Bhagwan Shree: on Gurdjieff, 32; personality and influence, 47–8; wealth, 47–8, 58; life and character, 48–51, 63, 219; beliefs and teachings, 51–6, 62–3, 75; disciples and followers, 51, 55–9, 223–4; 'Dynamic Meditation' technique, 54; narcissism, 54–5, 222; moves to Oregon, 57–8; collecting, 59; decline, 59, 151; arrest and deportation, 62; 'illnesses', 151, 154; on need for religion, 176; on fictions and sanity, 199; corruption, 207; authority, 210, 222, 232; *The Supreme Understanding*, 47
Rajneesh Foundation, 55, 57
Ranch Apocalypse *see* Waco
Rank, Otto, 117–18
Read, Sir Herbert, 23
Reavis, Dick J: *The Ashes of Waco*, 17
Reddy, Balgur Venkat, (Meera's guardian), 230
Redwood Valley, California, 6
Rée, Paul, 187
Reinach, Salomon: *A History of Religions*, 147

reincarnation, 76, 163, 201
resurrection, 204–5
Revelation, Book of, 14–15, 79, 139, 166
Ridout, Alan, 225
Robertson, Revd Marion Gordon ('Pat'), 167–8
Robison, John: *Proofs of a Conspiracy*, 168
Rodriguez, Alfonso, SJ, 136
Rofé, Hosein, 27
Röhm, Ernst, 3
Roland, Romain, 189
Rothermere, Mary Lilian, Viscountess, 28
Rowbottom, Ralph, 47
Rowse, A. L., 185
Russell, Bertrand, 69

Sachs, Hanns, 118
Salomé, Lou Andreas, 120
San Francisco Gun Exchange, 11
Sanders, E. P.: *The Coming of the Kingdom*, 139, 142–3
sanity, 152–3
'Sapper' (Herman Cyril McNeile), 168
Sarmoun brotherhood, 26
Saurat, Denis, 33
schizophrenia, 29, 155–7, 190–2; *see also* paranoid schizophrenia
schizotypy, 191
Schopenhauer, Arthur, 72, 88, 92, 98–9, 158–9
Schucker, Thomas, 232
Schuré, Edouard, 68
Schweitzer, Albert, xiv
science: discovery in, 176–83, 193, 206–7; and scepticism, 205–6
Scruton, Roger, 104
sensory deprivation, 19
Seven Seals (Book of Revelation), 14–15
Seventh Day Adventist Church, 13
sex and sexuality, 52, 55–7, 112–14
Shah, Idries, 27
Shaw, William, 16
Sheela, Ma Anand (Rajneesh's administrator), 58, 60–2
Shree Rajneesh Ashram, Poona, 54
Silberstein, Eduard, 116
Silverman, Sheela: *see* Sheela, Ma Anand
Snow, C. P: *The Search*, 179
Spielrein, Sabina, 97, 103

Spinoza, Baruch, 73
spiritualism, 101
Stalin, Josef V., 3, 105
Starbuck, Edwin D: *Psychology of Religion*, 197
Steiner, Rudolf: educational work, 67–8, 80–1; ideas and beliefs, 67–9, 71–81, 129, 171, 204; charisma, 68–9; life, 69, 72–3; visions, 69; and thinking, 70–2; cosmogony and natural world, 73–5, 81, 200, 204–5; 'creative illness', 73, 161; on spiritual world, 77–8; writings, 80; achievements, 81; Jung on, 85–6; mental state, 155, 170, 198; and science, 198; integrity, 207; self-belief, 211; devotion to others, 222; *The Philosophy of Freedom*, 71
Stekel, Wilhelm, 117
Stern, J. P., 219
Stoen, Grace, 9
Stoen, John Victor, 7, 9
Stoen, Tim, 7
Storr, Anthony: *The Dynamics of Creation*, 183; *Human Destructiveness*, 160; *Solitude*, 183
Subud, 27
Swedenborg, Emanuel, 101
synchronicity, 100–1, 157

Templars, Order of, 167
Temple, William, Archbishop of Canterbury, 96–7
Tennyson, Alfred, 1st Baron, 230
Teresa, Mother, xiv, 50
Tertullian, 205
Theosophical Society, 76
'things-in-themselves', 72
Tomalin, Claire, 42
transference, 114, 216–17
Troxler, Ignaz, 67
Tsuang, Ming T: *Schizophrenia: The Facts*, 89

Uncertainty Principle, 99
Unification Church ('Moonies'), 209, 223

Velasco, María de, 130
Vermes, Geza, 139, 146
Voragine, Jacopo de: *Lives of the Saints*, 131

Waco, Texas: Ranch Apocalypse, 4, 12, 14–15, 17–18
Wagner, Richard, 187, 219–20
Waldorf School Movement, 67
Walker, Kenneth, 23
Wallace, Alfred Russel, 76
Wallas, Graham, 178
Wasco county, Oregon, 61
Weber, Max, xvi
Webster, Richard, 117, 209
Weishaupt, Adam, 167
Whitman, Walt, 185
Wilson, A. N., 139
Wind, Edgar, 102
Winnicott, D. W., 90
witch-hunts, 167
Wolff, Toni, 91, 97
women: as Divine Mothers, 228, 231
Wordsworth, William, 138, 185
'Work, The' (Gurdjieff's), 25, 28, 39
Wright, Frank Lloyd, 39–40
Wright, Olgivanna Ivanovna (*née* Lazovich), 23, 39–40

X, Michael, 8

Yates, Dornford, 168
Young, James, 23

Zen, 28
Zoroaster, 139–42

Printed in the United States
117189LV00002B/2/A